Puffin Plus

Mischling, Second Degree

Ilse Koehn was born in Berlin in 1929. In 1937 her parents were suddenly and inexplicably divorced. Ilse spent most of her wartime childhood in various evacuation camps, both in Germany and Czechoslovakia, and became a member of the Hitler Youth Movement. Returning to Berlin in 1944 she lived through the last, terrifying days of the war with her maternal grandparents, the Derecks.

Ilse learned the truth about her past when she was fifteen years old. Her beloved grandmother, Oma Koehn who had disappeared mysteriously in 1943, was Jewish, and had died in Theresienstadt concentration camp. Ilse herself was a 'Mischling', a child of mixed race. It was to protect their grandchild from a terrible fate that the Derecks had forced Ilse's parents to divorce. They gained custody of the child, and concealed everything from her.

Ilse's father survived the war because his was an essential occupation – repairing high voltage wires. He and Ilse's mother remarried and Ilse returned to live with them. She trained to be a graphic designer, and moved to the United States in 1958 to pursue her career.

Ilse Koehn has worked as an art director for an advertising agency, and lately as a freelance book illustrator and designer. She now lives in Connecticut with her husband who is an art director, and her stepdaughter.

Writing this book, which took the author ten years, meant a traumatic re-living of her childhood experience. It is a memorable document.

ILSE KOEHN

MISCHLING, SECOND DEGREE

MY CHILDHOOD IN NAZI GERMANY

PUFFIN BOOKS

Puffin Books, Penguin Books Ltd,
Harmondsworth, Middlesex, England
Penguin Books, 625 Madison Avenue,
New York, New York 10022, U.S.A.
Penguin Books Australia Ltd, Ringwood,
Victoria, Australia
Penguin Books Canada Ltd, 2801 John Street,
Markham, Ontario, Canada L3R 1B4
Penguin Books (N.Z.) Ltd, 182–190 Wairau Road,
Auckland 10, New Zealand

First published in the U.S.A. 1977
First published in Great Britain by Hamish Hamilton Ltd 1978
Published in Puffin Books 1981

Made and printed in Great Britain by
Cox & Wyman Ltd, Reading
Set in Intertype Lectura

Contents

1

1926-36 · The Derecks

Mutter Dereck was used to hearing flattering remarks about her daughter's slightly exotic beauty. She usually replied with a sly, cackling laugh, 'Yes, I know, she's the flower on the dung-heap.' To her, this statement was not in the least derogatory, since she regarded her dungheap, the compost pile, as a gold mine — indeed, referred to it that way.

'That's why we called her Margarete. It was probably the Huguenots in the family that gave her those big brown eyes and black hair.'

When asked about Grete's voice, she would shrug her shoulders. 'Who knows? Who cares? Everyone on my side and her father's had tin ears, as far as I know.'

Grete's rich alto voice had attracted the attention of her teacher in school, and through him she became a member of the Berlin Children's Choir. When she finished school, the choirmaster went to see her parents, to urge them to let her study music. He was received coldly.

'Music? She will have to earn a living,' her machinist father said bluntly. He stood there huge and awkward in the wooden clogs he wore at home. 'Music!' He spat out the word like a piece of wormy apple. 'That's for the idle rich. We are workers.'

'Her head is full of raisins already,' Mutter Dereck added as she wiped her hands on her apron and threw a sideways glance towards Grete.

Grete cried for a bit, but she knew her parents too well to have shared the choirmaster's hopes for her. Dutifully she became a seamstress and tailor's apprentice in a Berlin fashion house. She was not unhappy. Earning money would soon allow her to be independent of the parents she feared.

She found friends among the young members of the Social Democratic Party, to which the elder Derecks belonged. She and her friends had heated political discussions that often lasted far into the night. A new era was beginning, they thought, free of oppression, with opportunities for all. They, the young Social Democrats, would work for a democratic Germany. Let that Adolf Hitler rant and rave. Who was he but an obscure tramp, a house-painter from Austria? He and his party, the Nationalsozialistische Deutsche Arbeiter Partei — called Nazi for short — were brown-shirted, jack-booted misfits and hoodlums.

Hitler, the illegitimate offspring of a cleaning woman, had founded the party in 1920. Now in 1926 his followers numbered in the thousands, but few Germans regarded them as a real threat.

Grete was a very active party member and belonged to several committees. She even spent one of her vacations attending a seminar on women's rights. She worked hard, they all did, but they still found time for parties, barbecues and singing. Ernst Koehn played the guitar. His tenor harmonized with Grete's alto. They fell in love.

The Derecks were not pleased with their son-in-law, who was eleven years older than Grete. True, he had a good job as an electrician for the Berlin Light and Power Company, but that was the only thing in his favour as far as they were concerned.

'Sure, he's good-looking, charming, plays the guitar,' Mutter Dereck said to her neighbour, 'but what does that get you? And books, books, books,' she sneered. 'Studies after work, he does. If he has so much energy left over, why doesn't he come here to help? God knows we could use an extra pair of hands.'

And then there was Ernst's mother, Oma Koehn, the widow Koehn, born a Rotenthal. Jewish?

'I don't believe in organized religion, Frau Dereck,' she had answered Mutter Dereck's question archly, using the formal address. 'I don't belong to any church, don't go to any.'

'We don't either,' chuckled Mutter Dereck, as if her question had been a joke. 'Wouldn't have time for it anyway. By the time others go to church, I've already fed the animals and practically done a day's work.' And she added rather pointedly, 'Well, that's what happens when you own a house.'

The widow Koehn did not own a house. She lived in an apartment surrounded by fine furniture and thousands of books.

Grete and Ernst preferred to move in with Oma Koehn rather than with the Derecks. However, they soon bought a parcel of land and began to design their own house. The young couple could not afford an architect, but Ernst learned to do architectural drawings well enough to satisfy the building inspectors. They had barely enough money to pay for the raw materials, so they determined to build the house themselves. They carried stones, mixed mortar, put up walls, hewed beams, cut glass for window-panes. There was nothing they would not tackle. 'What we don't know, we can learn' was their motto. They even designed and built their own furniture.

The room with the south-east exposure would be for the child they both wanted. It would be able to look out at the hazelnut tree. Grete planted climbing roses under the window. The child would wake up to the sweet scent of roses.

In August 1929 a healthy eight-pound child arrived and was named Ilse. She was not christened ('We are Free-thinkers'). Only a simple entry in the birth register: Ilse Margarete Koehn.

I know now about the years of political upheaval in Germany, know that my parents were among the hundred thousand workers who demonstrated against Hitler; know that the democratic parties were unable to unite against him; know that on 30 January 1933 Adolf Hitler was elected German Chancellor and soon began to call himself 'Der Führer', leader of Germany. In May the Führer outlawed the labour unions and in July all political parties but his own; and he immediately began his hate campaign against the Jews and the boycott of Jewish shops. On 7 April 1933 when he had been in office only five weeks, the first anti-Jewish law was decreed, and others followed in rapid succession. By October 1933 'non-Aryans' were legally excluded from institutions of higher learning, from the government, and from the professions.

Hitler ordered the big bonfire in front of the Berlin university where his followers burned all 'un-German' books – books whose authors were either Jewish or in opposition to Hitler. My parents crammed most of their now forbidden books into two huge crates and buried them at night in our garden. I know all of this now, but don't remember it.

I do remember my sunny room – it seems the sun was always shining during those years. It made Oma's gift, the blond Biedermeier furniture, sparkle. I remember watching the birds while still lying in bed and the roses that climbed up through my window. They were pale-pink roses of an exceptionally sweet fragrance. Our garden was full of flowers, every imaginable kind, and there were hazelnut, cherry, apple and pear trees and even a peach tree.

The only tears I remember shedding were for 'The Ugly Duckling'. That it finally became a beautiful swan did not console me at all for the misery it had had to suffer.

I longed to go to school; in preparation I remember having to recite 'My name is Ilse Koehn ['a good German name you can be proud of – old Pomeranian stock,' Vati said]. I live at Number Twelve Twenty-eight Street in Waidmannslust.' I was so happy when I started school.

'When they ask you what your religion is, say Dissident. It means Free-thinker and that's what we are. We did not have you christened because we consider ourselves enlightened. Enlightened, class-conscious workers. When you grow up, you can make your own choice.'

The only Dissident among Lutherans and Catholics, I was quickly nicknamed 'Pagan'. It did not bother me. I thought that my classmates were perhaps a little jealous because I could go home early when Religion was the last class. I wondered if this was the reason my German teacher, Frau Katscher, didn't like me, because she also taught Religion. But then Frau Katscher only liked the rich girls. I enjoyed school.

Some Sundays we went to Tegel Lake, where we met my parents' friends in a garden café. Willy Schmidt, the former union leader, and his wife, Frieda, were always there, and Hans and Lotti Koller, the journalists. There were the Gerstens with their children, Alla and Rolf. 'The Roosters', Axel and Vera Hahn, came and Else and Hans Wagner, the actors. When they were around, there seemed to be more laughter, less solemn talk. They all talked a lot, over coffee and cake, while we children swam or had fun on the swings and seesaws.

On the way home, Vati always carried me on his shoulders and the three of us sang quietly.

On one such Sunday night the balloon he had bought me bounced against his cigarette and burst. When I cried, he yelled angrily, 'Stop it! Life isn't all balloons.'

'But she's only a child,' Mutti said.

'We must bring her up to see real life, life as it is, not as we would like it to be. It's never too early to learn that!'

Vati had never sounded so harsh. I was scared, sensing that it wasn't my crying but something else – 'real life'? – that made him so angry.

I was six years old in 1935, happy and ignorant about what was going on in Germany. I had no idea that our Sunday outings were one way for the former Social Democrats to gather without arousing suspicion. My parents did not tell me that the Nazi Party held a congress in Nuremberg. At that congress, on Sunday, 15 September 1935, the Führer announced three new laws. These, with thirteen supplementary decrees (the last published 1 July 1943), were the so-called 'Nuremberg Laws'. The first one declared the swastika the official emblem of the German state. The second imposed special conditions for full German citizenship that excluded all Jews. The third, the Law for the Protection of German Blood and German Honour, prohibited marriages between German citizens and Jews. Marriages contracted in violation of this law were declared void; even extra-marital relations between German citizens and Jews were prohibited. The law also forbade Jews to hire female Germans under forty-five years of age as domestics, and Jews were not allowed to display the national colours. Any violation of these laws could be punished by a jail sentence.

These laws affected millions of Germans. The basic definition of a Jew was published 14 November 1935. The later regulations defined the different categories of *Mischlinge*, the mixed offspring of Germans and Jews. The three basic designations were (1) Jew (2) Mischling, first degree (3) Mischling, second degree.

A Jew was anyone with three racially full Jewish grandparents, or a person who belonged to the Jewish religious community, or who joined it after 15 September 1935 when the law became effective.

Also categorized as a Jew was anyone married to a Jew, or who married a Jew after 15 September 1935. Offspring of such marriages, including illegitimate offspring of either person, were categorized as Jews.

A Mischling, first degree, was anyone with two Jewish grandparents, provided this person was not of the Jewish faith or married to a Jew.

A Mischling, second degree, was anyone with one Jewish grandparent, provided this person was not of the Jewish faith or married to a Jew.

The law stated as irrefutable fact that a grandparent was Jewish if he/she was racially Jewish, even if that grandparent was not of the Jewish faith and did not belong to the Jewish religious community.

Only after the war did I find out that Oma's parents had been Jewish. But Oma had become a 'Free-thinker' and married the 'Aryan' Willem Koehn. This made their son and daughter 'Mischlings, First Degree'. Vati's marriage to Mutti, an 'Aryan', was now a 'mixed' marriage and I, the offspring, was as of 14 November 1935, a 'Mischling, Second Degree'.

My small world didn't change that day, or the next, or the

next. I was blissfully ignorant of all these laws. Vati brought home toys and candy. No one smashed windows in our quiet Berlin suburb.

Hitler was building up the armed forces. They took a loyalty oath to him personally, and in March 1936 they marched into the Rhineland. They occupied what had, under the Versailles Treaty, been declared a demilitarized zone. There was no enraged outcry from other nations, only mild diplomatic protests.

My parents, I remember, talked about Germany. They said that a dark time had come for our Fatherland; they never mentioned the word Jew.

And then it was the spring of 1936. That year Vati's sister, Tante Ruth, and my cousin Dieter came from Italy to visit and see the Olympic Games. Dieter was ten years old and I adored him. Who else could boast of a cousin who spoke Italian and English as well as German, studied piano at the conservatory in Milan and was sure to become a concert pianist? Dieter made me clay animals, and taught me to run up a down escalator. Tante Ruth and Dieter took me sightseeing in Berlin and I had such a good time that I barely noticed that Grossmutter Dereck came to visit us more frequently. In fact, she came almost every day, but always left just before Vati came home. She'd tell me to 'go and play', so I would not hear what she told Mutti. But whatever it was she said, it made Mutti cry.

2

1937 · Break-up

What had happened? I did not understand, and I was frightened. Sitting behind my father on his bicycle, I awkwardly tried to hold on to him. Awkwardly because he wore a ruck-sack on his back. It contained some of my belongings – a dress, some underwear, a toothbrush and Peter, the big teddy bear, whose head stuck out. We had picked things at random and they weren't folded or packed very well. Mutti would have known how. But Mutti was in a sanatorium suffering from a nervous breakdown.

'She will soon be well,' Vati said. It did not sound convincing. And now we were going to Tegel, where I was to stay 'for a few days' with people named Ertel. All I knew about them was that Vati worked with Herr Ertel. The memory of my stay with them is blurred by tears. They were kind people, and tried their best to make me feel welcome. That made it only worse. How could I ask, 'Why has Vati left me with strangers? When will he come to take me home?' without sounding ungrateful and rude?

After two days which seemed an eternity, Vati came. His normally open and friendly face was a stony mask. He did not look like my Vati at all.

'Mutti is still in the sanatorium,' he said. 'We will visit her soon.'

My insides hurt as if they were being shrunk, and when he added, 'We are not going home,' I felt a sudden impulse to run and cling to Frau Ertel. Then I felt so guilty that I didn't even listen to what else Vati had to say. Quietly I took my place on the baggage rack of the bike, too miserable to ask where we were going.

Oma's house. Oma at the top of the stairs, tall in her black dress with lace collar. Oma, white-haired, seventy-eight years old, ancient to me and frightening. We are going to live with Oma for a while. How long is a while?

'Oma, why is Mutti sick? Oma, how long will it be? Oma, when will Mutti be healthy again? Will we go back to our own house then?'

Oma pats me on the head. 'Child! even if I had the answers, they would be over your head.'

Over my head, that's easy. I'm little. Whenever Vati and Oma talk seriously, it's either, 'Don't talk in front of the child' or 'It's all right, it's over her head anyway. She doesn't understand.' How can I understand if nobody explains anything to me? I'm not used to that. Vati and Mutti always answered my questions, explained everything. But now, when I see Vati at night – he leaves in the morning before I wake up – he talks of everything but when we will be home again with Mutti.

'Ilse, stand still! How can I brush your hair when you dance around like an Apache?'

'What's an Apache, Oma?'

'An Apache ... Never mind, I'll tell you when you come home. If we don't hurry, you'll be late for school – and you still have to change your dress.'

'Why can't I wear this one?'

'Because I have not washed and ironed it yet.'

'I've only worn it once!'

'Don't argue! I don't want anyone to say that just because I'm old I can't take care of you.'

I think Oma is overdoing it. I mean, a fresh dress *every day*!

I still went to the same school. Oma lived no farther from it than we did, but on the way there were more interesting things to see now. Mansions and beautiful gardens. There was one neglected, abandoned one where I could easily squeeze through the fence. Sometimes after school I sat there among the tall grass and wild flowers, thinking of Mutti and our garden. I couldn't stay too long because Oma and our coffee ritual were waiting.

When I got home, Oma's sewing table by the window was already covered by a hand-embroidered tablecloth. I set the table with the happy Butzen-design dishes. I was careful, very careful, particularly with my favourite, squat little marmalade jar. It had been only my second or third day at Oma's, when I had broken one of her tea glasses, one of the set from the silver tray. Oma had turned beet red with rage and chased me around the table with, of all things, a pillow! Finally, out of breath, we had stopped and stared at each other. Oma stood as if frozen in mid-motion, about to strike the deadly blow. It looked so funny that I began to laugh. And Oma? She started laughing too, then fell into her chair with a sigh and I jumped into her lap. The ice was broken, we were friends.

Oma had made coffee, ersatz coffee, and buttered my rolls.

'Can't I have margarine too?'

'You are growing. You need butter. Margarine is better for old people.'

Oma puts fresh flowers on the table, then the newspaper. Everything has to be in its proper place before we sit down. We talk about school and Apaches. She makes me get the dictionary and books with pictures of Indians. Then comes the paper. I know what a masthead is, a byline, an essay, an editorial. Oma has explained them all. Every day she flips past the first few pages. These are the ones that have pictures of the Führer and Storm Troopers and SA and Nazis, words I hear more and more often.

'Not for children,' she says categorically. 'On with your job, let's hear what the countess is up to.'

I read aloud the daily instalment of the serialized novel.

Oma hardly leaves the house. I do most of the shopping. She does take me to the movies, though, and sometimes comes along to the butcher, Mellmer. Herr Mellmer's speech is so predictable that we have a game, anticipating his exact words.

'My, my, Frau Koehn, the little one is getting skinnier every

16

day. I guess we'll have to do something about that!' Oma mimics.

'No!' I say.

'What do *you* think he will say?'

'Nothing, because he won't be there today.'

'He'll be there, and moreover, he will give you a slice of liverwurst.'

'If he's there, he'll be out of liverwurst,' I say, just to be contrary.

But he's there, and says, 'My, my, Frau Koehn, the little one is getting skinnier every day. I guess we'll have to do something about that' and hands me a slice of liverwurst. Oma gives me the 'What did I tell you?' look and we both grin. And then Mellmer suddenly says something unexpected: 'How come you two are always so happy?'

When Vati and I went to visit Mutti in the sanatorium, it was the longest train ride I had ever taken. It was one of those summer Sundays when everyone wears bright clothes and the whole world seems to be happy. But we weren't. My heart felt like a stone. Vati looked like one and the huge building was forbidding. Even the trees in the surrounding park were so tall and dark they seemed ominous. We passed white-smocked women. One was screaming hysterically, another babbled incoherently. I clung to Vati's hand. I don't know what I expected, but Mutti looked the way she had always looked — very beautiful and loving. The three of us strolled in the park, almost as we used to when we took walks in the woods. But then a loudspeaker announced that it was time to leave. As we passed through the gate, Vati kept his head turned away.

'I told you not to take the child along, Ernst! It's too much for her,' Oma said. 'Next time you go alone!'

Next time? There was no next time. Mutti came home. Home to her parents, the Derecks, in Luebars.

'You have to understand,' said Vati, 'that we love each other very much. And we both love you. Grossvater and Grossmutter

17

Dereck have succeeded in making your mother divorce me. And maybe it's better that way.'

I feel my eyes getting larger. Tears come. 'But Vati!' The scream inside me comes out as a feeble sob. 'Vati! If you love Mutti and she loves you . . .'

'You will see her on week-ends. I know it must be confusing to you. It is. Makes no sense – and yet it's better.' His body suddenly shakes. Vati is crying. 'Someday you'll understand.' It comes out muffled as he leaves the room. I am left standing there alone with tears streaming down my face. I don't understand. I don't understand.

The best time of the day is after dinner. Vati talks about his work and his colleagues in a way that makes Oma and me feel we are there. He demonstrates how he and all the other men in overalls stood dumbfounded while his boss, known as the 'Little One', rolled up his sleeve and retrieved a tiny screw out of a huge barrel filled with dirty oil. We laugh when he shows us how someone awkwardly, laboriously, leaned over a box to fix something when it would have been much easier to go around to the other side. If only the evenings were longer. But he already has the guitar in his hand – time to go to bed. He will sing to me: 'All the flowers are sleeping under moonlit skies . . .' I fall asleep, seeing our hazelnut tree at home, and I dream that we are all there again.

Saturdays Vati comes home early. I always run down to greet him, but never as fast as on paydays. That's when he goes treasure-hunting in secondhand bookstores. Even Oma comes half-way down the stairs to look expectantly at his bulging briefcase.

'Well,' he says, taking off his coat and pretending not to notice that we are on pins and needles, 'what's for lunch? Shall we eat?'

'Did you find something? Did you find something for us too?' we say simultaneously.

He affectionately pats his briefcase, smiles. 'What do you think I have here? Nothing but *jewels*, wait till you see.'

Oma waves her hand impatiently. 'Don't keep us in suspense, Ernst! Show us!'

But Vati makes not the slightest move to open his treasure chest. Instead he embarks on a minute account of the stores he visited. Describes a special edition of *Faust* that old Gerlach had kept for him. 'Parchment, leather binding, beautiful.' And he looks as if he were still seeing it. 'Collector's item. But twenty mice?' When a price awes him, he uses one of the many Berlin slang words for money. 'I was tempted, but . . .'

Finally, he takes out the books, one by one. As if at an auction, he calls out title, author, publisher, praises any special feature such as a leather spine or illustrations. At last in possession of our treasures, we have lunch, but afterwards everyone disappears into a favourite corner for a few hours of undisturbed reading.

'One penny for the Winter Help programme! One penny! One penny!' The Hitler Youth accompany their shouts with the furious rattling of small coins in tin cans.

'Ilse, shut the window! There they go again, collecting – so Hitler can buy arms and make war.' Vati sounds mad.

I don't understand. 'But,' I say, 'they are collecting for the Winter Help. That's to buy food and clothing for poor Germans.'

Oma and Vati exchange one of those 'Only someone who is deaf and blind could believe that' glances.

'Food and clothing! *Ja!*' Vati is sarcastic. 'People will believe anything. They fall for the same swindle, the same lies, over and over again. Any idiot can come and promise them the blue from the sky, and off they go, marching merrily towards their own slaughter.'

Oma sighs. 'Yes, we've seen it all before. We gave the Kaiser our gold in return for tin medals inscribed with "I Gave Gold for Iron." '

'Cannon instead of butter,' Vati says. 'To think that I was only seventeen at the beginning of the World War. A mere child, it seems to me now. But the young fall easily for slogans. I even volunteered to fight for the glory of the Fatherland.

Glory? Hell! I was lucky to come out alive, with nothing worse than frozen toes and ears. But here's the next generation eagerly waiting its turn to become cannon fodder.'

'A penny! A penny for the Winter Help!' We can hear them even with the windows closed.

Week-end evenings are horrible. When Vati goes out to visit friends, Oma falls asleep early and then my world feels like a dark, empty hole. I always beg Vati to take me along, and sometimes he does. We walk hand in hand, and the loneliness is not so bad, we are at least partially a family.

I like going to the Gerstens', because of Rolf and Alla. Alla is nineteen, beautiful and so nice, I cannot imagine anyone not liking her. Rolf is twelve. He piles a mountain of pillows on the coal-bin for us to snuggle in. The gas lamp throws a soft, eerie light on Alla's blonde hair and the manuscript of a play she is reading to us. The tea-kettle sizzles over the red coals. Alla has a different voice for every character in the play, and the kitchen becomes a fairyland. Vati and Herr Gersten talk and then play chess. Vati and I will go home very late and Oma will be at the top of the stairs, saying, 'Irresponsible, Ernst! Absolutely irresponsible of you to keep the child out so late and awake so long.' I slip past her, leaving Vati to deal with her anger, knowing he will say, as always, 'You are absolutely right.'

It was at the Gerstens' that I first heard the word Boergermoor. Herr Gersten said it, and it had something to do with their eldest son, Erwin. It sounded as if something dreadful had happened. There was a feeling of terrible depression and impending doom. I wanted to find out more. But Alla, as if sensing my thoughts, firmly led me away. 'Come on. Grown-ups always talk about such depressing things.' Over my head again, I thought bitterly, not for children. I did not know how right I was. After the war I found out that Erwin had been thrown into Boergermoor concentration camp because he had been overheard calling Hitler an idiot.

Vati had accompanied me part of the way. Now, for the last few hundred yards, I was alone on my bike. I felt strange, uneasy, and found myself pedalling slower and slower, looking back to the corner where he had left me.

Suddenly I was in front of my grandparents' house. There was Mutti, and we were in each other's arms. Grossmutter was there too. When I turned to say hello, she grabbed me by the shoulders, inspected my collar, checked the buttons on my dress, almost as if she were trying to find something wrong. Inspection over, she muttered, 'Guess it's all right. Apparently *she* does take care of her.' I knew she meant Oma. 'Don't see *how* she can, though, at *her* age.'

'Really, now!' Mutti protested. 'Stop it, Mother! Ilse looks fine. She looks healthy and *clean*.' Mutti hugged me. 'I've missed you so much!'

'I've missed you, too.'

'Grossmutter baked a cake especially for you. We'll have coffee and cake, then you and I will take a walk in the woods.'

'Grete! I promised Frau Lampert you would have her dress ready for a fitting tomorrow!' Grossmutter said in an offended voice.

Mutti looked startled. 'But Mother! How could you? You knew Ilse was coming! Couldn't you have made it Tuesday?'

'She needs it for the wedding, and you haven't even started!'

'How could I? You know I haven't had time!'

'You still have Leni's dress to do and if you don't start today, you won't be able to get it done ... Well? Do you intend to grow roots here? Come on in, let's have coffee.'

'It's not that much work,' Mutti whispered into my ear. 'Maybe we'll still have time for a stroll.'

Grossvater was already at the table. He barely looked at me. I said, 'Hello, Grossvater, how are you?'

'You're pale and skinny, as usual,' was his reply. 'You should eat more,' and then he devoted himself to the cake.

Mutti had a large room upstairs. I saw that it was furnished with the bedroom set from our house. I wondered where all the other things were, the furniture Vati had built and . . . But I did not dare ask. Instead I sat opposite Mutti, threaded needles for her and took out basting stitches in the hope that she would be done soon.

'I am going to school again,' she told me with pride. 'I was an apprentice in one of the finest couturier salons before I married your father. Now I'm studying to become a master tailor. But Grossmutter – ' her voice became a whisper – 'she makes me sew for the whole neighbourhood. I wish she wouldn't promise people things without my knowledge. I barely have time to do the work for school. And they don't pay very much either. I guess they think because they know me . . .' She did not finish the sentence, but instead inquired about the Gerstens.

Should I tell her what I had heard about Erwin? But what had I heard? Boergermoor? I decided to just give her their regards.

'Will you be finished soon?' I asked as meekly as possible, but I already knew the answer.

'I'm afraid not.' For the first time since she had started, Mutti looked up from her sewing. I could not help noticing how tired and unhappy she looked. I felt I must reassure her.

'It's all right, Mutti! I just wanted to be with you.' That was not entirely true, but she did not notice the false tone in my voice. Her face brightened and she said eagerly, 'Next time we will have fun. We don't have to take a walk. Maybe we could go swimming together – anything you like.'

'Yes.' I was getting late and I cast a furtive glance at the clock. 'Mutti, I will have to leave soon. Vati will be waiting for me at the corner.'

'Oh, good,' she replied and sounded as if a great weight had been lifted from her. 'Then I don't have to worry about your riding back alone. Will you tell Vati something for me?' I nodded. Her face was bent down over the sewing. 'Tell him I love him.'

'He says he loves you, too.'

'Someday we will all be together again.'

I knew better than to ask when. There was apparently no answer, and it would only make her cry. I was glad to go back to Vati and Oma.

'Ilse, Bilse, no one wants her ...' Willy Schmidt always makes me laugh, and when *he* laughs, his white whiskers spread out and cover his face from side to side. Vati has taken me along. I am allowed to sit at the table. Willy puts a coin on the table. 'Watch this!' he commands and quickly moves his hands over it. Thinking that he has distracted me, he says in a very different tone of voice to Vati, 'We've heard about Erwin,' and then quickly to me, 'Where did you say it was?' I point. 'No. Wrong! Watch again!' His hands move once more over the coin, but he keeps talking to Vati about Nazis. This time I point to the right hand, but instead of repeating the trick, he absent-mindedly hands me the coin and keeps right on talking. 'We Social Democrats ... Weimar Republic ... Stresemann ... unions ... parties ... participatory democracy ... Nazis ... Nazis ... Nazis ...' My head begins to swim, his voice gets louder.

Frieda, coffee pot in hand, stops. 'Willy! Willy, not so loud!'

'I'll talk as loud as I want to in my own house!' Willy shouts. 'I'm still the master here!'

Frieda rushes to the window, glances around, from there goes furtively to the door. She opens and then closes it quickly. But this agitates him so that he gets up and starts pacing about the room.

'In my own house, on my own piece of land, I cannot even say what I want to without having to see whether someone is snooping around, listening, waiting for an opportunity to de-nounce me?' He shakes his fist angrily. 'These damned, mis-erable dogs, that's what they are! Cowardly miserable dogs! Scum that has every reason to fear the light of day. And they think they can take over Germany, rule it? Not if I can help it!'

He looks around with a wild expression on his face, becomes aware of my presence, smiles. 'Ilse, have you heard of the guy who went hunting in the desert?' There follows a funny story. I laugh, but also wonder who the 'miserable dogs' are.

Axel and Vera Hahn are my favourite people. They always come unexpectedly, and when they step through the door, the rooms suddenly vibrate, resound with laughter. Axel, tall and blond, has the stature of a Viking. Vera, just as tall, has short black hair and a figure that a Greek goddess might have envied.

Vera jumps, lets out a mock scream. Teetering at the edge of the carpet is a mouse. As I bend down, another one appears, then another and another. Each one smaller than the one before. A whole family of wind-up mice.

'For you, Ilse! We brought them all the way from Russia.'

Oh, joy! And even the tiniest one has whiskers, is perfectly formed. Let the grown-ups talk. I can busy myself with the mice. But there it is again. Though they speak in low voices, I hear 'Erwin' and 'Boergermoor.' They mention other names. I don't want them to talk politics. I want them to laugh, tell stories, sing.

No one even notices when I take down the guitar, place myself next to Vera, offer it to her.

'Maybe it's not too late, Ernst,' she is saying. 'It's never too late, I believe that, and we have to do something, right? We have to *organize*! We can't just idly stand by and give the Nazis free rein!' I desperately want her to take the instrument, but she is leaning over the table, talking with great intensity, unaware of me. 'There are still enough of us left, Ernst, and we should fight!'

I can see I'm getting nowhere. No one smiles, their faces are grim and worried. Tossing manners aside, I slide the guitar under her arm into her lap. At last she looks at me. Then at the guitar as if she's never seen one before. Will she scold me? She frowns, her fingers drum on the wood and then, finally, she smiles, moves her chair back and takes proper hold of the instrument. Tentatively she picks at the strings, tunes up, and in her deep, resonant voice sings: 'Even if burgers, and sceptics should scoff, For us the sun will keep shining!' We all join in the refrain. It is a song of the Social Democrats. I know it well. Oma closes the window.

After a few songs Vera hands the guitar to Vati, asking him to play certain songs. How well they play and sing. Still, something seems to be missing. I become painfully aware that it is Mutti.

Oma, the only one who is not singing, smiles. 'Sing some of the beautiful Russian songs,' she pleads, and Vati hands the guitar to Alex. His song, soft at first, almost moaning, gets louder, faster, wilder, and I'm swept away on the sound. They switch to Spanish, Irish, Italian songs. They are exuberant and then Alex cries out, 'One for Ilse!' The guitar is back in Vera's hands. She sings alone and I think that no one else in the whole world, not even Vati, can sing children's songs as she does. She knows my favourites, asks me to join her in the refrain. I'm out of breath, but she isn't, slides into one of the political songs, then into the 'Internationale'. I know the words, but I do not sing, looking anxiously from one to the other. Sure enough, the clouds are rolling in again. The ominous, threatening, invisible thing is in the air again and before I have time to think about it the singing stops. They lean over the table. The guitar has been carelessly put aside. Vati says, 'Alex, what you propose is suicide!

'So — let's all go about our business,' Alex retorts bitterly. 'Let's not risk our necks. Is that what you are saying? You of all people?'

'I did not say let's not risk anything.' Vati is angry. 'But there's a difference between risk and suicide. Yes, we should and will act, but it must be thought out, carefully planned. We can't go about this like enthusiastic kids. Alex, this is serious — and do you realize how many people's lives you are playing with?'

Alex looks down, his voice still bitter. 'Back to the old debating society, ha? We know where *that* got us. Talk, talk, talk!' he shouts. 'Talk and resolutions and more talk! That's what got us into the mess we are in. Talk and no action! Leave the action to the Nazis, they are good at it. Their action sure speaks louder than words.'

I retreat in a corner with my mice.

It was a nice afternoon. Oma and I were reading when there was a sharp knock at the door, instantly followed by a staccato of louder, authoritative pounding. When I opened the door, I faced what seemed to be a grey wall moving towards me. I had the nightmare feeling that it would come close, closer, and crush me.

It consisted of two huge women dressed in long, identical grey coats with big black handbags and laced boots. Ugly, flat, black boots. They had pallid faces, and their hair was tied back so tightly they seemed bald.

'That must be her!' said one, pulling me up against her enormous body by one of my pigtails. She held it painfully tight, using her other hand to part the hair on my head this way and that. Then she released me with a push that made me stumble backward against Oma.

'At least she doesn't have lice!' she declared. 'Is this the child?' she demanded of Oma as if she had caught her with stolen goods. But she did not wait for an answer. 'We are social workers,' she continued in that same tone. 'We've come to see whether the child is being properly cared for. Where does she sleep?'

Oma pointed, and both women went over to my bed, lifted the cover, looked under the pillow, the mattress, pulled the bedclothes apart and left them.

'Where do you keep her things?'

Again Oma just pointed and immediately they descended on the chest of drawers. They burrowed into my underwear, my scarves and mittens and my small belongings. Having made a mess here, too, they stomped over to the closet, and in passing hit Oma with one of their monstrous bags. There was no apology. How they yanked at the clothes, all but ripping them off their hangers! And not only mine, but Oma's and Vati's as well.

Shoulder to shoulder, they steam-rollered their way to the kitchen. 'Is this where you prepare her meals?'

Oma said nothing, watched as they went through cupboards and looked into drawers and pots.

What were they looking for? Why didn't Oma tell them to leave? But now apparently they were finished. They walked out of the door, barked, 'You will hear from us!' and, still side by side, marched down the stairs. I closed the door, tried to look at Oma, but she hid her face as she put things back in order.

Not long after their visit, a letter arrived from my grandparents. Without comment, Oma quickly dropped it into her drawer. This heightened my curiosity, since she normally showed me what little mail she got. When, a few days later, she went to see a neighbour, I did what I knew I should not do. I opened the drawer. In the letter my grandparents informed Oma that they had applied to the state to be given custody of me. My heart began to pound. I knew it would mean living in Luebars.

Soon afterwards Vati told me about it. 'It will only be temporary,' he said. 'I'm still fighting to get you back.' As if I was already gone! Pushed around like a ping-pong ball, and how can you cry and be miserable because you've been told to live with your mother, whom you love? 'A few days,' 'a little while,' 'only temporary'! Didn't I belong anywhere any more?

'You will soon be going to high school here in Hermsdorf,' Vati said, as if this solved everything.

3

1938 · Luebars

I kick the rusty old pail angrily. Sure enough, Grossmutter materializes out of nowhere. 'What did you do that for? Don't you know I still need it to cover the rhubarb?' She walks into the garden with the pail, shaking her head.

No, I don't know. Nor do I care. Ugly, ugly, I think bitterly, everything here is ugly. Things are rusty, broken, cracked, frayed. It does not matter to Grossmutter, she still has a use for everything. I think about Oma, try to imagine her here, but can't. Oma would not eat off a plastic tablecloth, or from unmatched, cracked dishes. Oma throws a plate away immediately when she finds the slightest chip. What a difference! All the beautiful books in Oma's house; here, not a single one. I can't even read here. When I try to hide somewhere with a book, Grossmutter always finds me.

'You'll ruin your eyes! All this nonsense, stuffing your head with dreams. What good is it? Help me weed. Take the apple baskets down to the cellar. Go get me some carrots. Be careful not to tread on the spinach plants. Schoolwork? You can do that later. I never learned anything useful in school! Do this, do that.' I never have a moment to myself. And no friends here. I wonder whether Inge and Waltraud miss me. Strange, at Oma's I still had time to play outside. Waltraud and Inge are my best friends. They're in high school already. One more year, then I'll be there, too. One long eternity of a year.

I don't see much of Mutti. She comes home late and tired; so does Grossvater. During dinner we listen to the news on the radio. Hitler has invaded Austria. 'God knows where this will end,' says Grossmutter. 'What next?'

'War is next,' Grossvater says without looking up from his

plate. 'Better put in some more potatoes, there's room behind the bee shack.' He heaps food on my plate. 'Eat, eat! Who knows how long we will have this much? Put something on your ribs for the lean times.'

'I don't want any more.'

'You haven't eaten anything!'

It's the same every night. The radio commentator saves me. He starts talking about the great Führer, the great Germany that's in the making. That makes them even angrier than my not eating.

'Shut that garbage off,' Grossmutter commands.

'Mutter! If someone were to hear you!' Mutti looks frightened.

Right after dinner, Grossvater goes up to bed. I still have homework to do. 'Nights are for sleeping,' he says. Mutti has to argue with him every night before I'm allowed to do my schoolwork. 'Don't stay up so late. The electricity bill is high enough as it is. Good night.' The door slams shut. The way he says good night, he might as well say jump off the roof. Why couldn't they have let me stay where I was? Why did they bring me here? They are obviously no happier having me than I am being here. But I can't say this to Mutti, or anyone else, for that matter. I have no one at all to talk to.

I can listen, but the only place where I hear anything is at Tante Martha's. She is Grossvater's sister and owns a grocery store. Grossmutter is annoyed that I don't come back right away when she sends me there. She expects special treatment from Tante Martha, but it's impossible. The store is always crowded and there's not a chance that all those big women with their enormous handbags will even let me through. They push me around and, if anything, I have to wait longer. Children may as well wait, they have nothing to do anyway. In a way, I don't mind; it allows me to listen, observe how suspiciously they look at each other, how they quarrel, how they complain and gossip about someone's sons – those bums who are so full of their own importance now that they work for the State. 'Work? They haven't done an honest day's work in their lives!' There's always at least one who seems to get a mountain of food. Every bag and package that Tante Martha piles up on the counter is enviously observed by everyone.

There's talk about the latest nuisance, this business of having house wardens, block wardens and so on.

'They have to know where you are in case of fire,' says one woman, whom I call 'Red Hand.' Since I don't know their names, I invent names for them. 'Fire? Don't make me laugh,' says 'Rabbit.' 'They just want to know about every nook and cranny. When they have it all written down, there won't be a place left to hide. Not that we have any reason to hide,' she adds quickly, casting a furtive glance at her audience. 'That superintendent of mine,' she continues. 'Well, I won't say it here. He has been dying to have a good look at my apartment. I've never let him in, but now I have to. Now he is the house warden! Can't fix a leaky faucet, that one. Only thing he can do is look important. You should have seen how he ogled my closet! God knows what he thinks I keep in it. But I know how his wife, that dirty slut, would like to get her filthy paws on my furniture. Those two would surely like to settle themselves in my nest. Can't say I blame them, considering the hole *they* live in.'

I look at her and find it hard to believe that this woman has anything of beauty, anything anyone would envy her for.

Rabbit continues without pause, 'I know all about them, and he knows I know. But not a chance. I won't give him a chance to have us conveniently "disappear"! I "Heil Hitler" him right out of the door. Give him his own medicine. Yes, sir! I love our Führer ... and Heil Hitler to you all!' The last is said almost triumphantly.

There is some uneasy laughter and, to judge by the faces around me, no one is quite sure whether she is joking or really means it.

Rabbit has left with her groceries. Now a quiet, whining voice takes over: 'My husband has just been named house warden. He doesn't like it, but what can he do? He has to report about the people in our house, the space they occupy and everything. But he wouldn't denounce anyone! Not my husband, he wouldn't hurt a fly.'

'Shut up! Why don't you shut up!' says Red Hand. 'No one has accused your husband of anything. Who's talking about *him*?'

It's finally my turn. The talk has turned to children, recipes. . . . At least I'm not missing anything important.

The important news comes out of the radio. Prime Minister Chamberlain, French Premier Daladier and Mussolini have come to Germany, to the Führer's home. On 30 September 1938, they sign a peace agreement in Munich.

'See!' says Mutti at dinner. 'You were wrong, always predicting the worst. There'll be peace after all.'

'Grete, you are stupid!' Grossvater's tone is sharp. 'What do *you* know? Nothing. To believe the hogwash that comes out of that box!' He gestures towards the radio. 'Propaganda, nothing but propaganda! Who knows what the hell is really happening? What deals are being made? There will be war, and the worst is yet to come.'

4

1939· High School

March 1939. German troops have moved into Czechoslovakia, and on the 15th are in Prague. Fanfare and trumpets, the radio blares nothing but marches, interrupted only for special newscasts. There are trumpets in my head, too. These are my last days in grammar school. I am excited. Today Vati comes to school to get the necessary transfer papers from Frau Katscher. I will be going to high school, see Inge and Waltraud again, pass Oma's house every day. I will be able to visit her as often as I want to.

'Why would you want to send her to high school?' Frau Katscher is incredulous. 'Why?' she repeats. 'She is only a worker's daughter!'

'Ilse is at the top of her class. Isn't that so?'

'Yes, but – ' says Frau Katscher.

Vati is adamant, raises his voice. Frau Katscher continues to insist. Her voice is shrill. 'Workers' children should finish grammar school, then go to work. There is no point in giving them a higher education. Why would you want your daughter to learn Latin, English and such things?' she asks.

'So that she can go to the university and continue her studies, of course!'

'Never!' replies Frau Katscher with finality. 'She will never make it. Even if she goes to high school. I am a *teacher*. I *know* – and only over my dead body will you have her transferred.' Her face is red with anger, her bosom heaves.

Vati takes me by the hand. We leave without another word, go to the principal's office. He gives Vati my transfer papers with compliments and good wishes.

Next we go to the Lyceum in Hermsdorf to see Frau Director

Francke, the elderly principal. I answer her questions with growing confidence. I no longer doubt that I will be accepted. Vati sits down to fill out a form. I imagine myself a pupil here, but suddenly Vati puts down his pen, looks at Frau Director Francke and says: 'I can't answer "yes" to this question.'

He hands the form back to her. They look at each other. Silence.

I don't understand. Would not understand even if I read the question: 'Are you, your wife, your parents, her parents, your grandparents, her grandparents, Aryan?'

Director Francke sighs deeply. 'Yes, Herr Koehn, we live in dark times.' Her hands absent-mindedly crush the paper, make a ball out of the form, drop it in the wastebasket. Vati gets up, ready to leave, but they begin to talk. I don't understand. To judge by their faces and voices, it's about politics. Now they are shaking hands; we say good-bye.

'Herr Koehn?' Her voice is almost inaudible. 'I hope it goes without saying that what we have talked about will remain between us.'

'You can rest assured,' Vati replies.

We are almost through the door when she calls after us, 'School starts Monday, eight a.m., Herr Koehn. Ilse will be in Class One C.'

Vati is deep in thought, obviously does not want to be talked to. All I can think is: I'm accepted, I'm accepted.

There should have been a picture of the Führer on the wall. It was the law. In the grammar school there had been one in every room. Here there were none. The only picture in the entrance hall was one of chubby children smiling dumbly as they danced on a very green lawn, the work of Hans Thoma, the painter after whom the school was named.

Frau Beck, my classroom teacher, was tall and thin. A kindly old spinster. What little hair she had was combed severely back and rolled into a tight little knot at the nape of her neck. We called it 'the onion'. She always wore grey, seemed grey herself.

She spoke hesitantly, as if afraid her listeners might take offence at her thin, whining voice.

Small and voluptuous Frau Brand ('*Doctor* Brand, if you please!') also wore grey, as well as a silver maple leaf on her ample bosom. In contrast to Beck, Brand was a forceful person who kept rigorous discipline in her Latin class. The maple leaf would bounce up and down when she became excited. One of her passions was woollen underwear, those long-legged bloomers that she insisted we must wear the moment the temperature dropped below forty degrees Fahrenheit. She was not above lifting our skirts to check on us.

Geography, history and English were taught by Frau Hoffmann – properly Dr Hoffmann, but, unlike Brand, she did not make an issue of her title. Hoffmann looked like a little bird, small, skinny, with straight, black, slightly oily hair. We never saw Hoffmann in anything but brown velvet. Hoffmann smoked. Not in class – that would have been unthinkable. But we knew she did, just as we knew that Brand heartily disapproved of cigarettes and lipstick.

Unlike Frau Katscher, who had started class with a brisk 'Heil Hitler' followed by a prayer for Führer and Fatherland, Beck, Brand and Hoffmann simply said 'Good morning' when they came in. Their lessons were delivered in a monotone that made us keenly aware of the many, many years they had taught the very same things. They refrained from political comments, but allowed themselves an occasional sigh when the subject came up, and a few remarks of annoyance when air-raid drills began to interrupt classes.

Dr Lauenstein was the only male teacher. Young and tall, handsome too, he was quite a contrast to the ladies, who were all in their fifties. He alone wore the Nazi Party button, shouted 'Heil Hitler' when he entered the classroom and spent the next fifteen minutes expounding on the Führer's 'Blood and Soil' philosophy. Old German soil soaked with German blood, as he put it. He was unbearably bombastic when he talked about the superior Aryan race. When he finally turned to Goethe, there was always a sigh of relief. No one, certainly not I, had any idea what he had been talking about. But when he dedicated himself to 'the great Goethe' he held us spellbound, made us see and feel the beauty of Goethe's language. He seemed wonderful then.

In September 1939 Hitler invaded Poland. Britain and France declared war on Germany. We were at war. Vati and even Grossvater had been right.

To aid the newly liberated Germans, schoolchildren were asked to collect clothing and sell candles. Beck handed out the candles without a comment.

Everyone in school talked about the war. Brothers, fathers, uncles were drafted or volunteered for the armed forces. 'We'll show those dirty Poles! They can't do this. Not to us! We'll avenge every atrocity ever committed against a German,' said my classmates.

It was the exact opposite of what I heard at home. At both homes. I had tried to question Grossmutter, only to get her stereotype reply: 'I told you schools teach nothing but nonsense!'

'But it's on the radio too!'

'That's why we always turn it off! Cock-and-bull stories. Now go get me some parsley!'

My family said that Hitler was leading Germany to doom and destruction. Hitler said he was leading us to glory, and my classmates seemed to believe him. They eagerly listened to the radio broadcasts that in my home were shut off. Why did we have to be so different?

I wished there were someone in my class I could talk to. Inge was not the right person. She had told me jubilantly that her father had become a Storm Trooper. I hadn't seen Waltraud, but I knew that her father wore a uniform. It seemed that suddenly everyone in the street was in uniform. Only Vati still wore his old grey loden coat. I decided to try Uschi Bohr, my new friend. We both lived in Luebars and biked to school together. One day, on the way home, I asked her tentatively, 'Isn't it strange that Lauenstein is the only one who says "Heil Hitler"?'

Uschi didn't even look at me. Her strong legs, in often-mended knee stockings that were too short, kept pedalling evenly.

'What's strange about that?' she asked. 'So all the old spinsters say "Good morning!"' She mimicked Beck's meagre, shaky voice. 'They're from yesterday, day before yesterday. That's all. They still long for the good old time. Anything new scares them. That's why they're so boring. Now, Lauenstein — he's exciting!' She turned to look at me, pigtails flying, her cheeks flushed and rosier than usual. She brought her bike close to mine. 'Don't you think he's handsome?'

I nodded, thinking of something else. 'Will you please go by and tell Grossmutter that I'll be late?' I said. 'I want to visit Oma.'

Oma did not explain either. 'Why are we different?' I wanted to know. But she said quite firmly, 'We are not different. Just because our opinion of Hitler is different from most people's does not make us different. Don't confuse a difference of opinion with being different. Don't *you* start on that too. I hear and read enough of these stupidities.'

And I thought stubbornly that I knew we were different, I was different, and I wished Oma would explain.

The doorbell rang. I opened the door and faced old Herr Michaelis, the landlord, wearing a house-warden badge. He glanced over my shoulder into the corridor, obviously trying to get as complete a view as possible. Smiling slyly, he said, 'Is your grandmother home?' His tone implied that he knew she was, and I knew he knew. The house was not large; we could always hear each other's footsteps.

'May I come in?' he asked, all but pushing me aside to enter. 'Ah, Frau Koehn! You don't mind, do you, if I come in for a moment?' He waved a stack of papers at Oma. 'Lovely tea set you have there ... Ah, yes, you see, I have to fill out all these forms and need a lot of information from you. Ah, my God, that at my age I still have to do so much running around. But what can I do? It has to be done, I guess, sooner or later ...

and after all, if, God forbid, we were trapped in a fire, you understand I'd have to know where everyone was.'

Oma opened her mouth for the first time to say coolly, 'You mean you intend to rescue me in case of fire?'

It seemed a ridiculous proposition indeed, looking at Herr Michaelis – old, barely managing to walk, if walking it could be called, breathing hard from the effort of coming up one flight of stairs. But he ignored Oma's remark and tottered into the living room. Uninvited by Oma, he sat down in a chair with a big sigh of relief and proceeded to make himself at home. Pushing the flower vase aside, he spread his papers all over the table. Carefully he licked a pencil. Oma was still standing. Oblivious to this, he began, 'Now let us see' – pause and paper-shuffling – 'Ah, yes, here. How many persons in this household?' Oma did not answer, but he continued. 'Three? No, two, I guess. The girl here' – he gave me a quick look – 'she does not belong, I mean officially, to the household,' he mumbled. 'Lives with her mother, right? Wonder ... should I put that down? Guess not.'

'It is not necessary, Herr Michaelis,' said Oma. 'She is registered with her mother in Luebars.'

Herr Michaelis had trouble controlling his unsteady hands. Carefully he drew the figure two in a box, saying, 'Two persons, then. Two persons in this household. Now, the head of the household would be your son, I suppose. His first name?'

'You know that as well as I do, Herr Michaelis. I have been living in this house for forty years. Longer than you have.' Oma was still standing.

Undismayed, Herr Michaelis printed. *Koehn – Ernst.* 'And your first name?' Oma's answer came clipped: 'Edith, last name Koehn, born Rotenthal.'

Michaelis, occasionally licking his pencil, put it all down. 'Religion?' he wanted to know.

Oma said, 'We are Dissidents or Free-thinkers, as you like. We don't belong to any church. Anyway,' she went on, 'what does my religion have to do with a fire in the house?'

Herr Michaelis did not answer. He bent his head so low that

his forehead touched the pencil. 'How many rooms?' he finally asked, answered himself, and wrote. Now he got up, walked slowly, clumsily towards the bedroom door, opened it and stood staring so hard I half expected the dresser drawers to open by themselves. Oma came up behind him. He turned and headed for the corridor and kitchen.

'This shelf under the ceiling. What do you keep there, Frau Koehn?'

Oma, who was close behind, passed by him, then turned to face him. 'Would you like a ladder to look for yourself?'

He was taken aback. 'Oh, no, no, no, that won't be necessary. You know, of course, that nothing is to be kept in the attics.'

'Herr Mi-cha-e-lis' – Oma's voice was super-polite, cool – 'this is merely a shelf, as you can see, and not an attic. Only my son's violin and my winter draperies are kept there.'

'Ah so, ah so,' he muttered, making first for the kitchen and then going back to the living-room. Oma stood aside to let him pass. He sat down; Oma too sat down, opposite him.

'Your son has not been drafted, has he?' He looked past Oma's right ear, shifted, looked past the left. Herr Michaelis never looked directly at anyone.

'My son is past draft age, Herr Michaelis. Besides, he is needed here.'

'I see.' More careful lettering. 'Where exactly did you say he worked?'

'I didn't.' Oma's voice was cold and cutting. 'I don't know *where* he works, but he is employed by the Berlin Electrical Company, if that's what you mean.'

'Well, but it's strange, isn't it, that you don't know where your son works?' He seemed almost happy to have finally caught Oma at something.

'There is nothing at all strange about it, Herr Michaelis. He works in the field, as they say. He goes wherever there is a problem. He is a specialist on one-hundred-thousand-kilowatt cables. If there's a power failure, he is able to fix it.' Oma sounded proud.

Michaelis looked up, impressed. 'I didn't know that.'

Oma looked as if she was about to say something, but kept quiet. Michaelis gathered up his forms, taking his time. I felt like pummelling him, wanted to push him out and scream, 'Oma! Don't tell this nasty, stupid man anything! Oma!' Instead I was frozen to the spot. Michaelis was still shuffling papers. Finally, unsteadily, he got to his feet and walked to the door. Oma followed slowly. Thud! She closed the door after him. She walked to the window and stood there looking out.

I expected her to say that she'd ask Vati to tell Michaelis to mind his own business. But she was quiet, lost in her own thoughts, and I couldn't think of anything to say.

5

1940 · Hitler Youth and Bombs

'A Hitler Youth girl came today,' said Grossmutter. 'You are on their list and must go to a meeting this afternoon.'

'I don't want to go!'

'You go!' she said categorically.

'Why? Why do I have to?'

'Because I say so. We don't want any trouble.'

'What trouble?'

'Stop asking so many questions. I said you are to go.'

While still in Hermsdorf I had wanted to join the Jungmaedel, as the ten-to-fourteen-year-old girls of the Hitler Youth were called, because of Inge and Waltraud. They had told me how much fun they had, singing and playing all kinds of games. When I mentioned it to Vati, he had looked at me as if I were a ghost, then yelled, 'Join an organization of those pigs?' Then Vati calmed himself and he sat down beside me. 'Listen,' he said, 'it may be true that all they do is sing and play games. But their very songs and games are designed to teach you the Nazi philosophy. And you know that we do not believe in it. Young people are impressionable and the Nazis use their enthusiasm for their own ends. There are things that you are too young to understand. When the time comes, you and I will have a long talk.'

Farmer Neuendorff was ploughing his field as I walked to Luebars for the meeting. The village was seven hundred years old and the Neuendorffs, Ratenows, Quades, the founding families, were still tilling the soil. I knew I wouldn't have anything in common with their daughters.

There were only about nine of them, and the dislike between them and me was mutual and instantaneous. The meeting was short, and at the end the leader said, 'I need someone for an important courier service.' How they all begged. Eighteen hands reached for that letter. I just wanted to stand aside, to get out of there. But no. 'You look the most responsible,' the leader said, handing me the letter. If looks could kill, I'd have been dead.

Grossmutter was furious when I told her. 'How dare they send a little child all the way into town?' I'm not so little, I thought, and now, of course, I wanted to go. 'It will take hours,' she said. 'And, besides, I had counted on you to help me in the garden.' I was not sure whether she was actually worried about me or merely angry that I had to leave and couldn't help her. But when I had changed buses for the third time and was caught in traffic and crowds of rushing people, I began to think she was right. I'd never taken such a long and complicated trip by myself. I was afraid I wouldn't find my way home.

Clutching my directions tightly, I finally found the headquarters of the Hitler Youth. I was directed to an upper floor, Room 17. I knocked and went in.

At first I couldn't see anything. The room was dark and the blinds were down. Slowly my eyes adjusted; I made out a big desk in the middle of the room – nothing else. Because on the desk there sat, or, rather, lay a young man and woman. They must have been very high-ranking Hitler Youth because their uniforms were covered with emblems, medals and ribbons. But in what a state they were! Totally dishevelled. He had lipstick all over his face. Lipstick! The German woman does not smoke, does not drink, does not paint herself! The Führer's motto, even I knew that.

The room was full of smoke. Her skirt was crumpled and up to her hips. I could see her loose garters. Her stockings were hanging around her ankles and she wore only one shoe; the other was on the floor. They both seemed out of breath, but at the sight of me they started laughing hysterically. Shocked, I stood mute, letter in hand. The man, still laughing, took it, signed a receipt. The girl straightened her skirt. Beet red, I fled down the stairs, followed by their laughter.

That was my initiation into the Jungmaedel. Grossmutter bought me the black skirt, the white blouse, the black scarf and the brown leather circle that kept the scarf in place. The symbols of honour. We handed in the scarves and leather rings and had them presented to us at a big ceremony. Raised flag, everyone in line and formation, Hitler Youth band, loyalty oath. They had let me join, but to me it was already all meaningless. A big ballyhoo, a façade behind which I did not want to look. I went to one more meeting and then simply stopped going. No one said anything about it. No one came to get me. Apparently even the Hitler Youth had other things to worry about in 1940.

Germany is at war. The German armies invade Denmark, Norway, Luxembourg, Holland, Belgium and France. Italy becomes our ally. On 20 June France capitulates and signs a peace treaty. We are victorious, invincible. There's a feeling of euphoria everywhere. Everywhere except, of course, in my home. 'Shut off that rubbish, Ilse!' says Grossmutter when the radio blares forth yet another victory. 'They'll victory us right into the grave – mark my words.' But Grossmutter barters her preserves, fruit, eggs for things that come from the invaded countries. A pair of shoes for Mutti from Prague, soap from Belgium, silk from France. There are men from the neighbourhood in all those places, and they send things home, where their wives and mothers trade over the backyard fences. That's also where the women vent their anger against the air-raid drills, the new laws that require a pail of water or sand on every stair landing. Silly nonsense! As if enemy planes could ever get to Berlin, the capital. But then we have a 'real' alarm, and they are a bit upset because the first bombs have fallen.

They fell in Neuendorff's field, about five hundred yards from my grandparents' house. The bomb site was the biggest attraction in Berlin. For about a week the stream of sightseers seemed endless, though there was nothing to see but four big holes. Bomb fragments became the hottest, most sought-after items for children. One of them was worth a whole collection of movie-star or soccer-player pictures. Especially one with a bit of outside paint on it. That rated as high as an autographed picture of submarine hero Guenther Prien.

Grossmutter is in the kitchen when I return from Tante Martha's one day. I can't wait to tell her what I have heard: 'They are going to send all the children away!'

Grossmutter slaps the roll of dough into a ball, flattens it, kneads it, looking at me. She does not have to look at what she's doing. Her hands know. They have kneaded dough for so many loaves of bread, cakes, biscuits, have grabbed the kettle, shuffled the coal underneath it, reached for the potholders, lifted lids, peeled, pared, sifted, stirred uncountable times – so that only an occasional glance is needed.

'Who says?' she wants to know, pressing the dough into a cake form, and wiping her hands clean on her apron.

'Some women at Tante Martha's.'

'Nonsense.' She bends down and puts the cake in the oven.

'But one woman said she knew for sure. Her brother is a high official.'

'Bah! Nothing but rumours.' She looks into the living-room, where the clock is, then at me. 'Anyway, don't worry. You'll stay with us. If I were to believe everything I hear, I'd go crazy. Get me some carrots, I better start the dinner.'

I walk through the garden, look at the sparse green of the berry bushes, see the cracked, rusty pail over the spot where the rhubarb will come out. Notice the neat row of little spinach plants, the crooked, tar-roofed rabbit shed, the uneven cement in the courtyard and the four wooden clogs by the stairs. I see it all as if for the first time. Stay here? In Hermsdorf? Sent away to where? Spring 1941. This August I am going to be twelve years old.

6

1941 · Camp One

In April I was in Czechoslovakia — in Radoczowitz, to be exact. Ilse Koehn, a tiny, unessential part of the Kinderlandverschickung (KLV) or Children's Evacuation. *Germany protects its future, its youth* — that's what our parents had been told so that they would allow us to be evacuated. *The whole school will go!* But out of the five hundred girls at Hans Thoma School, only eighty of us are actually here. All the teachers? We have Beck, Hoffmann and Lenz, the music teacher. *Under the supervision of the teachers, school will continue normally.* Mutti had talked feebly about safety, Vati said that a dark future lay ahead and I would be better off with 'all the others'. Every one of his sentences had either begun or ended with that phrase. I didn't want to go. They said they didn't want me to go, so why did they let me go? Maybe they wanted to be rid of me. No. They love me. I know they love me. But why? I'm crying, and that won't do any good. I look at Beck, who is staring out of the window. 'I will look after your daughters as if they were my own.' That's what she had said to our mothers. Well — I wish I could think of a really mean word for her.

We, the first transport of one thousand Berlin children, allegedly being sent to East Prussia. Another lie. What a to-do there had been at the station. Garlands, banners, Hitler Youth bands. Military, Hitler Youth and Nazi Party dignitaries. Even Baldur von Schirach, the Reich Youth leader, was there, shaking hands along the train. Mine too.

So here I am. Trapped in the wilds of Czechoslovakia. It took us twenty-four miserable hours to get here. The snacks and chocolates given us by our mothers hadn't lasted that long. We are hungry and thirsty. 'The children will be provided for.' If that's their idea of providing . . .

I dip my pen into the inkwell for the umpteenth time. 'Dear Vati and Dear Oma' is all I have on paper so far. That's another thing: I will be the only one who has to write *two* letters when writing home.

The whole, miserable trip comes back to me now. We left Berlin at ten in the morning, but stopped within an hour, rolled on for a bit, were put on another track, moved slowly until nightfall, when the train suddenly picked up speed. At midnight we crossed the border from Germany into Czechoslovakia. By that time everyone was aware that we were headed in the wrong direction. Beck's hair, for the first time, was in a mess as she ran back and forth, trying to find out where we were going. Lenz had lost her smile and Hoffmann looked more frightened than any of us. When we reached Prague in the morning, they got off the train, but told us to stay where we were. They barely made it back in time. Prague. That's where Rita and Hilde came aboard. The two Hitler Youth leaders who were to be in charge. We arrived in Ricany at ten in the morning. Children still on the train had to throw our baggage down to us. Even my new accordion, Vati's gift to console me for the piano lessons I was going to miss. Ricany. There wasn't even a station platform, only a sign and a shack at the edge of the woods. The middle of nowhere. That's where we stood and waited for a whole hour while Rita and Hilde searched for transportation. A nasty mixture of rain and sleet fell and covered the ground. We were wearing light summer coats. It had been warm in Berlin.

They finally returned with an old man dragging a handcart. I feel my face getting hot with rage at the thought of it. My tears fall right on the word 'Vati'. 'The childen can carry their bags. It's only a forty-five-minute walk,' Rita announced as she piled her luggage and Hilde's and the teachers' on to the cart. *Only* forty-five minutes! There wasn't even a road! We stumbled, slithered in single file through primeval woods. No house, not a sign of civilization. I had never seen any place like it. After a while I was last in line, behind all the others. My suitcase was too large, packed with clothes for at least half a year, as we had been told. And I also had the accordion. First I carried one and pushed the other, alternately. Eventually I was kicking both. My new accordion! But I was in a panic. Those ahead of me looked smaller and smaller, finally disappeared. I was alone. Never had I felt so lost, abandoned. Vati and Mutti wouldn't even know where to look for me. They believed I was in East Prussia. It would take them eternities to find out. It would be too late. This thought got me going again. I made it, caught up with the others in Radoczowitz. A few thatched-roof houses and one hotel, that was Radoczowitz. The hotel was to be our camp. It hadn't been planned that way. The owners, an old Czech couple, had to be roused from their sleep. They didn't want to let us stay. They left us standing in the small entrance hall, insisting that they had been told to expect boys, not girls. And certainly not today. Next Sunday.

Rita phoned the Gauleiter, the military governor of the district of Prague, who eventually turned up at noon. A bald, fat man in glittery uniform, he embraced and kissed Rita and Hilde, but ignored Beck and Lenz, who had practically thrown themselves at him. He ordered the Czech couple to let us stay and prepare some food for us. He departed muttering in the general direction of Beck and Lenz, 'Little organizational error. These things happen. Straightened out now.'

It was Rita and Hilde, not the teachers, who assigned us to our rooms. I share mine with Hanni, Ruth and Sigrun. I don't know much about them, but I like them. The room is small. Four bunk beds with rough army blankets, one table, one closet and a washbasin. By the time we got in there and put our bags down, we were too tired and miserable to feel anything. But it's hitting me now that all this really happened, that it's not a nightmare from which I will wake up to friendly surroundings. This is real. As real as the shots we heard last night, and as real as Lenz's voice when she screamed, 'No lights! Please, no lights!' But this morning they are denying that anything happened.

'It was nothing.' Beck looks away from us. I stare at her back and that knot of straggly hair. She does not know much more than we do, that's obvious. As obvious as it is to us that *they*, the Hitler Youth high command, never meant us to go to East Prussia, but had planned all along to send us here to Czechoslovakia, a country that ceased to exist when our troops moved in. Now it's called the Protectorate of Bohemia and Moravia. Few parents would have consented to send their children here, knowing, or at least suspecting, that the local population would be hostile to all Germans, even children.

Heads bend over letters. Except for the scratching of pens, it is totally quiet. Somehow I've put it all on paper. Twice! I'm sure, though, that I have ended my letters in the same way as everyone else: 'Please come and get me! Please come and take me home.'

Beck, pale and tight-lipped, collects the letters. She will mail them for us, she says.

At the dinner table we sit as if struck by lightning. The soup is getting cold. Rita, wielding two fistfuls of letters, is screaming, 'These are no good! How dare you write such hogwash, such nonsense, such . . .' Words seem to fail her and her face is red with anger. 'You will sit down right now and write again. You will write that you have arrived safely in a beautiful resort area and that you are living in a nice hotel. You will only write pleasant things!'

Beck, Hoffmann, Lenz, at the head of the long table next to Hilde and Rita, say nothing, stare vacantly into space, avoiding our eyes.

'There's no reason for you to look so sad!' Rita shouts so that my eardrums hurt. 'Everything is fine. You don't know how good you have it! How dare you worry your parents needlessly! You have exactly one hour to write new letters. I assure you that I will not let *one single line* pass that might upset your parents!' Pause. Silence. Then Rita speaks again in a more normal tone of voice: 'Later we will take a walk. When you hear me whistle, line up in front of the camp. In uniform, of course. What a group!' She shakes her head, looks from one to another. A timid sob breaks the silence. Then another. It's contagious. I'm crying, everyone is, as if the sluices have been opened.

Hilde jumps up, waves her arms frantically. 'Stop it, I say! Stop it! I won't stand for this! You are Hitler Youth. This behaviour is unworthy of our Führer! What is the Führer's motto for his Youth?' She points to someone at the far end of the table. Startled, the girl leaps to her feet, opens her mouth. No sound comes out.

' "Tough as leather, hard as Krupp steel, swift as greyhounds!" ' Hilde shouts impatiently. 'If you're not now, you soon will be, I can guarantee you that. What's needed here is some order! And discipline. You may even come to like it – and me.' Uncertain laughter. 'Now go write your letters.'

I can't imagine ever being able to like her, or anything here. I hate her, hate it here. I want to go home and don't even care whether it's Hermsdorf or Luebars.

May–June 1941. Torn clouds swiftly pass the cold moon. Hanni Knaak snores. It's not bad, just a slight wheezing. In the bunk beneath, Ruth lies all curled up. Ruth Schubert, the wild one, the star athlete. Below me, Sigrun stirs.

'Sigrun? Are you awake? Sigrun?'

No answer. Sigrun Knust, meek, slow-thinking, a follower. We are a good group in Room 18. It took us a while to fully realize that we are trapped here. God, all the silly escape plans we hatched. Two of the older girls actually ran off during the first week. I wonder where they are. Probably they were caught before they even got to Ricany and were sent to a 'special work camp for incorrigible girls'. That must be worse, though it's hard to imagine how. Our motto here, the sentence you hear a hundred times a day: 'One can get used to anything.' Whatever idiocy or chicanery Rita and Hilde cook up, we shrug our shoulders and say, 'One can get used to anything.'

Our room is the envy of the camp. Minimum punishments. Toilet cleaning – brr, who wants to do that? Yes, we got wise to *their* games. I am the decorator and expert bedmaker. Sharp, perfectly square corners (I use a triangle), absolutely no wrinkle. Even Rita's eyes pop. The drawings on the wall are mine, and it was my idea to paint a bedsheet and use it as a tablecloth. We always have fresh flowers. Ten extra points for Room 18. Hanni is in charge of underwear. She alone is able to fold even flannel nightgowns into regulation squares. I shake my head. *They* actually check whether all folded garments are the same height and width – with a ruler! Sigrun cleans. She leaves no speck of dust on the curtain rod, nor even on the baseboard behind the bed. Ruth does the shoes, and the soles are as shiny as the tops. I wouldn't want to do that. But she says she likes it. Even after *their* silly war games, when the shoes are muddy. That ugly, sticky clay mud typical of the area.

One can get used to anything, even to being awakened at one thirty in the morning by *their* whistle. Uniform inspection and silent night march because someone talked or giggled during the newscast. Five minutes after the newscast, Room 18 lines up, not a button loose. *They*'d rip it right off. Four abreast, we march in formation around the village square. *They* don't dare lead us farther, since that first time when we were shot at in the woods. How *they* ran, faster than any of us. Now we are not allowed out of camp at all. We must stay in the courtyard or indoors. Beautiful resort area – what a laugh!

One can get used to anything, even to flinging ourselves to the ground when *they* yell, 'Down!' Doesn't matter if there's a puddle. We remain flat until we hear the command 'Up!' If this isn't insanity, what is? If I were to tell Grossmutter, she'd tap her finger to her forehead: 'Stupid, you know.' Mutti wouldn't believe it even if she saw it. Vati would stop them at once. He'd scare the living daylights out of them. He can shout loud enough to make walls shake, without straining himself. But what's the use? They're not here and I can't even write them about it.

Do they wonder why I constantly ask for money? Money for shoelaces, buttons and thread, money for paper, ink and toothpaste. I have to vary the reasons. Grossmutter is so practical she would send me the actual things rather than the money. And if I wrote them that I spend it all on toothpaste, they'd

49

think I was crazy. But Blendax toothpaste is my own personal triumph over the damn fleas. Just thinking about them makes me scratch again. God! My whole body is covered with bites. I swear, nothing itches as badly as fleabites. One night when I thought I couldn't stand it any longer, I was so desperate that I knocked on Beck's door. Thought she might show some compassion. 'I will look after your daughters as if they were my own.' *Denk'ste, Pustekuchen* – that's what we say when we mean, 'That's what you think.' She shut her door in my face with a not very compassionate, 'What am *I* supposed to do about it?' Looking around for something that would cool my skin, stop the itching, I discovered Blendax toothpaste. I've been covering myself with Blendax every night. I bet the Czech in the small general store on the square doesn't understand this sudden run on toothpaste.

July–August 1941. Night-time is the only quiet time here. I don't mind being awake. Today was house-cleaning day. Everything had to be scrubbed and all mattresses dragged down to the yard to be aired. And it was my idea to ride down on the mattresses instead of carrying them down the steep staircase. Everyone enjoyed it. It was great fun while it lasted. Naturally, Beck, Lenz and Hoffmann picked this day to check on us. For once they weren't 'not feeling well' and staying in their rooms, and had no 'important business in Prague'. Result: we have a week of night marches. So what? One can get used to anything. Besides, I'm lucky. The kids could have blamed me, beaten me up. Others have been beaten by their peers here for less.

Getting used to not having school sounds easy. But it isn't. Even the worst students here now long for classes. *School will continue normally.* Isn't that what they said? No one here is stupid enough to believe what's written on the bulletin board. Geography, German, Music, even Latin and English. It's all listed, in case there's a camp inspection, I suppose. But we haven't had a lesson in anything since I don't know when. Except in music – if you want to call singing schmaltzy folk-songs a music lesson. When Lenz starts on her favourite song, the one about red clouds in the sky and warm wind in the firs, pandemonium breaks loose. We hate that one the most, and mimic Lenz's high-pitched voice, but she always continues unperturbed. Maybe she's deaf. Respect for the teachers? Not us. The one time Beck attempted a German lesson, I drew pictures all around my dictation, but at least I wrote something. Most of the others just ran around, noisily borrowing pencils, erasers and what-all from each other. But now we all wish we had school. That's what teachers are for. Ours don't do anything except go to Prague. We sometimes wonder what kind of 'important business' they have there.

Maybe it's not nice, but I gloated, like everyone else, when they too caught head lice. And it was funny when we all lined up in the yard to have our heads dunked in Cuprex, the remedy they use. Beck, Lenz and Hoffmann, each with a towel over her arm, then the rest of us. Rita and Hilde, with much laughter, did the dunking. Our teachers didn't even smile.

How long have we been here? Eternities. How long will we be here? No one knows. One day runs into the next. It's boring. Hilde and Rita play outside with us when the weather is good. Ball and other games. When it rains, we sit in the large dining-room, sing Hitler Youth songs, play charades. We finished Hitler's book, *Mein Kampf*. Thank God. Rita and Hilde are really pretty nice. At least they are young, both in their early twenties, and they're lively, they laugh. Yes, aside from the night marches and uniform and room inspections, they're all right. They even sat up all night with Ruth when she sprained her ankle. They do their best to relieve the boredom. Still . . .

I imagine that I'm Karlson, the little servant girl who has to take care of the troll Goinguae's house in Ossian Elgstrom's *Die Kleine Magd Karlson*. Karlson is really Lillimor, the troll Goinguae is her father and the big white mountain is his bed. I wish my name was Lillimor and the troll Goinguae was Vati and he'd tell me to bring him fried tyres for breakfast and a red-hot automobile engine for lunch. I'm tempted to switch on the light to look at the pictures in the book. But my roommates would scream. The 'Roosters' have sent me the book for my twelfth birthday. I love it. It makes me both happy and sad and, yes, homesick.

September 1941. The light in the corridor makes the round glass window in the door look like an oversized orange. Sounds of sobbing and sniffling come from every one of the eight hospital beds. I have never been sick, not a single day in my life. Just because that rotten Dr Kuehne thought he saw some red spots on me. There were none! I should know! But what does he care? To him I'm just another number. Impotent and powerless, I want to scream, but we've done that already, to no avail. The door is locked. No one gives a damn.

Hardy did. Hardy, Hardy, Hardy, I still love Hardy. We all do. Everyone loves Hardy. I think back to when he first appeared in camp. Leave it to Ruth to be the first to go to see him when the news spread that we had a camp doctor. One aspirin for her non-existent headache and a scarf. That's what she brought back from the visit. He pretended to pull that magnificent scarf out of her sleeve and then he let her keep it. After that the whole camp lined up in front of his room, with unbelievable excuses. But he took it all in stride. Saw everyone, gave something to everyone. How embarrassed I was when my turn came and he asked, 'What's the matter with you?' Instead of using any of the hundred reasons I had made up, I heard myself saying, 'I just wanted to meet you.' And he laughed — wasn't angry at all and pulled a tiny silver whistle from my ear. I still have it. Hardy cared for every single one of us. At least, he made you believe that he did. I think he really did.

I reach under my pillow. The whistle is still there. Handsome young Hardy and all the tricks he knew. He would grab a pack of playing cards, throw them into the air and when he caught them again they were half the size they had been. The trick we liked best, however, was what he did with his Chinese box. He could open each side, the top and the bottom until we were sure that there wasn't a box at all. I will never forget Hardy, not as long as I live, nor the evening of entertainment by all and for all that he dreamed up.

Hardy made sure that everyone had a part in it. He taught even the dumbest, most untalented girls some little trick or act. He found cloaks for Beck, Lenz and Hoffmann and made them his assistants. What wonderful stage sets we built under his supervision. And costumes, out of nothing! He knew about all these things, and even mascara.

Hardy the doctor had only two remedies. Aspirin for everything from sprained ankles to headaches, and tetanus shots for scraped knees and elbows. The red blotches and feverish heads that many girls complained about, he blamed on female peculiarities. But Hardy had had only two semesters of medicine and was not really a doctor. When he was offered a job in his real profession, as an entertainer, he left. Everyone, even the teachers, cried.

Dr Kuehne, rotten mean Dr Kuehne, came a week later. He went from room to room to introduce himself, and when he finished his inspection, he raced to the phone and ordered seven ambulances. He had to make many calls. Apparently it wasn't easy and we hoped it would prove impossible, but that very afternoon, he shipped sixty-eight of us off to Bulovka Hospital in Prague. He said we had scarlet fever – and only two of us felt even a little bit sick. The rest felt fine. But he had to make himself look important. Ambulances! Off with you to four weeks in quarantine. Suddenly Beck, Lenz and Hoffmann kept a great distance from us. When they waved good-bye, their relief at being rid of us was written all over their faces.

Kuehne had protested vehemently, but he had been unable to keep Rita and Hilde away. They squeezed into the ambulance to say good-bye, cried with us, hugged and even kissed us. I won't forget that either. Since then no one has spoken to us. My stomach growls. We haven't had anything to eat, not since yesterday morning in camp. It will soon be morning again. The 'orange' is turning pale as the room gets brighter. I sit up and find myself looking straight into Ruth's eyes. The first ray of sun stabs the linoleum floor. Wordless, we stare at each other. Then suddenly, like two marionettes on the same string, we turn away, burrow under the covers in a new fit of crying.

Hours pass. I'm sure everyone is awake, but no one moves. Not a word. Around noon a key turns in the door; eight pairs of eyes follow the nurse who rolls in the food cart. Suddenly we all talk at once, bombarding her with questions. She hands out the trays, shakes her head, walks out. The door is locked.

'What is this? A prison? Why the heck don't you say something? Anything? You stupid goat!' It's Ruth's voice screeching. There is no way to vent our anger and frustration. We look at the food. A moment's silence and Hanni says, 'Maybe she's a deaf mute?' Then a scream, and another and another. 'Yeech!' 'Igitt! It's not possible! They can't expect us to eat *this*!' 'Look at it! Pfui — I'd rather starve!' Fat black bugs are crawling around among the peas on my plate. I count eight. Ruth wins — she has fourteen. And the only other thing on the plate is something that looks like mushy bread but turns out to be rock-hard on the inside. We all but throw the plates at the nurse when she comes to collect them. We point at the bugs, she raises her eyebrows, shrugs her shoulders, leaves. The breadlike things we keep to use in a throwing contest.

How many days have passed? Locked up. Prisoners, being punished for what? The scarlet fever that we don't have? These swine won't even allow us to use the bathroom. They make us use pots that are kept under our beds. I hate that. They have taken away our clothes to be disinfected! All we have are these stupid hospital gowns. 'Bulovka is one of the most modern hospitals,' Kuehne had said. But they've put us in the old wing, of course. Aside from our beds and a washbasin, there's nothing in this huge room. We have no books, toys, nothing at all to play with. On the other side of the window is Prague. Yes, we do have a view, a spectacular one, which makes us feel even more imprisoned. To be shut up, to have to look at the beautiful park across from us, the many gilded spires, church steeples, bridges and boats on the Moldau River makes me so mad I could . . . I don't know what. That's just it. Tough luck, Ilse. 'Real life.' Well, it's rotten. Vati and Mutti should have never allowed me to leave.

The highlight of our days? When we spot a couple kissing in the park. I wonder what it feels like not to be at all. Anything must be better than *this*. Yeah, we get three meals a day now. Not good, not bad. No more bugs.

Screaming and begging, we have at least got paper and envelopes from one of the nurses so we can write home. They still don't speak to us. Do they think they can drive us crazy? Actually, they might have succeeded if it hadn't been for Rita and Hilde. They have come to visit us twice, bringing full shopping bags. They can't come in, of course, so they stand outside our window, two floors below, and throw apples and oranges up to us. We can catch them. Luckily, they both throw well. They have also brought mail and parcels from home. We found out about the mail only a few days ago, when they allowed us out to use the bathroom. There was a whole pile of packages in the corridor in front of the doctor's office. When Ruth saw the letters, she just grabbed them and distributed them faster than you could say 'Here!' But the nurses bodily defended the packages, screaming in Czech, and the lady doctor came out and shooed us back inside. She's beautiful and we think she speaks, or at least understands, German. If she does, she kept it to herself. In three weeks she's been in our room twice! She and about a dozen other doctors and nurses, a whole procession, marched in and walked past the beds, and while they talked to each other in Czech, a nurse took our blood pressure. We've given up asking them anything. They just don't answer. We might as well be stones. When the nurse was through, they left. That has been the full extent of our medical care. And they refuse to give us our packages. Ruth – who else? – tried to snitch one. The nurse on duty not only took it away from her, but shoved her. Both screamed at the top of their lungs, the one in Czech, the other in German, until the doctor came. Now they lock the door of our ward again. Shit!

It's all over! We are free! Even the camp, that rotten old miserable camp in Radoczowitz, suddenly looks good. Feels like home. Beck, Lenz and Hoffmann beam, welcome 'their daughters' back. Sigrun, the only one of us to be spared

Bulovka hospital, has done a prize-winning job of decorating Room 18. We talk excitedly for half the night.

'I don't get it,' says Sigrun. 'I mean, why wouldn't they let you have your packages?'

'I could understand it,' Hanni interrupts, 'if they had given the contents to poor Czech children, but to just let everything rot there!'

Sigrun still shakes her head in disbelief as we describe in gory detail how the stacked-up parcels gradually turned into an ant-hill. 'Can't blame the ants – my mother bakes fantastic cakes.'

'You haven't tasted my mother's cherry-almond ring, that's my favourite, and that's what she wrote me she sent,' I say. Thinking of it makes my mouth water. I want to describe it, but Hanni interrupts. We constantly interrupt each other because there's so much to tell. 'Thousands, millions of ants – you wouldn't believe it.'

'At least we got even with them, a bit anyway.' Ruth says not without pride. 'When we left, I just had to kick that pile.' And Hanni continues, 'And then we all did the same, until everything was scattered all over the floor.'

'Didn't they make you pick it up?' Sigrun asks.

'No! We just left. The cars were waiting. But I wouldn't have anyway. I would not have touched those packages,' Ruth says boastingly. 'Let *them* do it. Let them eat cake with ants. May they choke on it.'

28 September 1941. Everything is packed. The camp is being disbanded. No one knows why. Tomorrow we go home. I am going home. To Luebars, I suppose. Yes, I'm happy, but not the way the others are. It would be different if I could go home to Mutti and Vati and *our* house. But I am a little uncertain, a tiny bit afraid of what I will find. I really don't know why.

7

1941-2 Berlin

Mutti! Mutti! Where is Mutti? I'll never find her in this chaos. Maybe she didn't get my letter. Everything happened so fast. We were divided into small groups and each group was sent back to Berlin by a different route. There is no fanfare, no garlands, no Reich Youth leader to welcome us back. Us? I'm the only one left; the three others in my group have just left. I could have gone with them, but I wrote Mutti I would meet her at Gesundbrunnen Station so she would not have to come all the way into town. Even from here it takes an hour to get to Luebars.

How could I have known there would be such crowds? I can see neither platforms nor trains, only people. Pushing, shoving people. Very few civilians. Most wear some kind of uniform and all are carrying luggage, bundles, boxes. Where are they all going? I was lucky even to be able to get off the train here. The crowd pushing to get on was so fierce that for one panicky moment I thought I wouldn't make it.

The charred skeleton of what used to be a big theatre pierces the dark sky. Big, fat clouds roll along. I've found a spot between two signs where I can sit on my suitcase, the accordion cradled in my arms. A small island in this maelstrom. Loudspeakers blare, 'Caution, caution! Express to Stettin on Track Three. Step back, step back!' Something hits me in the back as the crowd surges forward. And then I see her. She sees me too. We push towards each other; I lose sight of her, find her. Her arms are around me and the accordion. We are being kicked, shoved from all sides as we wrestle over who will carry my suitcase. Talk is impossible.

'Local to Oranienburg on Track Four!' Our train. 'Step back, step back!' We are being swept towards it, caught in a stream that is sluiced through the doors. Something pushes against the back of my knees, I can't fall, am held upright by those around me. People are wedged in between the doors. A final push with tremendous force from those still outside, and with a hissing sound the automatic doors close. The train moves. We are aboard. Mutti and I have been separated, can look at each other only when the train sways us all in a certain direction. I still have the accordion, but have no idea where my suitcase is.

Wollankstrasse, Schoenholz, Reinickendorf, Wittenau – the stations go by, the crowd is thinning out. Finally Waidmanns-lust. We get off without difficulty. Together at last.

'Ilse, I'm so sorry, I don't know what happened.'

'It's all right.'

'Oh, Ilse, please forgive me!'

'I'm so glad to be back, Mutti. We are together, that's all that matters.'

Mutti is so nervous. She hugs me, grabs the suitcase, puts it down again, straightens her hair, hugs me again. There are tears in her eyes. 'Ilse, I don't know how it happened! I looked everywhere.'

'I wasn't waiting long, Mutti, really I wasn't. I knew you would come. Everything is fine now.'

'Yes, yes, but . . . I don't know how to tell you . . .'

'Tell me what?' I am suddenly scared.

'About the accordion,' she says and begins to cry. Between sobs, as she nervously fingers her hair and hugs me, it comes out. She has left a new accordion, Vati's welcome-home gift for me, on a train. She has tried to locate it, phoned, run around, but of course it's gone.

'It's all right, Mutti, the one I have is fine.' What else can I say? 'How many basses did it have?'

'Twenty-eight!'

The one I have has only eight. You can't do much with it. Still, 'I probably couldn't play it anyway.' I try to console her.

'Did it have a real accordion case? One that is moulded around the keyboard?'

'Yes, it did,' she answers, more tears flowing.

'Please, Mutti, stop, it doesn't matter,' I say, thinking of the square box mine has. 'Please, Mutti! For the way I play, the one I have is just fine.'

'*You* will tell Vati?'

'Yes, I will. Don't worry about it, please don't.'

Her face lights up. She looks more beautiful than I have ever seen her. Her skin is flawless and as soft as it looks. The most prominent feature in her face is her eyes, large, hazelnut-brown eyes. Vati used to sing about a girl with hazelnut eyes and he'd look at Mutti and you knew he meant her. Mutti has an unusual face, exotic, mysterious. I don't know anyone who even remotely resembles her. Why am I so ugly? I would be happy with half her beauty. The dark-blue railway uniform she wears – I have just noticed it – looks terrific on her. She tells me about it, and while I listen I think how nice it is to just hear her voice and a joy to hear her laugh. Hans Wagner used to say she should have it insured, that hers was the most beautiful laughter in the world.

Mutti is talking animatedly. 'Can you imagine? One day! I had passed everything else. Only one day of oral examination left, and they wouldn't even allow me to take that. I passed everything with "Excellent". One more day and I would have been a master tailor. At least I had the choice of working for the railway or in a munitions factory. It's a law now that every able-bodied person must work. Some women I know were not even asked, just assigned. I don't mind the work at the ticket office, the people are very nice, especially my boss. He allowed me to exchange shifts today so I could meet you. Yes, I really like it, even with the occasional night shift.'

We are home, home in Luebars. Everything looks the same, though a bit smaller. Grossmutter, rotund as ever, with almost no waist, wears the same old, often-patched grey-and-white-striped apron. Her long skirt leaves only her ankles visible above what seemed to be a pair of Grossvater's old shoes. Her face is wrinkled, her grey hair pinned up in the back. She must have been pretty once, but was she ever slender? I can't imagine it.

'I can't stay, you know that,' says Mutti, seeing the coffee table set for three.

'You surely have time for one cup of coffee and a piece of cake!'

'Mother!' Mutti sounds exasperated. 'You know I have to catch the two-forty train, which arrives at three thirty-five, already ten minutes late for Frau Schmid. I must relieve her. She was nice enough to say she would wait. She doesn't *have* to do that, you know!'

Grossmutter shrugs her shoulders and starts cutting the cake while Mutti helps me carry my things upstairs. I did not know that Mutti would have to leave so soon. I am stunned. She has only just come all the way from town. First she had to go to town by bus and train to meet me, then the same trip of over an hour back and now she has to turn around and go right back again. The third time in one day.

'Do you like them?' she breaks into my thoughts. 'I picked them early this morning, something pretty to welcome you.'

A colourful bouquet of calendula, iris, baby's breath, asters and bleeding hearts sits on the table, next to a large bowl of grapes, apples, pears and peaches.

'All from our garden,' says Mutti with pride. 'Just look at those apples! Aren't they beautiful? I even took one from the 'Grand Duke,' Grossvater's favourite tree. I hope he won't mind. He counts them, you know.'

Besides the flowers and fruits there are chocolates and a brand-new box of water colours, a drawing-pad and books.

'Yes, it's all for you,' says Mutti. 'I missed you so and, besides, you were not here on your birthday.'

Everything is arranged so prettily, as only Mutti can do it. I don't even want to pick anything up for fear of ruining the arrangement; besides, more important than gifts, I have my mother back. I hug her, kiss her, never want to let her go again.

And then we both catch sight of the alarm clock at the same moment. Time!

Grossmutter, muttering to herself, wraps up a quarter of the cake for Mutti to take along. Mutti, here a minute ago, is gone.

'But you are much too big,' Grossmutter protests as I firmly snuggle into her ample lap, but I stay there while munching on the cake and long afterwards. I have to tell her all the things about camp I meant Mutti to hear. At last, freeing herself from me, she says, 'So, just as I thought. This whole evacuation thing came to exactly nothing. You would have been better off here, and God knows I could have used you. The garden, the house, the animals – it's all getting too much for me. I better make dinner now. You can take care of the dishes and then unpack your things. The laundry basket's in the cellar.'

She is moving about downstairs. I hear the veranda door, then, 'Here, chicky, chicky' as she feeds the chickens. I feel forlorn. Uncertain where to put what, I sit down on the bed, look at my presents on the table and start to cry. Why am I so unhappy? I'm home. No, it's not because of the lost new accordion. I hadn't expected it, hadn't even had time to look forward to it.

Suddenly I know. It's because there's no space for me here. Whatever small vacuum I may have left has been filled, much as dough slowly swells into the gap left by a spoon. My space here has been filled. Mutti has her job. I can tell she likes it. Grossmutter, Grossvater – everybody is occupied. They don't need me!

I hear his heavy steps downstairs, then his rough, loud voice. 'Did Ilse come?'

'Yes, she's here,' Grossmutter answers, then calls, 'Ilse!'

We eat dinner almost in silence. He is tired, has a headache, goes to bed. ' 'Night,' he says and 'Don't forget to pull down the blinds before you switch on any lights. Better yet, don't use any lights – you don't need lights to undress. We never had any when *I* was young.'

The only other two sentences he has said to me were familiar: 'Pale and skinny as ever. Didn't they give you anything to eat?' and 'It is good to have you back. Grossmutter needs help.'

'Hope they won't come tonight,' Grossmutter says, then adds, 'The aeroplanes, I mean. Hope we won't have an air-raid. And remember about the lights.'

I had forgotten about air-raids, and fear grips me as I feel my way upstairs, undress in darkness, slide into what used to be Vati's bed. Tick-tack, tick-tack. The luminous numbers of the alarm clock stare at me. A beam of moonlight squeezes through a narrow space between blind and window frame, sits on one of my crumpled socks like a bright little bulb. I shut my eyes, pull the cover over my head and roll myself into a tight, lonely ball.

'Child, child,' Oma says over and over again, hugging me. 'Child! And to think that we have not seen the end yet of all this madness!'

Oma's face looks drawn and it seems to me that worries, rather than anything physical, have bent her proud figure. She bustles back and forth across the room, picks up this and that, asks questions but barely listens to my answers. Finally she turns around to face me. She smiles, but it looks as if it has taken an enormous effort to settle her face into that expression.

Once more we sit at her sewing-table by the window, eat biscuits and drink ersatz coffee. The talk is disjointed because we look out of the window more than at each other. We are waiting for Vati. Vati knew I was coming, but . . .

'During the last air-raid they hit one of the main cables,' Oma says. 'He has been gone now for – ' she looks at the clock, counts – 'almost twenty-four hours. Ach, he has to work so much these days, he's hardly home, and when he is he's too tired to do anything but sleep. He should be here soon.'

And then I see him, his loden coat open, the shabby old briefcase under his arm. He crosses the street. I'm downstairs and in his arms in a flash.

Brimming with stories, I hardly touch my lunch. All the happenings, the pent-up emotions of the last half-year. But I don't get to talk, not with all the details as I used to. Question follows question, leaving time only for yes or no. You can't tell things that way. Vati, still swallowing a last bite, gets up and lies down. I know he is tired. Still I'm disappointed. I have to get back to Luebars, every minute is precious, an hour an eternity.

'Only for an hour, little rabbit. No, I have decided it's time for you to learn to defend yourself, develop some quills. That's why I'm going to call you Hedgehog from now on. I sent you one, a little stuffed one to the hospital, you know.'

'No, I don't know. I remember that you wrote about a surprise, but, you see, we never got the packages, they . . .'

Vati is wrapped up in his blanket. Only his closed eyes and nose are showing. There's one little grunt. He's fast asleep. Oma whispers, 'Yes, a Steiff hedgehog, very fluffy. We'll get you another,' and she settles into her chair with a book.

I try to read, but can't concentrate. Instead I watch the hands on the clock. They don't seem to move. I wonder what has changed. Even here I don't feel at home any more. No space, no time for Ilse. This very minute I wish I were with Ruth and Sigrun and Hanni. If I could talk to them on the phone at least. But only very rich people and stores have telephones.

I wake Vati up, on the dot. In good spirits, he pummels me and we chase each other around the table, like old times. That's Vati as I remember him, or almost. And then we talk about the Czechs and the parcels, and he says that 'we Germans' have done terrible things in Poland and Czechoslovakia. He tells me about the small Czech village of Lidice, where the Führer's Aryan supermen, the proud troops, put every man, woman and child against a wall and shot them in cold blood while they burned down the houses.

'Ernst!' Oma interrupts. 'Is this necessary?'

'Yes, it is,' Vati retorts angrily. 'It is indeed. I want Ilse to know why all Germans, anything German, will soon be something hateful and despicable to the rest of the world. Thanks to big Adolf and his henchmen.'

I nod. Oma, I can tell, wants to change the subject. She says, 'Waldmanns have arrived — safely!'

I don't know who Waldmanns are or where they have arrived. Vati stares into space, says nothing for the longest time, then, 'They are lucky — or are they? To begin again where you are no one, where nobody knows you. I don't know. For us the question of immigration doesn't even exist. They have connections, money, education. We live from hand to mouth, wouldn't even have the train fare to . . . Where would we go? We don't know anyone in a foreign country. I speak only German . . .'

Oma fiddles with her hands, looks down. I can't see her face. Vati goes on, almost defiantly, 'Even if by some miracle we could get to, say, Paris, then what? How could I get work? Where would we live? On what?' There's another long pause before he says, 'No! Our only chance for survival is here on our home ground. It's known territory at least.'

I'm not sure I know what he is talking about. Go to foreign countries? It's bad enough that I don't have a family like others, no home where I feel at home. Vati makes it sound as if I can't even count on Oma's place being safe and here. I want to embrace him, be physically close to him, but he and even Oma look distant, seem far away.

'Oh, Ernst!' Oma sighs again. 'I only hope your boss, the Little One, can keep you here.'

'Mother! We both know things will get worse. I'm already on his research team. Important work. The air-raids will continue, most likely get more severe. They need us to keep the electricity flowing. The Little One will do all he can, that's all I can ask, and more than most would do.' Vati's face brightens, he turns to me. 'And for the rest, little Hedgehog, we count on a little bit of luck, right? What happens without it?'

Dutifully I supply the end of that silly Berlin saying, 'Without it, you even lose water from a basket.'

'Come on, let's get you home.'

We bike to Luebars and say good-bye at the corner.

'See you next Saturday,' he says. 'But don't be too disappointed if I'm not there. I never know in advance, and when the Tommies hit one of our major lines, we have to go out, whether it's morning or night, Saturday or Sunday. You know that!'

Yes, I know, and I try to look understanding despite the fury inside me. Rage I can not easily define, except that it must be against those workshifts that won't even allow time for parents to be with their daughter after half a year of separation.

I am sitting on my bike, half leaning against a tree. Uschi Bohr is late, as usual. She wasn't home when I went to her house to find out what was happening in school. Her mother told me that half of the school was now being used as barracks by the army, therefore classes are held in shifts. Ours is the late shift this week.

'Sorry, I know I'm late.' Uschi, red-cheeked, pigtails flying, still wears the mended knee stockings, which now barely cover her calves.

We pedal furiously, no time to talk. There it is, good old Hans Thoma School. There are soldiers in battledress and bunk beds in the hallways. What confusion! I hurry after Uschi, glad that she knows where to go. She motions me to sit next to her.

'I've managed to keep a seat for you.' Her face is one huge smile. 'It wasn't easy.'

I smile back, trying to put all my emotions into one big grin. I feel like hugging her, and close to tears from gratitude. Uschi has saved me a seat. There is a space for me after all. How can I tell her what this means to me? Maybe she senses it, for she says, 'Glad you're back' as Beck enters.

'Good morning.'

'It's eleven thirty on my watch,' says Ruth behind me. We kick each other under the desk, and both look for Sigrun and Hanni. Sigrun, in the front row (typical), waves at us.

Beck looks around. 'I'm happy to see we are all here again.'

Hanni enters, grins, waves, takes her time finding a seat and sitting down.

'As I said,' says Beck, 'I'm happy all of us are here.'

'You should be,' I whisper in Uschi's direction.

'Quiet, please!' says Beck. 'We will continue today with punctuation and the proper use of the comma.'

Nods from those who have remained at home, whispers, remarks and giggles from the evacuees.

'I said *quiet!* . . . The comma! When do we use the comma?' Hands go up, Uschi's too.

'Have you had that?' I ask. She nods. Questions from Beck, answers . . . not from the evacuees. I raise my hand.

'Yes?'

'Miss Beck, we have not had punctuation!' Echoes from the other evacuees. What will Beck say?

'Well . . .' A moment of uncertainty, then: 'But you should know. Punctuation is most important. You should know.'

'Yeah, like how? Listening to the holy ghost?' Ruth giggles.

'Quiet,' Beck orders, 'or I will expel you from class.'

'Wouldn't make the least bit of difference, would it?' Ruth persists.

Beck either has not heard or decides not to pay attention. She goes on about commas, hyphens, quotation marks.

Can it be? I wonder. Can she go on like this, pretending nothing has happened? Radoczowitz and Bulovka Hospital already forgotten? Half a year lost?

The bell rings. Beck, sensing we will besiege her, is at the door in a few quick steps. 'Your history class is at the other end of the building. Quick, move on or you'll be late!'

But we, the evacuees, cluster around her, wedge her against the door frame, bombard her with questions.

'Read up on it, read up on it. You really should know these things by now!'

Pushing and shoving at the door.

'Move on! Move on!'

As I pass her, she gives me a little shove, then a soulful look and a pat on the head. That patronizing pat is enough to send me on my way. I am prepared for velvet-clad Hoffmann now.

But Hoffmann has decided to go back, repeat. 'Open your

books to . . . the Thirty Years' War. No, wait, not yet. When did it start?'

A moan from the class. Someone shouts, 'But we've had that already!'

Hoffmann, without lifting her eyes, continues. 'Then we will go over it again. It started how?'

Nothing has changed, except that recess is more fun since we can jump around on the bunk beds. Simultaneously with the bells, sirens go off. We all run in different directions, bump into each other, scream, laugh. Teachers shout, wave their arms. Soldiers put on their helmets and eventually succeed in lining us up and herding us into the cellar. By the time the last group pushes in, the All Clear is sounding. Naturally we take our time getting back upstairs. No one is in a hurry. There's only one class left anyway. Music.

'You want to bet Lenz will sing?' Ruth asks.

Hanni, Sigrun and I just roll our eyes.

'Is she still with her red clouds?' Uschi wants to know and 'Room 18' breaks up laughing.

Lenz, skinny Lenz with her saccharin smile, her long skirt and white socks in walking shoes, addresses us: 'My children!'

'I'm not your child,' I mutter.

'You don't think *I* am?' from Ruth.

'Isn't it nice that we are all home again?' says Lenz.

Eyebrows go up. Someone in the back squeaks, 'Red clouds in the sky,' giving it an extra, crazy tremolo. Laughter. Is Lenz offended?

'That's just what I thought we should start with,' she says, the smile never leaving her face.

Room 18 exchanges knowing glances, but Lenz is already at the piano, striking the first chord, and without looking up, she says. 'You know this is my favourite song.'

'Unfortunately,' from the back. Someone says in mock enthusiasm, 'Yes, yes, Frau Lenz, please let's sing your song.' 'Let's hear about the red clouds.' 'Yeah, and about the warm wind, please, Frau Lenz!'

Lenz turns on the piano stool, graces us with an apologetic

smile. Her high-pitched voice rises as she lifts her face heaven-
ward:

> 'Red clouds in the sky,
> Warm wind in the firs and
> I rejoice, re-joi-i-i-ice
> In the beauty of the morning.'

The class joins her, singing in every conceivable key. We
sound like a bunch of piglets being speared. We stop and let
her sing the last refrain alone.

> 'I rejoice, rejoi-i-i-i-ice
> In the beauty of the morning.'

There is nothing to rejoice about during the cold and dark
winter days of 1941. War and fighting everywhere. Japan, after
attacking American ships in Pearl Harbor, is at war with the
United States. Four days after that attack, on 11 December,
Hitler too declares war on America. Hitler is a megalomaniac,
says Grossmutter. Grossvater nods when she says that. Le
Havre, Scapa Flow, Spitzbergen, Tobruk, Crete, Ploesti.
German troops are everywhere, from France to Norway, North
Africa to Greece and Russia. The Dnieper, the Ukraine, the
Crimea. Russian names dominate the news as the Germans
drive into this immense country, all the way to the gates of
Moscow. Russia is cold, the Russian winter an enemy as bitter
as the Russian army. It's cold here too. All the lakes, even the
rivers are frozen. I want Uschi to go skating with me. Next
week we'll be on the afternoon shift again, then it will be too
dark. That shift has been shortened to three classes, but when
we get out of school it's pitch black outside and we are scared
riding home through the deserted streets. The few streetlamps
have blue lights because of the air-raids; they might as well not
be on, for the little light they give.

'I wish I could go, I love skating,' says Uschi, 'but you
know ...'

I know. Her mother is always sick, and Uschi has to baby-sit for her two small sisters, stand in line in the shops and even cook. 'Maybe if I talk to your mother . . .?'

Uschi's mother is in the kitchen. That tenement kitchen is so tiny there's barely room for us to stand. Everything seems grey, pinched, including Frau Bohr, who sits on the one chair. She looks as if she's going to cry any moment. But then she always looks that way.

'I don't feel very well,' she sighs. 'Uschi knows that, don't you?'

Uschi looks at her mother with pity. 'I know, Mum,' she says softly, 'but I thought maybe today . . . for just an hour . . .'

Her mother looks down, doesn't say anything. I plead with her. She remains silent. It's hard to imagine how someone so small can get up so heavily. As if she hasn't heard a single word, she moves to the stove, picks up a spoon as if it were a lead weight, uses it to fish around in a pot that's simmering on a low fire.

'Here, look!' On the spoon is a perfectly clean white marrow bone. 'Three soups I've made with this!' The way she says it makes me feel it is my fault. 'I hear there's been a meat delivery today. *I* can't stand in line!'

The last words sound like a wail. Her voice trails off. Dropping spoon and bone on the table, she sits down again, covers her face with her hands.

'I'll go, Mum.' Uschi pats her mother's shoulder and gives me an apologetic look that says, You see! What can I do? And repeats, 'It's all right, Mum. I'll go.'

'The ration cards are on the counter, don't forget to take newspapers to wrap the meat in,' says her mother with some strength in her voice. 'Not even wrapping paper. They have nothing! Nothing!'

She's still not looking up. I'm not sure she even knows I'm here. Is she crying? I say a quick good-bye, tiptoe out. 'Same time tomorrow?'

Uschi whispers back, 'Same time tomorrow.'

Left, right, left, right, my feet pedal automatically. Grossmutter would have let me go. I think of the bone again. Grossmutter keeps bones, but they never look like that, and anyway Grossvater grinds them up in a contraption he built especially for this purpose. The bone meal is fed to the chickens. My grandparents use everything, have everything. 'We have because we work' echoes in my mind. Grossvater is even tanning rabbit hides now. They are all over the cellar, stretched out on boards. And Vati and Oma? They never talk about food. Oma's soups, I have noticed, have got very thin, tasty but thin – and I'd rather not think about it any more. Oh, I've had all kinds of schemes, like taking food from here and bringing it to Oma, but I've abandoned them all. For one thing, Grossmutter is keenly aware of every morsel. For another, I'd feel ashamed – I wouldn't know how to give Oma something like that. It would be like saying, 'I don't like what you give me' or 'Your food isn't good enough for me.' I can't do that to Oma.

My thoughts return to Uschi; it makes me feel a little better, for Uschi eats my sandwiches and I hers. Mine are twice the size of everyone else's. Grossmutter's big slices of home-made bread and what she piles on them. There must be a quarter of a pound of butter on each one. She insists that I take two. I don't like butter, and I don't like the fat sausage on it. I like margarine and the funny, thinly spread fillings Uschi's mother uses. It had taken a while to convince Uschi that she was doing me a favour. I get scolded if I bring my school lunch back.

At home I hear voices and laughter. Grossmutter has her coffee circle today. That means the living-room will be warm. It is. Eight women, all from neighbouring houses, are assembled. There are mountains of cake on the table and the smell of fresh, real coffee pervades the house. They mend, knit, embroider while they talk and urge me to taste the cakes. I know the cakes are good. These women like to eat. They look it, too. I don't think there's one that weighs less than 160 pounds. They bake fabulous concoctions, try to outdo each other on the rare occasions when they get together. Slowly, deliberately, I work my way through the samples while the talk continues around me. Someone has found a factory where they give you sugar in return for sugar beets. Grossmutter immediately plans to take a load of her beets there. 'Ilse and I will have a full handcart.'

I'm leaning against the tile oven. We don't have central heating, only one of these ovens in every room. My grandparents are very stingy with the coal, though; this is the only one in use. I'm rarely warm enough. Mutti's and my room is not heated. Since we only sleep there, heating it would be like throwing coal out of the window, according to Grossvater. I sometimes try to sneak an extra coal or two into this stove, but Grossmutter always knows. She is teasing me now.

'Ilse thinks the oven will fall if she doesn't lean against it. I should think it's warm enough here.' Everyone agrees. 'Thin blood. That's what it is.'

I'm glad when Trude Kort interrupts her and they start talking about young Schmid, who has been collecting again for the Nazi Party. Knitting needles click, purl two, drop one. It turns out they all gave him something. No one wants any trouble. And they talk about the 'Nazi goat' who spies on everyone, and about the bunkers they are building up on Platanenstrasse. Air-raid shelters for civilians, mothers with small children, old people.

'It will be a while before they're finished, and . . . can they build them large enough for all of us? I wonder.'

'All of *us*? My dear Luise, what makes you think they're for *us*? They'll be large enough for the Party brass, that's all.'

'Sure,' says Grossmutter, pouring more coffee, 'these heroes are the first ones to have their trousers full.'

Laughter, during which I sneak out, tiptoe down the cellar stairs, for I just remembered something. I sing softly, 'We collect bones, scrap metal, rags, False teeth and paper bags . . .' as I make my way though the dim cellar. It's the official collection song. Quick, Ilse, I tell myself, don't bother with the light. I can't reach the light-bulb without a box; there's no switch, and I always forget later that the bulb is hot and burn myself. Above me, I can hear their voices. My apples for your preserves, cigarettes for coffee, coffee for butter, the usual bartering. Luise's voice is high above the others: 'I don't know, Alma, how you manage everything! I wish I had your strength. But I'm not well. Not well at all.' And Grossmutter's reply, 'I have no time to feel unwell.'

'We collect bones, scrap metal, rags, False teeth and paper bags . . .' The old jute sack I'm stuffing with rags is almost full when I hear Grossmutter's steps. The light goes on. I'm trapped.

'What are you doing there?' She yanks the sack away. 'What do you think you're doing?' And now she takes everything out again, examining each item with great care. 'Grossvater's jacket!' she exclaims. 'My aprons! And this! That's the cloth for the rabbit hutches when it gets too cold! What were you going to do with this?'

'I . . . I . . .'

'Out with it!' She is really angry now. 'What did you plan to do?'

'Tomorrow the collection is due in school. It's the last day, and – '

'These! You were going to take Grossvater's good garden trousers to school as rags?' She is fuming. 'Are you out of your head? And my aprons! I really believe you would have turned these in as *rags*! I caught you just in time. Heavens! To think that if I hadn't come down . . . What do you have to say for yourself?' Carefully she hangs the 'good garden trousers' back up on the nail, smoothes the patched aprons, which still look like rags to me. 'Don't you ever, ever do this again. Do you hear me?'

'But,' I finally manage to say, 'what am I going to take to school? I'm way behind in my quota, and my grades depend on it. Whom can I ask? The people I know have children themselves. They are not going to give me anything.'

'I'll find you something,' she says, sounding partially pacified. 'But don't take it upon yourself again to "find" things. Promise.'

I promise, but cannot help thinking how easy it is for her. There are enough things in attic, cellar, shed, all through the house, to fill my quota for years. Unlike Oma's neat apartment, where there isn't a single thing that could qualify as junk. Oma, trying to help me, keeps her daily paper, nicely folded, for me. She has already given me most of her pewter for scrap metal, and would even have parted with the fish dish, which happens to be my favourite pudding mould. The very idea made me both furious and sad. What a difference between my two grandmothers and their life styles.

'I almost forgot what I came down here for,' Grossmutter says, interrupting my thoughts as she gathers a few jars filled with cherry preserves. 'Trude is going to give us half a pound of butter for these so we can bake some Christmas cookies. Cookies for you, you ungrateful brat.'

All is well again, I know, because 'ungrateful brat' is one of her terms of endearment.

'Shoo!' she says, as if I were one of her chickens. 'Out, now. Out of here with you. 'I'll find you something later.'

The blare of sirens pierces the night. The long, even tone of an air-raid warning. I grope in the dark for my clothes, find the bag filled with documents and important things that goes down to the cellar with us. I feel my way along the wall in the hallway. No sound in my grandparents' bedroom. 'Grossmutter?' No answer. 'Grossmutter? Grossvater?' The noise of an aeroplane in the distance. I am frightened, begin to shout, 'Grossmutter! Grossvater!'

'Quiet! Let us sleep.' That's his grumbling voice. Someone turns in bed, then her voice: 'Go back to bed, it's only a warning.'

'I'm scared.'

'If you're scared, go to the cellar.' He sounds angry. 'Go down, for heaven's sake, but let us sleep. I have to get up in a couple of hours.'

I don't want to sit alone in that ugly cellar. Undecided what to do, I stay where I am, rooted in darkness, listening for every noise. Mutti is on the night shift again. Vati? When the All Clear comes, I sheepishly, quietly, steal back to my room and crawl into bed, wishing I at least had Peter, the teddy bear. I am sorry that I left him with Oma.

Spring 1942. The pile of earth next to the huge hole that Grossvater has dug is now a mountain. No wonder, since the hole is six feet deep and ten feet square. Wooden boards and beams are lying all over the garden. There's frantic activity. Our *Splittergraben* or underground bomb shelter is being built. Everyone is required to have one, and anyone without a cellar has to build a shelter as protection against bomb and grenade fragments. Our cellar is officially fit for twenty-five people, but Grossvater and Grossmutter have nevertheless decided to build a shelter as well.

The neighbours have followed the progress of the digging with great interest and discussed the matter at length. Their opinions ranged from 'Sure a shelter is better. Who wants to be buried under their own home?' to 'What does it matter where you are? If it's meant to hit you, it will.'

My grandparents reasoned that if the house burns, God forbid, it's good to have another shelter. And if it falls down from a bomb blast, the shelter should be far enough away so the house can't fall on it. They have measured the distance carefully, found just the right spot close enough to run to.

'That's what we've been thinking, anyway,' says Grossmutter, 'but who knows what will happen?'

She and Mutti have prepared great amounts of food, even one of our chickens and a rabbit. 'We have to feed those men,' said Grossvater. 'Part of the reason they're coming to help is that they know there's always good food in this house.'

The shelter, that little underground room, is almost ready. The men have just put in aluminium pipes, one for fresh air low down, and the one on top for used air. Now they are installing hinges on the door. The soil has been raked back across the top, and Grossmutter has already planted potatoes there.

'Catch two flies with one swat,' she explains to the crowd of spectators, neighbours who have come to take a look at the finished product. 'It camouflages the hill here, and we'll have something to eat besides. That's if we survive, ha, ha. Anyway, if it hits us, we'll at least be buried in our own ground.' As she cuts an eye section from the next potato, she laughs. The people standing around only manage crooked smiles. No one seems to think it's funny.

'But where do *you* go?' I demand of Vati, feeling guilty because I've never really thought about it. The house in Hermsdorf doesn't have a cellar, only the above-ground cubicle that Oma calls the coal cellar.

'Don't worry, Hedgehog,' says Vati after a moment's pause. 'We'll take care of ourselves, won't we, Oma?' Oma nods. 'And you just promise us to do the same. Keep your eyes and ears open. Be alert!'

While I wonder how alertness can help against bombs, Oma says, 'Yes, child. Be alert. Look around and don't panic, whatever happens.' Then she adds thoughtfully, 'I'm an old woman. It doesn't matter. But come have a look.' She obviously wants to change the subject. 'Have you seen the new radio Vati bought?'

A fine radio it is. The most modern and beautiful one I have ever seen.

'That's something, isn't it?' asks Vati with pride.

'Do you mean you can get all those stations?'

Vati laughs. 'You don't even know where most of these are on the map, I bet.' And then he explains, shows me the magic green eye that tells you whether you're really tuned in to a station. Suddenly, looking at the clock, 'It's almost time!' Oma gives him one of those 'Watch it, the child' looks. 'It's all right, Mother,' he assures her, 'Ilse is smart. She'll know when to keep her mouth shut.'

'The best thing,' adds Oma, 'is not to tell anyone about the radio. Don't mention it at all.'

First there are squeaks and beeps, then *boom-boom-boom*, pause, then the same drum sequence again, the last *boom* a particularly low, long-lasting one. Then a voice: 'London calling! London calling! This is Lindley Frazer for the BBC.' It is exciting. I hold my breath. Vati whispers unnecessarily, 'Hear that?' as the announcer continues in German.

'Low! Turn it low, lower, Ernst!' Oma sounds alarmed. She hands Vati her blanket. 'Here, better take this!'

The blanket covers us and the radio like a tent as we listen to a broadcast unlike any I have ever heard. This man, in faraway London, talks about German troops retreating from Moscow, Leningrad, of General Rommel being beaten in North Africa. He names specific army units, commanders, places that our 'victorious armies' have abandoned. I wonder how he knows, and suddenly I remember the posters that are all over Berlin. They show a black-cloaked, mean-faced man under the headline: 'Psst! The enemy listens!' I understand better now what I hear constantly on the German radio stations: 'Those who listen to foreign broadcasts and talk about our troop movements, are *the enemy within.*' In my mind I hear the hysterical voice of Propaganda Minister Goebbels: 'These despicable creatures are knifing the German people in the back. They must be erased from the face of the earth. Death by hanging is too good for them.' And now I'm more scared than Oma and wish Vati would turn the set lower still, but I am also fascinated and want to hear more.

'The tide is turning. Finally, my girl, the tide is turning,' Vati says. To my great relief, he switches to a station with music. 'Be on your guard, observant, alert. You know I would like to protect you, look after you, but I can't. You'll have to do it yourself. We'll survive. Right, Oma?'

Oma nods, but says nothing.

Vati goes on, 'We'll get through, no matter what lies ahead. We'll live to see Germany free again.'

When I say good-bye, Oma pleads, 'Please remember. Don't tell anyone about the radio, Ilse!'

I know it's serious when she calls me Ilse. I want her to know that I understand, but I don't know how. And on the way home I worry more, am more scared of everything. Afraid of bombs, afraid for Oma, who has no place to go during air-raids, for Vati, who may be out on the street, or that someone will find out he's listening to the enemy. Worry about Mutti, always away, and the cellar, where I don't feel safe at all. The shelter ... Forget it, I tell myself. If a bomb drops on that, good night! There is no safe place any more for anyone.

Sure enough, as if to confirm all my gloomy thoughts, we have an air-raid that night. At least Mutti is home. Stiff with fear, Mutti and I sit in the cellar, holding hands. But Grossmutter? She drops a basket of beans into her lap, saying what we used to say in camp: 'You can get used to anything. Who would have thought that we'd spend half of our nights in the cellar? But here we are.'

Outside, a noisy chorus of anti-aircraft guns. Grossmutter, undisturbed, shells beans. Grossvater is walking around upstairs. His steps quicken. He comes running down as we hear planes overhead.

'It looks as if they're headed directly towards us,' he says breathlessly.

Grossmutter, as if nothing is happening, says evenly, 'Here, why don't you give me a hand instead of cowering there? Might as well do something useful since we're awake anyhow.'

Outside, the world seems to fall apart. The noise is deafening. The house, even the cellar floor, shakes. Plaster is trickling from the ceiling. Mutti's voice, compressed by fear, is barely audible: 'I don't understand how anyone can do anything *now*!'

'Grossmutter is right!' yells Grossvater over the din. 'You two should do something too, instead of stealing from the Lord the very time of day – ha, ha, I mean night.' He laughs, a bit shakily, considering this a joke.

But Mutti and I clutch hands. I know she feels as I do, that if we make so much as the slightest move the next bomb will hit us. Grossvater leans against the door. Grossmutter throws empty shells into the basket, the beans into a bowl. They leave us alone.

Eventually the noise lets up and Grossvater goes on his inspection tour. 'You can see from the attic window,' he says, coming back. 'Looks like Siemensstadt or thereabouts. Whatever they hit, it's burning. The whole sky is red! Well, I guess that's all for tonight.'

Grossmutter gathers the beans in her apron and makes for the stairs.

'You can't go up yet!' we say, horrified. 'The All-Clear hasn't sounded. There might still be a plane around!'

'Then I'll come down again.'

Grossvater closes windows. We always open them so they won't be blown out. Glass is hard to come by. He locks the doors. Only Mutti and I remain in the cellar until the sirens scream ALL CLEAR. By that time the others have been in bed for at least half an hour.

There's seldom a night without an air-raid any more. Everyone is tired. For the first hour or two in school we talk of nothing but where the bombs fell last night, what they hit. The teachers join in. A hundred people killed in that one shelter? No, two hundred, five hundred. How do you know?

'My uncle lives there. But he never goes to the cellar,' Ruth brags. 'You know what happened? The whole wall of his house was blown off, just like that.'

'Was he hurt?'

'No, not at all! He had a glass on his night table and it was not broken. He said that he heard this fantastic noise, and when he stuck his head out of the covers, he looked into the sky. The wall was just not there any more.'

'Can you imagine! The whole neighbourhood watching you in bed?'

The class giggles, even Beck, who makes a feeble attempt to start her lesson, but is instantly interrupted by still another story of miraculous survival. These stories get crazier every day, and the best ones are told over and over again. Beck's next try at teaching is also thwarted. We insist that she discuss the 'all-expenses-paid vacation-harvest camps' with us. The information about how German youth can help in the war effort by helping to bring in the harvest has been posted today. Grossmutter will say there's plenty to harvest right here, but there's a camp on the Baltic island of Ruegen, and I know that's where I want to go. Not alone, of course. Uschi has to come too. I begin my campaign that very minute, talk of white dunes, beautiful beaches, the ocean. I get us worked up to a point where we are convinced that we absolutely must go. We already see ourselves swimming and collecting shells. Neither of us thinks about the harvest part of the deal. Anyway, what can there be to harvest? Ruegen is a sandy island, everyone knows that! We'll have four weeks of swimming, sun and beaches. That's what we think!

8

1942 · Camp Two

Americans are fighting the Japanese on the island of Guadal-
canal. In Africa, General Rommel, the 'Desert Fox', is mounting
a great offensive drive towards El Alamein. In Russia, the
German front stretches from Tallin in the north to Sevastopol
in the south, a distance of over two thousand miles. '*Das kann
nicht gut gehen*' (That can't turn out well), Berliners whisper,
shaking their heads. As if to emphasize the point, the
Tommies, as we call the British, drop a nightly load of bombs
on us. I've heard that they dropped 175,000 incendiary bombs
on Hamburg. And this in less than an hour.

We've got away, Uschi and I. There are no air-raids on the
island of Ruegen, not even alarms. Are we happy? *Scheisse*!
'Shit' is our favourite word, the worst we know, and the one
that best expresses our feelings. Do you prefer living in fear of
bombs to being in prison? But even that is a moot question. We
are here and have been told that no one, emphasis on *no one*,
leaves the camp. That's that. The camp is surrounded by a
barbed-wire fence ten feet high and it's miles from any beach.
We don't even get an ocean breeze, because the stench from
the potato shed overpowers everything. We work two-hour
shifts, but some can't even stand that. They just carried the
third girl away. I wish I could faint.

The potatoes, last year's, are piled sky-high, all the way up
to the stilt-supported roof, against a thirty-foot wooden wall.
This is what they call the potato shed. The potatoes are rotting
in the heat. Our job is to sort out the good ones and take off
the shoots. We work with our bare fingers. Most of the potatoes are beyond recall, a rotten, stinking mess that has to be
carried away in pails and dumped into holes that the other

shift digs. Harvesting, my foot! But then, this is punishment. The hundred girls from our barracks are being punished because someone moved during flag-raising. A week of potato-shed detail for one little movement.

The barracks surround a barren square with the tall, lonely flagpole in the centre. Every morning at six-fifteen, one thousand uniformed children march out of these barracks in perfect formation and form another square around the pole. Hands outstretched in the Nazi salute, we have to stand immobile while the Hitler Youth band plays, the swastika is raised, and the daily motto read and repeated by all of us. On command we turn and march back. 'No one moves, no one talks during all this,' Hanka, the woman commandant, told us the first day. 'I run this camp with an iron hand. There'll be discipline here.' There is. We might as well be in prison.

I am grateful for Uschi's unfailing good humour. I can't quite understand why she isn't mad at me for getting her here.

'There's one good thing about this,' she says. 'At least we can talk here in the shed. The fat pigs keep their distance, afraid the very stench could dirty their spic-and-span uniforms.'

The fat pigs are Eva and Anita, our counsellors, who all but burst out of their uniforms. No wonder they are so fat, since they stuff themselves with enormous amounts of buttered rolls, ham, eggs, meat and cake — all this in full view of a hundred desperately hungry girls. They gorge themselves on all those wonderful things, while we get one slice, one thin slice, of bread with jam for breakfast. Watery soup with another slice of bread for lunch. Mushy old potatoes with limp cabbage and a meatball for dinner. They always have dessert; we never do. They talk and talk, but we are not allowed to utter a single word. We must sit there, hands on the empty table, and wait until they have finished. *Scheisse!* All is *Scheisse* here. The toilets and showers are army-type and unpartitioned. The dormitories, two of them with fifty beds in each, contain nothing else, not even a chair. And they have no doors. Eva and Anita, standing in the open doorways, command us to go to bed. And a command is the last thing we hear at night. 'Eyes closed! Everyone face the door!' We do. Who wants to stand barefoot on cold cement for an hour? Uschi and I have already experienced twelve hours of this punishment for nothing worse than a giggle or a whisper.

We work in the surrounding fields eight hours a day – that is, when we're not on potato-shed duty. We march there in formation, come to a military stop in front of the toolshed, get baskets and pails and fan out to dig turnips or pick berries. Eva and Anita choose one of the few trees and park themselves in the shade while we work in the hot sun. When they feel the need to stretch their legs, I suppose, they whistle. This is the signal for us to stand at attention while they come around inspecting each one, looking for clues to whether we have eaten any of the currants or gooseberries. Those who eat are 'saboteurs of the German people'.

'LEFT-two-three-four, LEFT-two-three-four. Don't drag your feet!' It's easy for Anita to be fresh and perky. The troop marching behind her is anything but. We wear our oldest dresses and we are bone-weary and hot from weeding for four hours in the blazing sun. Talking is, of course, against regulations, but when Eva and Anita are out of earshot, it's possible, as long as you keep your face forward and talk out of the side of your mouth.

'Did you hear?' asks Uschi. 'That was my stomach growling. It's been doing it all morning.'

'I thought it was mine.'

'Hunh-unh. I'm positive it was mine. I'm even looking forward to that bowl of water they call soup here.'

'I'm so hungry I could eat a horse.'

'Stop telling me about all these delicacies. I can't bear it. Say, do you think we'll ever be able to walk normally again – stroll, for instance?'

'I don't think so, because I even goose-step when I go to the loo.'

'I know. I do too. Isn't it funny?' Uschi grins. 'And to think that I can thank *you* for all of this!' Our eyes move, meet. 'Oh, don't be mad,' she says. 'I didn't mean it that way. I would have come here even without you. I need a change of scenery. Don't worry. It's only another two and a half weeks.'

'Only!' And I groan involuntarily. Images of beaches flash through my mind. My stupid illusions and my stupidity, I think. I knew all about camps – sure, Ilse the know-it-all. *Scheisse, Scheisse, Scheisse.*

Scheisse, Scheisse, Scheisse. Luncheon rest period. I am lying in bed, eyes closed, facing the door. I seem unable to think of anything but that one word. Slowly I work my hand backward, wiggle my fingers in the hope that Uschi, behind me, will see and understand the gesture. Just 'Hi.' Instead, Eva's voice thunders through the room, bounces back from the walls. '*You!*' We all open your eyes, but no one moves. '*You two!* Uschi and Ilse! This is your rest period!! It means you're supposed to rest – lie still! One hour standing outside! Time you learned your lesson!'

We get up, stand against the wall in the hallway, facing each other, expressionless. 'Look at the two of you!' Anita screams. 'Slumped over like old bags. You are Hitler Youth, stand at attention, for God's sake!' They disappear into their room, slam the door, open it again.

'And no grimacing either!' says Eva. 'Maybe it's time we gave these two a good talking to?'

Anita nods. 'Yes, I think you're right. Come in here. Come *in*!' she yells, since we hesitate. They push us inside, where we stand awkwardly in our nightgowns and bare feet. They sit down.

Eva suddenly has a cigarette in her hand, lights it. Eva, the Super Hitler Youth, with a cigarette! Anita too is smoking. She leans back on her bed and smiles. 'Oh, sit down, for God's sake, and don't look so stupid. You are the only bright ones here in this whole bunch of dumb-bells. You know that and we know it too. Christ, what a bunch of idiots they've sent us this year. Unbelievable!'

She pushes a chair towards me, Eva one towards Uschi. We sit, barely perch on the edge of our chairs, not knowing what to expect next. Anita whispers, 'You are the only two in our dorm with brains. You know that, don't you?'

We nod. Uschi and I agree that it's true, but at this moment I am sure we look very stupid indeed.

'We need you, you see,' Anita says urgently. I don't see, don't understand, but keep my mouth shut. 'We need someone to take over for us tomorrow. You two will run the show. We'll announce it tonight. We'll give you our whistles, and that's really all you need. Hanka will be away tomorrow, she'll take the early train tonight ... won't even be here for flag-raising. Eva and I will also leave tonight – on different business.' They exchange a conspiratorial glance. 'Well, we'll tell you more later. You'll stay up late so we can go over your duties and then we, the four of us, will take a walk.' Another glance between them and a kind of smirk. 'Meantime, since you are now almost leaders, you should have some privileges. That's for you.' Anita points to the table and two bowls of pudding and two slices of cake. We've long been devouring the food with our eyes, need no second offer. It's all gone before you could say 'please'. And they keep talking, but I don't understand ... my head swims. I'm still in a fog when they shoo us out because rest period is over.

All afternoon my mind is a blur; I leave the weeds and rip out the salad plants, then try to put them back without anyone noticing. What's it all about? What does it mean? 'Don't breathe a word to anyone!' Why not, if they're going to announce officially that we are leaders for the day? What did they say about the fence? And Hanka coming back late, and be careful not to be seen, not to get caught or we'll all end up in the camp jail? Why? What are they up to? What kind of business?

Eva makes her speech after dinner. First she talks a lot about Hitler Youth, quotes the standard Führer mottoes: 'It's not shameful to fall, only to stay down,' and 'Tough as leather, hard as Krupp steel, swift as greyhounds.' And, without batting an eyelash, even the one I had secretly been waiting for: 'The German woman doesn't drink, doesn't smoke, doesn't paint herself.' Courteous and honest, valiant and clean are the Hitler Youth?

Inside my head, a little voice says, '*Scheisse*!' I hear only fragments of the rest of her speech. 'Only those who have learned to obey' will later be able to command. I have heard it all – even I could give that kind of talk. 'Leadership qualities' and – ah, she's coming to the point – 'We have two young leaders in our group here . . . blah, blah, blah . . .'

Finally, while everyone applauds, Uschi and I are asked to stand up. Eva and Anita ceremoniously take off the symbols of their rank, the metal whistles on red-and-white cords, and put them around our necks. No one protests when we stay up while the others are sent to bed.

'Eyes closed. Everyone face the door!' We hear it, but don't have to do it. Uschi and I look at each other, but we dare not speak. We are waiting in Eva's and Anita's room, apprehensive. What will the instructions be?

'I'm sure you both know what to do!' They speak simultaneously, laugh and close the door. 'You'll march our barracks to flag-raising,' Eva says, while Anita lights a cigarette, 'Ilse in front, Uschi in back. Breakfast, out to the field, the usual. What else is there to say?'

'Better let them go over it step by step,' Anita interrupts between puffs. 'Ilse! You first.'

We do, but I notice that they are not really listening. They are combing their hair, applying lipstick with great care. Lipstick!

Uschi is describing how we will return the tools, when Anita suddenly says, 'Ready?' and Eva replies, 'Ready! Come on, young leaders. Now comes the fun. Let's go. And remember, no noise! We have to be very careful.'

'You have the flashlight?'

'Yes, yes. Come on, let's go.'

The night air is cool and the stars clear and beautiful. I'm scared. We slink through the shadows behind the barracks, crawl through bushes.

'Damn! I think I tore my new blouse,' whispers Eva.

'Never mind. No one can see in the darkness.'

'But what about tomorrow?'

'You'll take it off anyway.' Giggles.

Suddenly we are at the fence. Eva, blowing her cigarette breath into my face, whispers, 'This is where we'll be coming back tomorrow. Now listen carefully. If Hanka should come back earlier, one of you will have to come here and flash the light three times.' She hands me the flashlight. 'Got it? Only if she comes back early. And make sure nobody sees you! We don't expect it, but – well, you know what to do. Good-bye. And remember, don't say anything to anybody.'

'But where will you be? Where are you going?' I stammer, feeling stupid for being so afraid.

'Never mind. Very urgent business.' They both giggle as they climb over the fence, which at this spot has already been bent practically to the ground. 'Get back and don't let anyone see you.'

We slink back the way we came. Somewhere in the distance a boat motor is being started. Men's and women's voices mix with its putt-putt, then slowly fade away. 'That must be them,' I say to Uschi, and we both freeze in our tracks as the Hitler Youth sentry in front of our barrack coughs.

Once we are safely inside, we talk. 'Where do you think they went?'

'It sounded like one of the boats from the air base across the bay.'

'Of course! That's it!' I almost scream out this discovery. 'Of course. They have a date with some air-force boys.' I feel both better and worse, now that I understand. Better because I at least know why I have to keep my mouth shut, and worse because I am afraid of a whole day ahead of us and what might happen. What if someone asks? I'm a poor liar. What will we say?

But the morning goes well, and the youth in charge of the fields sends us to pick berries without asking about *them*. When we return, he doesn't count the baskets, which is just as well, since you don't bring back so many when you both eat and pick. We try to spread Eva's and Anita's food portions around, but it's impossible. By general consensus, we get all the meat, and only the meat. Mashed potatoes and dessert are spooned out to everyone. It amounts to less than half a bite. Rest period is not as quiet as usual, because we forget to give the right commands. As the afternoon progresses, Uschi and I get increasingly nervous. Everything that even vaguely resembles a train whistle or the clickety-clack of wheels has us looking at each other with an unspoken question: 'Is Hanka coming back early?'

When Eva and Anita return, we heave a sigh of relief. We stay up late with them in their room, devouring the mountain of cold cuts and plum cake they put before us. But their flushed, happy faces make me envious. I wish *we* would have a free day. One free day of fun.

Anita must have guessed my thought. She startles me with, 'Soon we will take you to a beach for a day. Very soon. But tomorrow morning, first thing, we'll march to the infirmary. You'll all have your teeth checked.'

My rotten luck. Tomorrow is my birthday. But no one knows it. Not even Uschi.

'Crowning glory! Hurrah! They even make us march to the infirmary. It's a wonder we didn't have to put on uniforms. Where is their sense of order and discipline today?' Uschi says mockingly.

I am so glum I don't answer her, only nod. This is my thirteenth birthday. What a way to start it. The sky is cloudless and blue. A perfect day for the beach! But here we are, lined up to have our teech checked. Mine feel all right. I hope nothing is wrong.

A fierce-looking elderly man, white coat over his uniform, appears. 'Let's start with the smallest one,' he says, pointing to me. I turn, hoping it's someone else. 'I mean you!'

I follow him inside, sit down in the dental chair, scared of all the shiny instruments. But he leaves me with, 'I think I'll turn you over to my nephew.'

The nephew comes in and I like him instantly. He is very

young, can't be more than twenty years old, smiles broadly and doesn't even wear a white coat. It can't be too bad, I think, willingly opening my mouth. And he tells me funny jokes. I have a hard time keeping my mouth open because I have to laugh. I laugh and don't pay any attention to what he is doing. Laugh until I hear an awful crack that seems to split my head. More cracks, head and eardrums splitting, as my mouth fills with pieces of tooth. Teeth? And then I become aware that he's standing in front of me with a baffled look on his face and a pair of bloody pliers in his hand. Jumping out of the chair with a scream, I collide with a nurse. Both of them press me back into the chair and hold me while the pliers are applied once more. Then I'm free and I race out of the door, blood running down my dress, my favourite dress, and tears streaming down my face.

Everyone outside shrinks away at the sight of me. I run, run, run to our barracks and fling myself on my bed. I cry and cry and cry. Arms over my head, I lie there until the others come back. Remain during lunch and rest period. I am still in the same position when they all leave for afternoon work. Everyone leaves me alone. And I don't move until shortly before dinner, when, knowing they'll all be back soon, I finally pull myself together. I write two frantic letters, one to Vati, the other to Mutti. I go to the bathroom, look in the mirror. That's enough to give me another crying spell, but I wash myself and my dress and know that four of my perfectly good molars have been broken off right at the gum line. Our only chance to get out of here is the letters, now hidden under the mattress. How can I mail them?

Beach day. Today is beach day. I carry the letters hidden in my underpants. Uschi and I have plotted for days what to do when we see a mailbox. She will pretend to stumble and lean on the mailbox to steady herself. Hiding behind her, I can lift my dress, pull out the letters and drop them in while everyone will think I am holding her.

We see it at the same moment and lag behind, which is relatively easy because for once we are not marching in formation. Everything works according to plan. By the time Anita reaches us, looking suspiciously from us to the mailbox and back, the letters are safely inside.

We are enjoying ourselves today, I more than anyone. We climb over the dunes, jump, swim far out into the ocean, roll around in the soft white sand. One happy day. I almost forget my tongue. It's raw from constantly scraping over the jagged remnants of my teeth. What a wonderful day, and the letters are mailed. I am convinced that it can be only a matter of days before Vati or Mutti will come to take us away from here. I know that Uschi isn't hopeful – she thinks her parents won't believe what I wrote and will want her to have the rest of what they think is a vacation. They have even less money than my parents, and spent all they could scrape together to buy her a bathing suit, the suit she wears for the first time today. But I know my parents will manage somehow. I've written that they've got to think up an 'emergency'. The only way we can be released is an emergency.

Days pass. I have calculated every possibility – how long the mail may take, how long it could take to get proof of an emergency, how long to get here. I am beginning to wonder. Maybe the mail burned up in an air-raid? What then?

We are on our way to the fields when I see one lonely figure coming across the barren square. 'My mother!' I shout and run as I have never run before. So does Uschi. We both reach her at the same time. As my mother would tell it for years to come: Suddenly, before she knew what was happening, two girls were clinging to her as if for dear life. My mother, white with fatigue, had left right after work and travelled all through the night. On arrival, the camp sentries had shown her into Hanka's office, where she had shown Hanka the notarized doctor's certificates. One claimed that Grossmutter had broken a leg and needed me at home immediately so we could continue with our war effort, i.e., raising vegetables and poultry. The other document certified the critical illness of Uschi's mother. The daughter Ursula, it said, must assume the role of woman of the house instantly.

'Luckily,' says Mutti, 'we know Dr Wegner. He is such a nice old man. Still, I doubt that even he would have done it if I had not been able to give him a pound of sugar and a pound of butter. He looks so thin. I guess no one is looking after him.' She is feeling sorry for Dr Wegner, I know. That's just like Mutti, I think.

Hanka had been suspicious. Two sudden emergencies? Involving two girls who are friends? She had engaged my tired, gentle mother in a screaming and shouting match, from which Mutti emerged triumphant with our release papers. Mutti shudders as she describes Hanka. 'But I would never have left without you two. When it comes to my child,' she says proudly, 'even I can become a lioness.'

We have barely time to catch the next train back. Finally we sit huddled, one on either side of her. We are crying, all three of us, crying with relief and happiness. Uschi is possibly even more grateful to my mother than I am. Mutti says she had a tough time convincing Uschi's parents. but she had managed that too. Snuggled close, like two chicks under the wings of their mother hen, we fall asleep exhausted.

9

1942 · Berlin

September–October. German troops have reached the River Volga and raised the Nazi flag on Elborus, the highest peak of the Caucasus Mountains. Bitter house-to-house fighting is reported from Stalingrad.

'Wait till winter!' Grossmutter glumly interrupts the victorious radio announcements. 'Hitler is going to bite out his teeth on the Russian winter. Mark my words.'

'Don't say things like that.' Mutti, as usual, is frightened when Grossmutter makes such a remark.

'I say what I think,' Grossmutter replies. 'You're much too scared for your own good. What's the use? What comes comes.'

Grossvater, already in bed, shouts from the bedroom, 'Quiet! Let me get some sleep! And you better go to bed, too!'

It's still dark at four-thirty in the morning. It seems that I've just closed my eyes, but Grossvater is already stompnig through the house, shouting for us to get up. And this is Saturday, Mutti's first day off for a long time. Almost all the men where she works have been drafted, and she's been on many, many shifts. But obediently we get up. He wouldn't let us sleep anyway. When we come down to the kitchen, he has gone and Grossmutter is ready to leave. She wears heavy wool stockings, an old pair of Grossvater's shoes, her patched jute apron over a long skirt and a kerchief. She's the picture of a stout, poor peasant.

'You can't go like *that*!' Mutti says, shocked. 'Your stockings have holes and they don't even match!'

'Who cares?' Grossmutter shrugs. 'The mosquitoes and

berries won't mind. Would you rather see me in silk stockings and high heels?'

'But – ' Mutti begins meekly.

'Come on, come on!' Grossmutter urges, picking up two pails. 'Grossvater's already way ahead . . . and don't make such a face. You'll soon be glad that we have when others don't. It's going to get worse, and God help those without then. We will have. I will see to it!'

We trot after her into the early dawn. Grossvater, only a dark speck on the road, disappears into Luebars village. It will take us two hours to catch up with him. By that time we will have reached the dense woods in the distance, where we will gather mushrooms and wild raspberries. It's going to be a long day. There will be hours spent among thorny berry bushes buzzing with mosquitoes, and then the long way home carrying the heavy pails. When we get home, Grossvater won't shout for us to go to bed. We'll spend most of the night cleaning the berries, cooking them, boiling them down to jam and pouring it into the waiting glasses. Long rows of glasses that I have washed and set on damp towels so they won't break. After the glasses have been steamed tight, they'll be stored in the cellar, the jam preserved for years to come.

The day and night work out just that way. The only thing I haven't figured on are two alarms, during which Mutti and I cower in the cellar while my grandparents go right on working.

This morning there was a soldier in battle dress with Beck when she entered our class. He told us, as if we didn't know, that the south of Berlin had been badly hit last night. He ordered us to go home, put on our Hitler Youth uniforms and report immediately to the places he read from a list, to help with relief work. I am to go to Lilienthal School in Lichterfelde. I'll not be with Uschi, unfortunately, but with a new girl.

'Complete idiocy!' says Grossmutter. 'They're crazy to ask children to do that kind of work!'

'But, Grossmutter,' I reply with indignation, 'we'll only be making sandwiches and taking care of little kids whose houses have been bombed out. And I'm not a child any more.'

'Yes, you are!' She shakes her head. 'And I shouldn't let you go. All the way to Lichterfelde! It will take you two hours to get there!' Grumbling, she makes sandwiches for me to take along and gives me money for the train.

Looking back, I see her standing in the open door, still shaking her head and saying, 'I shouldn't let you go. I really shouldn't.'

So far our part of town, the northern suburbs, has remained almost untouched, and I'm shocked at what I see as I walk from Lichterfelde Station to Lilienthal School. Whole blocks are burned out; everything around me is in ruins. The school has become a temporary shelter for the homeless. Long lines of people are trying to get in. Their faces are haggard, distraught, and they clutch their few remaining belongings or sit on them.

The Red Cross is there, and army trucks are bringing huge containers of soup. They can't get through, and neither can I, because the crowd is jamming the doors. I finally find a Hitler Youth leader and report for duty, and she leads me through a back door into a huge kitchen. About twenty women are preparing sandwiches around a table. I am told to help. Someone steps out and I take her place. Slice after slice of bread to be buttered and passed on. Butter one, pass it on. I don't know whether I've been here for hours or days. Pick up another, butter it, pass it on. New mountains of bread and butter are constantly brought in. There is no time to look up, no time to think. Quicker, faster, butter it, pass it on. Suddenly, 'Here, you! We need someone at the soup!' and I stand behind a table ladling out soup, seeing nothing but outstretched hands with empty bowls or cups. Soup, more soup, one container replaces another, but the line of people has no end. I'm pushed aside, someone takes my place. Back to the kitchen, back to buttering sandwiches. I don't see faces, don't know what time of day or night it is. I'm oblivious to everything but the slices of bread that appear in front of me. I butter them mechanically, shove them to the next pair of hands.

The sirens! Alarm! The lights go off. Pandemonium and

shouting. 'Cover! Everyone take cover! Into the cellar!' Flash-lights point into the shoving, yelling, screaming mass of humanity that stampedes in one direction. Individual voices rise above the others: 'Paul! Paul! Where are you?' 'Help! Help! I'm being trampled to death!' Screams, children wailing and then the noise of falling bombs drowns out everything. The walls shake, and shrieks pierce my eardrums as the frenzied mass pushes in complete darkness towards the cellar. I don't know where I am, don't know where I'm being pushed to. Suddenly I find myself in the cellar. Hundreds of others are already there, and more and more are coming, demanding to be let in. Frightened eyes turn to the ceiling. Will it hold? I think I'm being kept upright by those around me, for I can't feel the ground with my feet. The realization that I don't know anyone here hits me. For the first time in hours I think of my parents and of how worried they must be. But Vati doesn't even know I'm here. Mutti is at work, may have stayed there tonight again . . . so this is the end. Alone. Alone in a mass grave. Suddenly there's movement in the crowd. All Clear. The raid is over, and we have survived. Someone hands me a stack of blankets before I'm even aware that I'm out of the cellar. No time left for thinking, as those newly made homeless come staggering in. This neighbourhood has been hit again. I help set up cots, pour coffee, carry blankets, make sandwiches, try to locate lost children. I have lost all sense of time when someone grabs my arm and yanks me away from the table. It's a young man in Hitler Youth uniform. He speaks sternly, angrily: 'Haven't you been here since yesterday?'

'I . . . I think so,' I stammer, and then he wants to know where I came from, why I'm here, etc. It's like an interrogation. I wonder what I've done wrong.

Suddenly he smiles. 'Do you know that you've been here for twenty-six hours? That's insanity! You are to go home immediately. That's an order! Children should not even be allowed here.'

'But I'm almost fourteen!' I say. Maybe he thinks I am much younger. 'I am almost fourteen years old.'

'Old indeed!' he says, shaking his head. 'Go home. Promise me you'll go home. Right now.' He gives me a friendly little pat on the head.

Dazed and tired, I ride the train away from the smouldering ruins, away from last night's horror, away from the screaming, pushing, frightened people, from the unending lines of out-stretched hands. Hands reaching for coffee, soup, sandwiches, blankets and coffee, coffee, coffee. It all blurs in my mind as I blink at the familiar and intact houses of Luebars. Sun shines on the last pompoms and asters in the front gardens. No sign of war. Then I'm home, safe in Mutti's arms, and the last twenty-eight hours become unreal.

October 1942. The war in Africa is not going well. Hitler has told Rommel to 'fight to victory or death'. Victory or death, what kind of order is that? I am standing in line at Kulewski's bakery. The line moves slowly. The woman behind me knits a sock for her son in Stalingrad. 'It's begun to snow there,' she says, 'I'd better finish these fast and send them. God knows how long the mails will take ... and these damn Russian winters! Victory or death.' She mumbles to herself and keeps knitting while her feet move automatically as the line advances. Among the eighty or so people waiting here there are few young women. Most are children or old people. One very old man, he must be eighty or over, leans heavily on a cane. Everyone looks grey, weary. We are all resigned to standing here for some time. Three or four women seem to be squatting strangely. They have brought folding chairs, but these become visible only when the line moves. Then hands reach under broad behinds, drag the chairs a yard forward, and the women sink back, hiding the chairs again. The one in front of me reads, doesn't look up. The one who knits uses her needles to scratch her head occasionally and mumbles something about her son. Now she makes sideways swimming motions, trying to disentangle herself from the wool. What with the knitting, the needles and the two shopping bags on her arm, it is no easy task. A neighbour helps her, and as the line shuffles another yard forward, a hole is left for the two to step back into when their battle with the wool is won.

Talk is scarce: last night's raid, the expected sugar delivery at the grocery. Yawns and exclamations. 'I'm so tired. Wish they'd let us sleep one night. Just one night. But no. Alarms every damned night.' All the usual topics, including children – how they are getting more nervous every day from lack of sleep, and how good it will be for everyone to have them all away from here. One less thing to worry about. These statements produce nothing more than nods, more yawns and an occasional 'Ach.' It has all been talked over, discussed from every possible angle, and everyone is so used to the idea by now that there is nothing more to be said till it actually happens, till the rumour becomes reality.

A few days later the evacuation of all Berlin schools, teaching staffs and pupils is announced and made compulsory. No one is surprised. Now everyone knows what's what and preparations can begin. Some try to send their children to friends or relatives in rural areas, but few succeed. The red tape involved is almost insurmountable, and the final obstacles are the friends and relatives themselves. These are no times to take on additional responsibilities. Who needs another mouth to feed? And who knows for how long?

Departure date for Hans Thoma School is 21 October, destination Harrachsdorf, a tiny village on the Czech side of the Riesengebirge. A popular ski and resort area, we are told. 'How long will we be there?' 'Till final victory, of course,' runs the standard joke. We've been told to pack for at least a year and to bring linens, comforters, towels, warm clothing. Grossmutter knits me a sweater after unravelling one of hers, and Mutti takes a day off to search for a pair of ordinary shoes for me. We have a special coupon entitling me to one pair of light street shoes with rubber soles. That's what it says. But every store we go to has either no shoes at all or not my size. What good are the coupons? We ride from one end of town to the other and finally find a pair. It's the same with everything else. You can't even get an eraser any more, and I mean one made of artificial rubber. The real ones? I don't even remember those. Unbeknownst to Grossvater, one of his old jackets is made into one for me. Everything, including flatware, is eventually crammed into two suitcases. I am packed.

'You should have gone to a dentist. Oh, Ilse,' says Mutti, 'why didn't I make you go? What will happen to your teeth?'

'There'll probably be a dentist in camp,' says Grossmutter.

Mutti has asked me often to make an appointment, but I didn't do it, what with alarms every night and going tired to school — that is, when I went there instead of waiting in line somewhere. And, last but not least, I had not been eager to sit in a dentist's chair again.

'They don't hurt, Mutti. Really they don't. Grossmutter is right I'm sure there'll be a dentist in camp.' Actually, from what I know about camps, there will not be one. And that's just fine with me.

Vati and Oma, when I say good-bye, don't even ask about my teeth. They seem distant — we don't talk to each other as we used to. Vati is called to work an extra shift. We have only fifteen minutes together. What is there to say? Keep a stiff upper lip, be alert, take care. The same things he always says. Oma, when I embrace her, is so fragile she seems nothing but skin and bones. It scares me. Vati too is thin. He's always been slender, but now he's skinny and grey, haggard and tired-looking. He walks me down to the garden gate. 'Little hedgehog, take care of yourself. One other thing — Oma may not be with us much longer. If you find a little cross on the bottom of one of my letters, you will know that she's gone.'

10

1942-4 · Camp Three

All the Berlin schools are being evacuated. All except two. These two, rumour has it, are being kept open for the children of Nazi Party brass, though officially they are supposed to be for hardship cases. I don't know of a single one. Uschi's parents tried in vain, then at the last minute switched her to another school in the mistaken belief that this one would stay. Now she's already in East Prussia. I miss her.

The train winds through the mountains and our noses are pressed against the windows. Never before have I seen such tall pines. We will get off in Polaun, the railway station closest to Harrachsdorf. We, the Hans Thoma School: 176 girls and five teachers. They are Drs Lauenstein, Hoffmann, Pfaffenberger and Lenz and Beck. Dr Pfaffenberger, the mathematics teacher, has only recently come to our school after being bombed out in Lichterfelde. Frau Director Francke and Dr Brand, being past retirement age, have stayed behind.

Two horse-drawn carriages from the hotels meet us at the station. The station itself is only a small wooden shack, almost invisible under the tall trees. The lady teachers and the younger girls and baggage will ride to Harrachsdorf. Lauerstein will walk with the older ones. We will meet at the Babitz Hotel in two hours.

The Hotel Babitz has four storeys, but is cheerful and cosy. We like it right away. The soft green meadows that surround it like a natural carpet run to the bank of a rocky stream. All around us, the tall pines rise with the mountains into the sky. It is quiet here. The only noise comes from the bubbling water and the wind and, of course, from us. The little river is called Mummel, a funny and appropriate name. We jump from rock to rock, waiting for the teachers to assign our quarters. They call us in, tell us that the younger ones, up to the age of fifteen, will stay here at the Babitz. The older ones will live at the Pension Gertrud, a much smaller hotel. There are not many of them. Anyone over seventeen is either on work duty (*Arbeitsdienst*) or has been assigned to some other camp as a Hitler Youth counsellor. Dr Lauenstein will be in charge of Pension Gertrud, with Beck as second in command. Pfaffi, as we call Frau Doctor Pfaffenberger, will be in charge of us here, along with Hoffmann. Lenz, though not given any command, will also stay here. The old crowd, our Room 18 from Czechoslovakia, huddles together. Sigrun and I are assigned a two-bed attic room, Hanni and Ruth have the one next to us. I would rather be with Hanni or Ruth.

After unpacking, the four of us stand at our window, look out at the clear, starry sky, breathe the fresh air that smells so delightfully of pine, and are suddenly utterly depressed. The mountains become barriers locking us in. We feel trapped, not knowing how long we will be here, alone and much too far from home. The uncertainty of the future, of everything, does not make it any better. Soo-y-ing, a new girl, joins us. I wonder how she feels. Her mother is dead – there are rumours that she was a dance-hall girl. Her father is a Chinese businessman. He left Soo-y-ing in the care of Frau Director Francke, and since Soo-y-ing attended the Hans Thoma School, she is with us now. I like her immediately.

We assemble in the dining-room to hear the house rules announced. The mood is glum. Pfaffi and Hoffmann seem as depressed as we are, stuck here in a small mountain village far away from everything. The nearest town is six hours away by train, and even it is a hamlet by Berlin standards. Hoffmann is used to going to plays, the opera; camps are not for her. She's said so, and old Room 18 knows so. She is glad that Pfaffi is taking over.

Frau Doctor Pfaffenberger, a small, solidly built woman, commands respect. She does not hesitate to give a shove here or a pinch there as she walks back and forth among the long tables where we sit. After she says, 'Quiet!' you can hear a needle drop. Our two Hitler Youth counsellors – by state requirement, every camp has to have them – introduce themselves as Irene and Helga. They give the usual speech that ends, 'Let us hope we will get along, and after breakfast tomorrow morning there will be a uniform inspection and a march through the village.' Helga wants to say something else, but Pfaffi, who's been sitting there with a stony face, interrupts.

'That will be impossible, as I have scheduled classes for that time.'

We perk up our ears. Nothing has been said about classes. Fascinated, and quiet for a change, we listen to the argument that follows. This is clearly a power struggle. Under the Hitler regime, Hitler Youth counsellors have more authority than teachers, particularly high-school teachers, who have the reputation of being either non-political or silently opposed to Nazi rule. No one has switched on the radio since we arrived; no one has said one single 'Heil Hitler'. Political indoctrination is the main function of the counsellors. Pfaffi loses her first fight and marches off with an angry red face, hair bouncing. But we know this is only the beginning. Frau Doctor Margarete Pfaffenberger, mother of a boy and a girl our age, is a highly intelligent, shrewd woman and a personality not easily dominated. Irene, twenty years old, and Helga, twenty-two, are no match for her. They know it, we know it and Pfaffi knows it best of all.

At the uniform line-up the next morning, Lauenstein appears, all six foot two of him resplendent in uniform, his medals glistening in the sun. Irene is beautiful and Helga too is more than ordinarily good-looking. Both have splendid, well-developed figures. Lauenstein, after having taken them in with a long interested glance, is at his most charming when he introduces himself. He is obviously pleased with our counsellors and the line-up of uniformed Hans Thoma schoolgirls. He is not sparing of praise. But before he leaves to look for Pfaffi and Hoffmann, he executes a movie-style 'Heil Hitler' complete with outstretched hand and heel-clicking.

Harrachsdorf's twenty or so buildings stand in a row on a cobblestone road. With the exception of the post office, school, general store, bakery with café and the burgomaster's residence, they are all hotels or pensions. Herr Erlebach is the burgomaster and he owns everything. The Hotel Erlebach is the largest, and the only one still open to the public. All the other one-time hotels now serve either as children's evacuation camps or as homes for wounded and convalescing soldiers. Except for one old woman, soldiers and other German children are the only persons to be seen on our march through town. The old woman does not return our greeting. We break formation to let her pass with her big basket on her back. She is dressed all in black – long skirt, long jacket and big shawl tightly wrapped around her head. She keeps her eyes on the road and walks past us, gnarled hand on knotty stick, as if we were non-existent.

I remember what Vati had told me about Lidice, and I wonder about the local people here. Are they Czech? Czech-German? How do they feel about everything being taken over by us? But there isn't much time to think. When we get back, Irene and Helga herd us into the dining-room for a singing lesson. They want us to sing Hitler Youth songs that, it turns out, no one knows. We are dismissed only for lunch.

After lunch we have to write down the words Helga dictates, while Irene hums the melody:

> 'A young people rises
> Ready to attack.'

'Only thing I want to attack is my luggage upstairs,' Ruth says to me, talking past Sigrun.

> 'Raise high your banners, comrades!'

'I can't concentrate and write when you two talk!'

Goody-goody Sigrun. Ruth and I exchange glances behind her back. Ruth, pointing to her watch, continues as if she hasn't heard. 'Do you know that as of right now we have been here exactly twenty-four hours? Twenty-four hours, and we haven't even had time to unpack or write home!'

> 'We feel the new age coming,
> the new age of young soldiers.
> Heroes of the past exhort us –
> Germany! Fatherland! We are coming.'

'Germany! Fatherland! We are coming,' over and over again until dinner. The teachers are in the dining-room, and when Pfaffi announces free time for the rest of the day, the cheer is deafening and unanimous.

Noise and commotion, everyone is running around. 'Anyone have some extra writing paper? I can't find mine.' 'What was the name of that big hotel?' 'Where did we change trains?' 'How tall are the trees here?' In and out, doors open, slam. Our room is like the centre of Berlin during rush hour.

'Quiet!' Pfaffi shouts. 'If I catch anyone slamming a door, one week of potato-peeling!'

'Here we go again,' I say, but am glad finally to be able to write without interruption.

Sigrun suddenly whispers, 'Do you suppose they'll censor the mail?'

We look at each other. 'Pfaffi?' Never. If Helga and Irene get that idea, Pfaffi will intervene. I don't know why, but I feel that Pfaffi is on our side. She doesn't like being here any more than we do.

The next day is cold and rainy. The right weather to unpack, clean, put things in order.

'Order! There will be order!' says Helga. We watch, amused, as she gets up from the breakfast table to demonstrate 're-porting'.

'Whenever Irene or I enter your rooms, you will stand at attention.' She draws herself erect, outstretched arm raised, begins, 'Heil Hitler! Lagermaedelführerin [Girl-Camp-Commandant, her official title], Room Number whatever-your-room-number-is reports four girls cleaning ... or whatever you happen to be doing at the moment.'

Everyone laughs. Helga turns crimson, shouts, 'There's nothing funny about it! Nothing at all.'

A voice in the background, very slow, very surprised. 'You mean we have to do that *every time* you come into our room?' Some giggles. 'Even while we brush our teeth?'

General outburst of laughter.

But Helga is serious. 'That's right! Even if you're brushing your teeth. No matter what you are doing, you will report in the proper manner to Irene and me and, of course, also to Frau Doctor Pfaffenberger and to Frau Doctor Hoffmann.'

'Not to us, thank you,' comes Pfaffi's cool voice. 'That won't be necessary,' and as if on signal, Pfaffi and Hoffmann both get up and leave the room, while Helga shouts:

'Well, it *will* be necessary for *us*! And you all better get started. We've put mops and brooms on each floor. Inspection after lunch.'

There are plenty of nasty remarks on the way up, but few brooms. Sigrun, an old hand at this, secures a brush and a dustpan for us, and Ruth and Hanni get a mop. We four believe that we have an edge on most of the others. We know all about inspections, we think. But where to begin? The room is so tiny that when you open the door and step in, you are in front of the washbasin. To get to the old-fashioned wardrobe, you must close the door. The wooden wardrobe, divided into two, has room for six hangers – maybe ten, with a lot of squeezing – and three shelves. That's it. There are two beds with a foot of space in between, barely enough to get through to the window and the little table that is wedged between them. This is our home now.

Sigrun kicks her suitcase under the bed. I do the same with mine, and do my bed-making number while Sigrun folds, pushes, squeezes, beats the mountains of belongings into submission. She manages to get more into the wardrobe than seemed possible. The rest gets stuffed back into the suitcases. There just isn't enough room. Still, when the lunch whistle shrills, we are more or less pleased with our efforts.

Lunch passes quickly. Low voices buzz as we try to find out

from one another what we may have forgotten to do. Afterwards we rush upstairs to put this last-minute information to use.

On the lower floors, doors open and close. Inspection has begun. 'They can't look under the beds here,' Sigrun says, and I reassure her, 'Impossible. No room.' My mind is on the stupid reporting. We picked matches and I drew the short one, so I will have to make the speech. Here they come.

The door opens and in file: Helga, Irene, followed by Pfaffi; Hoffmann must remain outside. There is no room. Five people in so small a space. Our noses almost touch. I have to turn sideways to recite, 'Lagermaedelführerin, Room Twenty-eight. Two girls ready for inspection.' I try not to look at Sigrun, knowing we'd both burst out laughing.

'Thank you,' says Helga, but does not add, 'At ease.' We remain standing erect, stiff, transfixed.

'You call this clean?' Helga holds a blackened finger under my nose. She has just run it over the top of the wardrobe. The question is rhetorical. Sigrun and I stand mute. We watch her wash her hand, then pick up a toothbrush. Thunder.

'Whose is this? And the other one equally filthy! You must use up a lot of toothpaste, to judge by this!' She holds the water-glasses against the light. 'Disgusting!' Now she squeezes past us to the window, gets her finger dirty again on the curtain rod, mutters 'Pigsty,' sees the wardrobe, so far hidden by the open door and Sigrun, 'Open it! . . . Pfui! Not girls, pigs. You are pigs!' She is holding up one of my shoes, which, granted, has a bit of meadow under the heel, but is otherwise as shiny as a mirror. She drops the shoe, kneels between the beds, pulls out the suitcases. Helpless and furious, we watch our private belongings being exposed. There they lie, naked to four pairs of curious eyes. Pfaffi suddenly shows some interest, and even Hoffmann draws nearer to get a better look at Sigrun's frayed, dirty old rag doll with the moth-eaten hair. There's my little teddy bear, my water colours, Oma's hand-embroidered tablecloth, books, photographs of our families. It all lies there and the silence is embarrassing. Awkwardly Helga gets up. On her way out, however, she stops to run a finger over the top of the mirror. Of course her finger comes away black and she finds her voice again.

'What kind of upbringing have you had! High-school girls! You better start cleaning. *Cleaning!* And while you're at it, check all your clothing. Loose buttons, holes in socks and the like are unacceptable here!' They all troop out. She closes the door behind them. 'There'll be another inspection tonight!' we hear her shout in the corridor.

Sigrun and I, as if on cue, sit down on the floor, back to back, in front of our suitcases. We hear each other sob, quietly, ashamed at first. Then, realizing that we feel the same, we turn towards each other, clutching doll and teddy bear, uttering children's curses. One by one, we pick up our possessions, put them away carefully, lovingly. The doll and the bear are wrapped in our best handkerchiefs, as if to make up for the tremendous injustice done them. When the suitcases go back under the beds, our tears have stopped. Defiantly, we start cleaning all over again.

At the dinner table everyone sits with hanging head. Sigrun and I are not the only ones with red eyes. Some girls are sobbing quite openly during Helga's barrage of abuse. She has sent the dessert back to the kitchen. 'You don't deserve it until you've learned to live like Hitler Youth girls instead of animals.'

The crying is contagious and a wave of sobs sweeps over the tables until Irene gets up and says almost soothingly, 'For heaven's sake, stop. You will learn. We will show you how. Stop that crying right now.'

Pfaffi and Hoffmann get up and leave. Not a single word from them.

Helga and Irene are in a different mood when they make their rounds again. They demonstrate how towels should hang, both ends exactly equal; they fold and refold garments, show how it's done. Toothbrushes have to stand at attention. That is, they have to stand at a certain angle in their glasses. The worst is over. We get a 2 rating. Considering that 1 is best and 6 worst, 2 isn't bad. A rating of 6 gets you a week of potato-peeling and/or kitchen duty. The way Helga and Irene inspect, there won't be any need for volunteers for a long time to come.

The third day starts with a quiet breakfast. We only get noisy when Helga stands up to speak. What has she thought up now?

'There will be uniform inspection after breakfast,' she says. 'Uniform inspection and line-up twenty minutes from now, out-side on the lawn.' Helga sits down and finds herself unexpectedly addressed by Pfaffi.

'Fräulein Helga!' Pfaffi's voice is cool and pointedly polite. 'I greatly appreciate your and Fräulein Irene's efforts to help me create some order here. You should, however, check with me before announcing any plans. This morning – '

'But, Frau – ' interrupts Helga, getting up.

But Pfaffi says sharply, 'I am not finished, Fräulein Helga. Would you please extend to me the common courtesy of letting me finish my sentence? Courtesy is a virtue stressed in the Hitler Youth, is it not?'

Helga bends her head and turns red. She sits down again and Pfaffi goes on: 'After breakfast, the children will assemble in the dayroom and we will try to work out a reasonable system for holding classes. That will take all morning, and probably a good part of the afternoon as well. We shall see. Now! Do you have anything to say?'

We watch as Helga pulls herself together, gathers courage. 'Frau Doctor Pfaffenberger, we only thought . . .' She stops, looks apologetically at Pfaffi, who answers almost soothingly, 'You can leave the thinking to me. I am trained in that field, and for more years than you are old, Fräulein Helga. I suggest that you and Fräulein Irene see me after lunch.'

'Frau Doctor Pfaffenberger!' For the first time, Irene opens her mouth. 'We have been sent here not only to help you keep order, as you put it, but to teach these girls the facts about our Führer and the Reich, to teach them the songs that they ought to know, and don't, and besides . . .' Irene now pauses. After having rushed through all this, she wants complete attention when she plays her trump. 'And besides, it is Helga as the Lagermaedelführerin who is really in charge here. That's what we were told. The rank of Lagermaedelführerin is higher than that of any teacher.' Irene cocks her head in a so-there gesture and sits down.

Pfaffi views her with interest, an amused smile forming around her mouth. 'Fraülein Irene, I am in charge here, and make no mistake about it. The responsibility for all these children – and, last but not least, for you – is mine. Very much so, I am afraid. I will be glad to enlarge on that later when you come to my room. Good day. Children! Everyone into the dayroom!'

Quiet little lambs follow Pfaffi and Hoffmann, silently jubilant, but we know better than to show it openly to Pfaffi. Pfaffi allows herself the vaguest hint of a smile. She has no need to shout for order or quiet. Presently she comes to the job at hand and we begin to think that maybe school will be held.

'Eight-eight!' screams Helga. 'Good catch!'

'Helga!' Sigrun has sidled up to her, points to her watch. 'It's dinner-time. Pfaffi will be mad.'

Helga pays no attention, throws the ball hard. 'Catch! Ooh, come on. Throw it! We'll have to see who is going to win!'

Helga and Irene are wild, as wild as any of us and as reluctant as we to break up the game. We play outside all day. What else is there to do? Pfaffi's attempt at holding classes has petered out. The old saying that nothing is eaten as hot as it's cooked comes to my mind. Sure, we have morning line-up, flag-raising, room inspections, but Helga and Irene are not as zealous as before. Most of the time we are outside in our play-ground on the meadow, or in the almost mystical woods of tall pines that rise high above a dark-brown carpet of pine needles. We wallow in the perfume of fresh wood that comes from recently felled trees. The trunks, thirty, fifty feet long, make ideal balancing bars. There are small rocks to collect and big ones to climb on, deer and animal tracks to follow and there is the Mummel. The river is right behind the hotel. Here and there its jumping, whirling waters flow over rocks and form falls.

'All right, let's go, everybody – and *we* won!'

Ravenously hungry, flushed and healthy-looking, we storm into the dining-room behind Helga and Irene. Pfaffi, in a good mood, accepts our pretence of being on time. Helga and Irene, almost as if they were the oldest daughters in charge of the small ones, tell about our adventures. If they leave anything out, hands fly up, and Pfaffi calls on us individually to fill in the details. We are lucky today. Sometimes, and you can always tell by her face, Pfaffi is mad. Then we all sit down as quickly and quietly as possible, and we feel sorry for our two counsellors, who have to concoct some excuse for our lateness. Then they take 'Mother's' wrath on themselves. Hoffmann never says anything. No one misses Lenz, who decided to move in with Beck at Pension Gertrud.

Newscast, as usual, after dinner. Pfaffi and Hoffmann leave as we gather around the radio. Our only interest is to hear whether Berlin has been bombed; everything else seems far, far away. Even Berlin is, and the newscasts never tell us what we want to hear: which section of town has been hit. It's always: 'The enemy attacked the nation's capital today, directing their attack mainly at residential sectors. The enemy has sustained heavy losses; thirty-two planes have been shot down, while we lost none.' You can get a pretty good idea, though, how heavy the air-raid was by how many planes were shot down. Tonight there is a change in the standard phrasing. For the first time we have not 'taken victoriously' yet another Russian town. Instead, our forces make an 'orderly retreat' for the purpose of straightening our front line. Retreat? It's the first time this word has been used officially. Are the Russians advancing? A heavy battle is raging around Tunis. The Desert Fox is not doing so well. We stand around the radio quietly, hearts heavy with fear for our families, for the future. One by one, we almost sneak out to go upstairs and to bed. No one speaks.

The first storm of the winter howls around the house, whistles through even the smallest crack in the window frames, bangs doors. Even the feather comforters are not warm enough. The sky is grey and the air smells of snow. We have an outbreak of acute homesickness. We know it is for this reason that Pfaffi announced a room-decorating contest to 'make the hotel feel more like home'. She and Hoffmann generously donated money. Helga and Irene went to Hirschberg, the nearest town, to shop for glue, coloured paper, plywood and coping saws. 'Have to keep the savages occupied,' says Pfaffi. We, the savages, are happy and busy with our preparations. The prizes are certainly worth a lot of effort. First prize is the job of mail pick-up. That's the most coveted one. You're the first one to know who has letters and parcels from home. Second prize, four weeks' exemption from kitchen duty. Third, extra portions of dessert on Sunday. The competition is fierce and everyone is so secretive that not even Ruth and Hanni will allow us into their room. As if we would steal their ideas! Pfaffi and Hoffmann are spending the week-end in Hirschberg; when they return, that's it. The deadline is near, every minute precious.

'I can't! I swear I can't. I'll ruin everything!' Sigrun's voice is belligerent.

I plead: 'You can! You know you can. Why don't you let me show you? It's so easy!'

'I don't want to!'

'But I can't do it all by myself! We'll never be finished in time!'

'Oh, yes, we will be, and you *can* do it. I know you can.'

'But why won't you help? It's the room that wins, not one of us individually!'

'I know! But I can't do this sort of thing and don't want to. I'll do all the cleaning, all your shoes too, keep the closet neat, everything for three months, if you do all this stuff and don't tell anyone.'

I am dumbfounded. 'You are crazy! Why would you want to do all the dirty stuff, and for three whole months? And what am I supposed to do while you clean?'

'Sit and read or draw,' comes her reply. 'That's what you like to do best anyway.'

Is there a note of bitterness in her voice? I am sawing the last silhouette, a simple scene of girls playing ball. I wonder about the crazy bargain with Sigrun, the solemn oath she has

109

made me take. I still don't understand it. They all know I do the drawings; what can she possibly gain? No one would have given it a thought. They'd assume that we did the work together, even if I did the original drawings. The girls come to our room and, when all else seems boring, ask me to draw and invent stories. I draw one girl and they say 'Doesn't she have a friend?' so I have to draw the friend and then they want to know about brothers, families, relationships. I have a whole population in my sketchbook.

Sigrun is lying on the bed. Is she sleeping? At least she could help keep me awake. I would, if everything were reversed. Or I'd read. She is right, I guess I'm never bored, not the way she is. As long as I have a book or can draw.

The day has come. Our room looks nice, the beds almost like couches. On the table is Oma's embroidered tablecloth and an arrangement of dried weeds and pine with a huge pine cone in the centre. On the walls are six camp scenes, black-painted silhouettes in wood. Sigrun thinks it looks great. I'm not so hopeful. I know that Hanni and Ruth have a carpet, a beautiful small carpet that Ruth's mother sent, and they have identical plaid wool blankets on their beds. God knows what the other rooms have done. The packages from home could have brought all kinds of things. Our room is nice, but very modest. But we win! Room 28, Sigrun and Ilse, because they achieved the most with what they had. We are the mail girls for three months to come. Strange – even before the cheers died down, we had offers of all kinds of things. Everything from cakes, dessert, chocolate to leather pocketbooks and pillowcases, velvet ones, all for the promise to tell about mail *before* official distribution after breakfast.

Sigrun and I promise each other never, under any circumstances, to allow ourselves to be bribed. Excepting for our own, we will try not to look at the names on the letters and parcels so that we won't even be tempted.

Winter, 1942–3. Snow has fallen, is still falling, covering village and valley with an even blanket. Only here and there a dark spot – wood neatly stacked under overhanging roofs. Those and billowing grey smoke are the only signs that there are houses, people, warmth somewhere in the mountains. The Hotel Erlebach's sleigh is in use. Four stout brown horses, bells tinkling on their reins, pull military personnel for joyrides through the village. The officers wear fur hats and are covered with blankets; still one can occasionally see their medals glistening. Everyone else, men, women and children, move about on skis. The village women, always wearing black skirts and carrying big baskets on their backs, speed over the hills with astonishing ease. Their tracks quickly disappear under the falling snow. More and more snow.

The Erlebach sleigh also goes to the Polaun station and brings wrapped up skis from Berlin. Those of us who've never owned any beleaguer the lumberyard where they make them. When I finally get money from home – both Vati and Mutti have sent some – the ski-maker has only one pair left. One pair of men's heavy wooden skis with poles that are taller than I am. Still, I am lucky to get these. One can't move without them. The snow already reaches the windowsills of the second floor. Eight feet of snow, and it's still coming down. We practise every morning on the nearest hill with a youth Pfaffi has hired. They can really ski, these villagers. We move about with ease now, though not necessarily with grace. Certainly not as gracefully as the black-clad old village women. Hoffmann, to everyone's surprise, skis beautifully. Pfaffi manages, but prefers to sit in her room reading and smoking ... and writing letters. She's trying to bring her daughter Renate here. Nazi officials have refused her requests again and again – it's bad for camp morale to have a mother and daughter together. Pfaffi is furious, says she is going to move heaven and hell if need be. No one here doubts that she will succeed. We wish her luck and yet ... every one of us would love to have her mother here. I'm glad Christmas is over. It was tough on everybody, despite the letters and parcels, despite the big party and the most magnificent tree I have ever seen, despite the good food. Frau Czoka and her hotel staff surely can cook and bake. They are good people, jolly, humorous and warm. It's nice to be hugged against Frau Czoka's big bosom, and she is not stingy with her love.

January 1943. We have lost the big battle for Stalingrad. President Roosevelt of the United States has met with British Prime Minister Churchill in Casablanca, French Morocco. It was in the news tonight, along with a short, ominous statement that there is heavy fighting around Tripoli. Later, on the way up to our rooms, Ruth said, 'They are getting together now. Trying to figure out how best to do us in.'

Just at this moment Gisela pushed past and added: 'But we'll show them! No soldiers are as good as Germany's. We have the best tanks, the best air force . . . the best everything.'

'Sure! Sure!' from Hanni, and you can never tell whether she is serious or joking. The last one into our room, she closes the door.

'God! Is Gisela dumb!' says Ruth, sitting down on Sigrun's bed, her usual place when we have our evening chats.

'Dumb?' Sigrun sounds piqued. 'What do you mean, dumb?'

Ruth hasn't expected this reaction. She looks startled, but only for a split second, then controls herself. 'She's just dumb, that's all. Whatever she says maddens me – because I don't like her.'

Sigrun, typically, has to persist. 'Don't *you* believe we'll win?'

'Of course I do,' Ruth says impatiently. 'And you're dumb too, for even asking me such a thing!'

'Sorry,' Sigrun adds belligerently. 'But I just can't stand to hear people say things against our fighting men. I mean, they are our fathers, brothers, uncles . . .'

'And grandfathers.' The last from Hanni. Ruth makes grimaces behind Sigrun's back, then gets up. Hanni does too. 'I'm tired tonight. I guess I'll go and listen to my mattress,' Ruth says. She knows that Sigrun winces when she uses slang. Sigrun does, but keeps quiet.

Outside, in the corridor, I can hear Ruth and Hanni whisper

before the door closes. Sigrun looks at me. 'What's got into her? Since when is she so sensitive? Why did they leave? If Ruth was tired, why didn't she go to bed right away?'

'I don't know,' I mutter, pretending to read and wishing for the millionth time that I could be with the other two.

It is still snowing. Will it ever stop? Even the biggest branches of those royally tall pines are beginning to bend. All day, every waking minute that we do not spend eating, we are on skis. We enjoy it, enjoy the open air and the snow. The local boys have a ski-jumping contest. We watch them, envious, from afar, when they leap fifty, sixty metres through the air. We climb half-way up the mountain, then shoot down, slalom around the woodcutters' sleds with their loads of tree trunks, zigzag in between the trees. Not for us the straight path. This sometimes ends in a rough embrace with crumbling bark. How I wish I had regular ski boots instead of Mutti's old winter boots, and bindings instead of string. Though I make the most elaborate knots, the skis still come loose. There, that should do it.

'Finally!' Ruth has come up beside me. 'At last I've caught you alone . . . meant to ask you something.'

'Shoot.' We ski easily next to each other. Ruth goes on without hesitation, knowing that I know what she's going to ask. 'Since when is Sigrun one of those Super-Nazis?'

'Since always! Didn't you know that? You don't think it's *my* Hitler picture that's hanging over my bed? It's there because it's the only spot where I don't have to look at it.'

'Never thought of it that way.'

'I was once invited to her house,' I tell Ruth, 'and their Hitler picture was as large as their dining-room table, I swear. Her mother served dinner in full uniform including the Führer's Mother Cross.'

'You're kidding!'

'No, I'm not. Ask her. Her father is a big Party wheel — polished boots, the whole bit. Even their tablecloth has Aryan runes on it. They are very "Blood and Soil".'

'What do you know!' Ruth seems really surprised. ' "Blood and Soil" – and jealous too. That bugs me. One can't ever talk with you alone; she always happens to come along. What did I tell you! Here she comes . . .'

Sigrun, trying to come to a smart stop, almost falls. 'Hey, you two! Why didn't you wait for me?'

'No one waits for anybody. You'll just have to ski faster. Look where Hanni is already!' And Ruth gives herself a big push with her poles, shoots down and I follow. Ruth slows down just long enough to say, 'She needs a baby-sitter!' And then the snow flies as we go down the hill at breakneck speed and stop in front of Hanni, who yawns as if she's been there waiting for a long time.

23 January 1943. Tripoli has fallen to the Allies. The radio announcer seems to sound particularly bombastic tonight when he talks about the 'heroic fighting of the Afrika Korps'. Helga, averting her eyes, leaves the room. Her father is or, rather, was a member of the Afrika Korps. We knew this morning when we picked up the mail and saw the official black-bordered letter. Her father has died for the Fatherland. So many of these letters have come. When we were still in Berlin, a girl whose father or brother had been killed would wear a black armband. No one does here. Not much is said. Tears are shed in the privacy of one's room. There is too much sorrow already; we prefer to go skiing, try not to think. What's the use? There's nothing we can do.

February 1943. In Munich a group of students has been arrested. Anti-fascist students who tried to organize resistance against Hitler. They called themselves 'The White Rose'. The radio announcer calls them abominable, a cancer on the body of the German people that must be eliminated, burned out. Ruth and I exchange looks. Suddenly I think 'Boergermoor' and hear Vera Hahn tell Vati, 'We must organize, Ernst! We can't stand idly by and give the Nazis free reign.' And I remem- telling Alex, 'What you propose is suicide.' And Vati and me under the blanket, listening to Lindley Frazer. The name had stuck in my mind. Vati in his old loden coat. Only Vati in an open loden coat when everyone else on the street wore a uniform. Why did I have to talk so much? Can I trust Ruth? Who trusts anyone? Come to think of it, Ruth said hardly anything, but I, smart-aleck Ilse, had to shoot my mouth off, tell her all about the Hitler picture, Sigrun's mother … Ilse, I say to myself, from now on you'll keep your big mouth shut. And don't think so much. We are all in the same boat here. The mail is slow. At this moment no one knows whether their parents are alive or dead, whether they still have a home. Don't think.

March 1943. A letter from Vati. There is a cross at the bottom. Oma had become very remote, but suddenly I miss her very much, feel a great sense of loss – and something else. Something that forms a lump in my stomach. I don't tell anyone that my grandmother has died. I am afraid.

I could not know that Propaganda Minister Josef Goebbels had written in his diary on 2 March 1943: 'We are now definitely pushing the Jews out of Berlin. They were suddenly rounded up last Saturday, and are to be carted off to the East as quickly as possible. Unfortunately our better circles, especially the Intellectuals, once again have failed to understand our policy about the Jews and in some cases have even taken their part. As a result our plans were tipped off prematurely, so that a lot of Jews slipped through our hands. But we will catch them yet.' *

Oma had not slipped through their hands. Six SS men came for her in the middle of the night. Oma had expected it. She was completely calm. 'By all means, gentlemen, help yourselves!' she said when they started looting her belongings. She stoutly refused to leave until morning. 'I know what to expect! Just tell me when and where the transport leaves, and I'll be there.' They finally agreed to leave, though one lagged behind;

* *The American Heritage Picture History of World War II*, by C. L. Sulzberger, American Heritage Press, 1966, page 322.

unable to resist the temptation, he pocketed a ruby brooch. 'You have good taste, young man,' Oma told him. 'This was the only piece of value I had left.'

At dawn the next morning Vati went with her to the railway station. Hundreds of old people, as well as Jewish munitions workers who had so far been protected, were already there, shivering in the cold. Vati was crying, but Oma was not. 'At eighty-four, Ernst, I have lived my life.'

The SS tried to push Oma up on to one of the army trucks, but Oma demanded – and got – a chair from which she could climb on to the truck herself. She never looked back.

She died soon after her arrival in the Theresienstadt concentration camp.

Early one morning five of us sneak into the warm kitchen, a small group of conspirators up and about while everyone else is asleep. Too bad that I had to tell Sigrun. Luckily, she didn't want to come, and has promised not to say anything to anyone. Typical, I think, no guts. Helga, heaving a sigh of relief, said, 'I wouldn't have taken her anyway; she's not a good enough skier.'

Helga, Ruth, Hanni, Soo-y-ing and I crowd around Frau Czoka and gobble our breakfast, eager to get going. Frau Czoka, bless her heart, has neat packages ready for us – second breakfast and lunch, plus apples and cake. We had to take her into our confidence, and she doesn't like the idea one bit. Makes no bones about it. 'It's dangerous! You kids just don't know how dangerous the mountains can be.' She shakes her head, time and again. 'It's not right! It's not right Frau Dr Pfaffenberger not knowing about it. I only pray that the weather will hold.'

She knows as well as we do that Pfaffi would never have given us permission to climb to the highest mountain ridge. But Pfaffi and Hoffmann are in Hirschberg and won't be back until night, and by that time we'll be back. We've planned this trip for a long time. We all agreed that to climb up to Schneegruben

Lodge, the shelter on the highest mountain, and then ski down would really be something. We've been waiting for Pfaffi to be away.

Rucksacks and skis on our backs, we walk past the village, taking a short-cut to where the trails start. We have trail and mountain to ourselves and everything is so beautiful we shout, yodel and sing. How wonderful living can be!

We are not even half-way up when at a quarter to ten a blizzard strikes. Blinding snow makes it impossible to see anything. Helga climbs a tree to push the snow off a signpost. Wrong trail. Our tracks, which we try to retrace, are already covered. Everything is white; the storm howls, and big branches drop additional loads of snow in our way. Where is the mountaintop? Where the valley?

Helga leads and we follow closely, five snow-covered figures stomping bravely through the wilderness. We can't afford to stop for lunch. The storm is nasty and, we know, dangerous.

At four in the afternoon, suddenly out of nowhere, only a few yards away, is Schneegruben Lodge. Sighs of relief.

The few people inside stare at us in disbelief and hurry to make room on the round tile stove to let us warm up. Someone treats us to tea after it becomes apparent that even our pooled money is not enough.

'Come on, let's go!' Helga won't let us rest, insists that we leave. It starts a heated debate, a debate that ends in complete agreement that it's madness to even try skiing down.

'They are not even mountain kids!' says one old man. 'I grew up around here and I would not go down today for love or money.'

'I wouldn't either!' says another. 'If they don't fall off the cliff, they'll get lost and freeze to death. I don't know which is more likely ... No, sir.' His eyes take us in, one by one. He shakes his head. 'The trail? The trail consists of two ice grooves from the woodsleds. Try to stay in them. Remember to try to stay in them. If you don't ...' He doesn't finish, turns around, walks off.

Other guests entreat Helga to stay, offering to put us up for the night. 'Why don't you phone down?'

We look hopefully towards the phone. But the phone is dead. The line's been broken. Happens in storms like this, they assure us. Helga, without further ado, herds us outside, makes us put on our skis, doesn't give us time to think.

'I'll go first, Ruth last. Leave about thirty feet between you. Break your legs!' (The good-luck saying among skiers.) 'Here I go!'

Try staying in the grooves, try to stay in them hammers in my head. The first part is the worst. Once we're below the timberline we'll be all right. My turn. Low, keep low and in the grooves or you'll fall into the abyss. Just then the snow stops; I can see the valley below. Don't look, Ilse! At this point, seemingly right next to me, the mountain drops straight down, and on the other side rises higher still. Oh my God, they might as well have shot me out of a cannon, and the trail is so narrow, one thin line, impossible for a sleigh to make it. My behind is as low as I dare without increasing this crazy speed or falling and ... the ground seems to drop out from under me as something dark races towards me. The trees! Timberline! I'm below it! Catching sight of something out of the corner of my eye, I swerve sharply left and add myself, rucksack, skis and all, to the pile-up in the snowdrift. We unscramble, find all our limbs intact, dance around in joy. Suddenly an eerie light. The moon! The moon illuminates the trail we've come down, shines on the narrow bridge on which the snow is piled and packed much higher than the rails. The bridge over the Mummel. Awed, we peek down; thirty feet below, the river still bubbles over its rocky bed. Slowly and respectfully we retreat. We have all come across this at breakneck speed. A cloud covers the moon like a curtain. We set off, staying as close together as possible because it's dark again. Our eyes have to get used to finding the gaps between trees as they stand out against the sky. We ski still at great speed, shout to each other for direction as well as courage. Round and down, through another curve, the way of all mountain trails. And then another pile-up in a huge snowdrift. Next to us there is something big and dark and a little red lantern.

'God! Can't you watch where you're going!' a deep masculine voice says. 'You've scared my horses!'

'Sorry,' says Helga, 'but not half as much as we've scared ourselves . . . and could you please tell us how far away from Harrachsdorf we are?'

'Half an hour or so!' comes the answer from the man, who is leading, as we can now make out, a team of horses that draw a sled carrying a huge load of long tree trunks. 'No more than half an hour for sure. Elbfall Lodge is only ten minutes from here, in the direction you're going. But watch out! There are three more sleds behind me.'

Elbfall Lodge, the one closest to camp. Practically home. Hurrah! And off we go.

'Get up speed! Get up speed!' Helga yells. 'This way we'll be able to make it all the way to the hotel without stopping.'

She need not have said it. We all know. If you do it just right, get the best speed you can make, you'll end up right at the door without stopping once. One last exhilarating half-hour of skiing . . .

Four weeks of potato-peeling and no dessert. Pfaffi was so furious, she lost her voice. We know she's right. Still, what are four weeks of potato-peeling in comparison to this experience? And Pfaffi was glad to have us all back in one piece, even if she didn't say so, and that also makes us feel good. Potato-peeling is nothing. We sit and giggle in the kitchen, reliving it all. Helga has joined us and peels potatoes, too, though Pfaffi didn't tell her to.

'Remember the bridge? I thought I'd die when the moon came out and I saw what I had led you over.'

'Yes! And remember the lumber sled with the red lantern? That could have been another disaster!'

'Yes! But, luckily, the man stopped the horses in time. These men really know what they're doing.'

'You bet! But tell me, have you ever experienced anything so absolutely glorious?'

'Never! Give me another potato! What? There are no more? It's almost a pity. Now we'll have to go in and join the others.'

7 March 1943. Essen has had the biggest air-raid of the war so far. Essen, that's where the Krupp steelworks are. Air-raids, air-raids, what else comes out of the radio? 'Subhuman Bolshevik hordes are being pushed back by the superior German forces ... our air force bombs England.' And then martial music. 'For we drive against England.'

13 May 1943. Tunis and Biserta are in the hands of the Allies. We have lost Africa. Thousands have been taken prisoner. The Desert Fox is defeated. Another fifteen thousand 'Bruttoregister tons' sunk by German submarines. Day in and day out, the same stories.

'What the heck are "*Bruttoregistertonnen*"?'

'That's how much a ship weighs. That's how they measure it.'

'Must have big scales! And how can you do that in the water?'

'Go away! You're stupid.'

'Last night the enemy again attacked the German capital.'

Everyone crowds around the radio. Anxious faces. But the announcer doesn't say which part of Berlin was hit, only 'The enemy incurred heavy losses. German fighter planes and anti-aircraft guns shot down forty-seven enemy planes. Despite these hideous attacks on residential areas, hospitals and other non-military targets, the morale of our people cannot be broken.'

Forty-seven planes shot down. How quietly the normally noisy crowd goes upstairs. Forty-seven. It must have been a terrible air-raid.

'Ilse! Draw something.'

'I don't feel like it.'

'Well, I don't really want to see anything either.'

'You want to play something?'

'No.'

No one talks about what everyone is thinking. You don't come out and say, I wonder whether my house is still standing or whether my mother and father are still alive. That's taboo! But no one can think of anything else.

May, June, July 1943. At last even the most stubborn patches of snow have melted away, and the splendour of the meadows has been breathtaking. Primroses, wild orchids, tall bluebells, violets and gooseflowers, camas, wood sorrel, gentians, cowslips and buttercups. Impossible to name them all. Impossible to make a dent in that multicoloured carpet. We brought them in by the armload. But now they are gone, mowed down along with the grass.

The Allies have landed in Sicily. Pfaffi and Hoffmann look grim. We sense that things are not going right. Yet it all seems remote, far away. Here in Harrachsdorf you needn't know about war. There is no trace of it. No plane, not even one of ours, has flown over this valley. Normally we would now be looking forward to summer vacation. Normally? Does anyone here remember what that means? We've been on vacation ever since we arrived here. Visits from parents are strictly forbidden, and no one is permitted to leave the camp. We are stuck here. This fact is slowly sinking in. The general mood is lousy. Zero. We are tired of *all* games. We are tired of parties, festivities, and Helga and Irene are tired of coming up with ideas to entertain us. Finally. I mean, how often can anyone look at me in pyjamas and paper hat as I tame imaginary fleas? We've seen each other's acts too often. Pfaffi and Hoffmann, lying in deck chairs outside, are bored too. But at least they can sometimes go to Hirschberg and see a movie. What to do? What to do?

I don't know how, but I suddenly know what we all need. A camp newspaper. Sigrun, when I tell her, is excited and willing to help. After long debate, we settle on a name: *The Mummel.* We draw the title page, write an editorial about general cleaning, even a first instalment of what is to be a serialized novel. It's about an old lighthouse-keeper. I'm not sure how it will develop – I'll worry about that next week. There is a poem that took us quite a while to compose. It glorifies our favourite dish, farina with browned butter, sugar and cinnamon. So what if some of the rhymes are a bit strained? I've drawn some caricatures, and we have a gossip column. Nothing nasty, just friendly ribbing. That part is done, and we like the way it looks, but a real paper has ads. What to do about ads? What about a buy-sell-exchange section? Of course, that's it. The packages come rolling in from home. By now we all have more stuff than we know what to do with. Under one pretext or another, Sigrun and I go from room to room, inquire whether the occupants have anything to sell or exchange. We are out of the door before they can question us. 'If you think of anything, just bring it to our room,' are our last words.

Leather-covered writing tablets, damask tablecloths, initialled silver, velvet-covered pillows, books – there is no end in sight. Our room resembles a warehouse, and the crowd outside tries pushing in against those wanting to get out. Sigrun and I write labels as fast as we can. There are things all over the floor, the beds, on top of the wardrobe, even in the sink. Everyone is screaming. My God, who could have foreseen this?

'What's going on here? Everyone back to their rooms! Now!' Pfaffi growls, viewing the scene with furrowed brows. 'What on earth is this?'

We wait until everyone has left, then tell her and show her our sample issue.

'That's great! Wonderful!' is her response. 'Tell you what: I'll exempt you from everything – all duties, everything but meals – so you can finish. You say you are going to have four copies, one for each floor? Sorry, but you'll have to produce six. Dr Hoffmann and I will want our own. You'll be able to have them ready by Sunday, I'm sure. Until then I promise to keep it a secret. I will announce it officially on Sunday after breakfast.' She looks about her in amazement. 'That's more than enough for your first issue. I'll see to it that no one disturbs you.'

It sounds easy enough, but six copies turn out to be a lot. The worst part is labelling and stacking the mountain of goods.

What a morning! There are loud cheers after Pfaffi announces that we now have a paper. Eager hands pass the copies along. There are chuckles and laughter about the gossip and cartoons, even the poem is praised. The old lighthouse-keeper, however, arouses no interest. The biggest hit, by far, is the ad page. Pfaffi has organized everything well. She had a large round table set up to display all the goods. Trading is brisk. Money and items change hands at an almost alarming rate. I have some misgivings, because the damask tablecloth Pfaffi bought belongs to Mutti. By the time I get home, she may have forgotten about it. I wonder what the other mothers would say if they knew that their daughters were selling family silver. But our parents are far away and by popular demand Sigrun and I have been asked to continue writing *The Mummel*.

It's not a bad deal. We two stay home when all the others go on a uniform march. We don't have to do kitchen duty, nothing at all but prepare the next issue.

August 1943. German troops have mounted a great offensive in Russia, but the Russians have retaken Orel. Nevertheless, we will win. Sigrun is beginning to get on my nerves with her dumb chatter. Listening to her, you'd think her brother was fighting the Russians singlehanded.

Yesterday Ruth whispered into my ear, 'We will win, provided we survive.' What did she mean? If she meant what I thought she meant, I could have said something. But I'm glad that I kept my mouth shut. Vati said the tide was turning. He wants Hitler defeated. I do too. I want to go home. I think that if Hitler gets defeated, Vati and Mutti will be together again. We'll be a family and live in our house in Waidmannslust. If we survive, that is.

American planes have attacked Ploesti. Ploesti is in Rumania. There are big oilfields there. I remember how jubilant the newscast sounded and how angry Vati was when the

Germans occupied it. 'This, unfortunately, will prolong the war,' he said. The RAF has launched its biggest air attack on Berlin to date. Most of the news is bad now and getting worse, but according to the newscaster. 'We sustained only minor losses.'

Sigrun and I are now working on *Mummel* No. 12. This, I hope, will be the last issue. I don't think there'll be any objections. We have something else to talk about.

There's going to be a parade. We are going to be in it. All the camps of Harrachsdorf will participate, and so will the convalescing soldiers. It's going to be the biggest event Harrachsdorf has ever seen. A very important person is expected. A new Lagermannschaftsführer. This is about the highest rank in the Hitler Youth and he will be in charge of all the camps here. The former one apparently has left. We've never seen him, only heard that he was a man in his forties who liked his uniforms to look perfect, sat around in the Hotel Erlebach drinking and couldn't care less about what was happening in the children's camps. The new one may be different. If he's anything like Hanka, good night.

Banners and trumpets. It seems that all the boys' camps have bands. I didn't realize there were so many of us here. German children, I mean. Formations of children reach from one end of the village to the other, and how spic-and-span we are today. Forward march! The sharp mountain wind carries the commands along. They echo back and forth in the valley. We are marching with nowhere to march to. Ruth and I giggle like crazy until Helga stops us and starts a song. Singing, we march to the end of town where the cobblestones stop, then turn and march back until we are at the very spot where we started. There's a platform in front of one of the hotels and lots of flags and men in Hitler Youth uniforms. But we are too far away, can't see much, hear nothing. We stand at attention; Helga says someone is giving a speech. Then the bands strike up again. Forward march! Back over the footpath. Lunch.

Which one was he? Which one was the Lagermannschaftsführer? No idea. Couldn't see a thing.

But this morning, as we lingered in front of the hotel, something really wild happened. A cloud of dust came roaring towards our house. When the noise died down and the dust settled, we saw a young couple on a motorcycle. They were a handsome young air-force officer and a blonde young girl wearing a tight blue sweater and pants.

'Hallo, all of you!' she said, laughing. 'I am Erika Ostermann, the new Lagermannschaftsführer.'

We were too surprised to say anything at all. She looked around, pausing at individual faces, and announced: 'I think I will like you. All of you.'

And then she kissed the air-force officer smack on the lips before walking into our house.

The officer and all of us stared after her. Then, turning to us and grinning broadly, he said, 'Something absolutely fabulous you're getting. If you are going to be her charges, I envy you.'

We were still standing there dumbfounded when she returned and they roared off the way they had come.

Erika has a private apartment in the village, but her headquarters, as she puts it, is here in our house. Everyone loves Erika. She is one of those rare, radiant people, a sun. She and Pfaffi have breakfast together every morning, around ten or eleven. Erika doesn't like to get up early and her schedule seems to suit Pfaffi. The two of them sit together for hours, talking and smoking. They seem not only to like but also to respect each other, despite the difference in age. Erika, after all, is only twenty-four years old. Yet, like Pfaffi, she commands respect. They rule together, never contradict each other. Helga and Irene show Erika the same respect they show Pfaffi.

It was three days before Erika assembled us, and then, since it was the first time that she had worn a uniform, we expected the official 'here-I-am-now-I-take-over' speech. Instead, she sent those of us who owned instruments to get them. Everyone else was asked to sing one note – A. Within half an hour she had divided us into five groups, one for each voice range, and then we had our first singing lesson. Three hours later we were able to sing the scale in harmony, almost.

'Abominable!' said Erika. 'But there are possibilities. With a lot of practice, that is.'

September 1943. The Allies have invaded Italy. We are still doing breathing exercises and the scale before breakfast. After breakfast, voice exercises. Erika insists that a note be held without quavering. We practice for three hours every morning, two more in the afternoon. Our other classes, few and far between as they had been, have now been completely abandoned. We still haven't sung a single song. Only the scale, individual notes and an occasional harmony for relief. Most of us love it; the few who do not, or who claim to be unmusical (a term Erika dislikes, since, in her opinion, there is no such thing as an unmusical human being), are allowed to take part in other activities supervised by Irene. Helga is indispensable to the singing. Erika says that she cannot do without Helga's beautiful voice. Erika has something to teach and we love being taught. Her love and passion for music are transmitted to us. She makes us feel we're accomplishing something.

Finally we learn a song and are able to sing it through without being stopped and corrected. Great jubilation. Erika orders a special dinner from the kitchen and tells Pfaffi she has a surprise for afterwards.

We have 'performed' for the first time. Great success. Even we were astonished how good the fourteenth-century folksong sounded. Our audience – Pfaffi, Hoffmann, Irene and the few drop-outs – were generous with their applause, even shouted 'Encore!' But we had no encore. Not yet, as Erika hurried to say, but now that the choir has been established, serious study can begin. Serious study? What have we been doing until now?

October, November, December 1943. Orderly retreat for the purpose of straightening the front line has become a standard phrase in the news. The city of Kiev is back in the hands of the Russians. Another winter here, another winter with ten feet of snow. It's not quite that high yet. 'What is not can still come.' The old saying rings true. It's snowing like blazes.

Our big battleship, the *Scharnhorst*, has been sunk. After dinner we all stood up – one minute of silence for all those lost in battle.

Silent night, holy night. Everyone was unusually quiet at Christmas. Fear is building up. What will happen? January 1944.

The fifth year of the war. Pfaffi has hung a map on the dining-room wall. She puts pins on places mentioned in the news, without comment and with a face totally devoid of expression. It's evident our armies are being pushed back – 'in orderly retreat'? They've been pushed back almost to the borders of Poland, and the Allies seem to have a firm hold on the bottom of the Italian boot.

February 1944. The Russians are in Estonia. How many German divisions are trapped inside the Dnieper River Bend?

We've been to a movie. A German movie, *Prague – Golden City*, that was being shown in a barn for the villagers. We had given Pfaffi such a hard time that she finally allowed us to go, but only in groups of ten and after we promised that we'd show the utmost courtesy to the villagers. Pfaffi knew best, and we shouldn't have gone. When we arrived, it was already dark and crowded. The outside wall of the barn was covered with leaning skis. Where had they all come from? No matter what we did, the villagers insisted on colliding with us, and never replied to our stammered apologies with anything but hateful stares. We had to stand, like many others. We didn't mind, but you couldn't see anything because of the smoke. All the men seemed to be smoking pipes. Everyone – men, women, and children – was chewing garlic. The smell was so bad we had to go out every few minutes. And afterwards all our skis were gone. We had stacked them in a neat tepee, separate from the others. We searched frantically in the dark, found them one by one, here and there. It took almost two hours to find all our equipment, and when we were ready to leave, a group of local boys came out of the dark. They ski'd around us, circled us, ran over our skis, jostled us. Finally they disappeared into the woods.

Another event: Ruth's mother came for a visit. While Ruth hugged and kissed this elegant woman, the rest of us watched in silent fascination. Then slowly, one by one, we turned and wandered off to our rooms. We sat numb for a while and then the tears came. Floods of tears of longing for home, for our own mothers, tears of anger and frustration over petty injustices. And, last but not least, tears because we realized that it was to avoid such outbreaks of emotion that parental visits had been strictly forbidden.

Ruth had to eat dinner with us while her mother ate alone at the Hotel Erlebach. Ruth sat at the table crying, and was slowly but surely joined by the rest of us. An angry Pfaffi ordered us to our rooms.

Ruth's mother had been walking up and down in front of our house, waiting for breakfast to be over. After Ruth left with her mother, Pfaffi delivered a fiery speech, forbidding us to write home and ask our parents to come. 'You all know that Ruth's mother got permission to come only because Ruth's brother was killed at the front.'

'So was mine,' Hanni whispered.

So many brothers and fathers have been killed. Pfaffi knew that too. She hurried on with her speech.

'You are here for your own safety, remember that! You are safe here and in good hands. You would not be safe right now in Berlin, the way things are there. I'm sure your parents are grateful that you are here. You should be too. I don't want to see any more tears! Do you hear me?'

How can we not hear? She's shouting loud enough to be heard in Hirschberg.

'And now into the dayroom with you for a German lesson. Dr Hoffmann will give you dictation.'

She says much more, but no one really listens. Nor do we listen to Hoffmann, who makes us write and rewrite her dictation while we look out into the snow. Ten feet of white snow. Hateful snow, hateful mountains, hateful white meadows, hateful, spiteful everything.

March, April 1944. Now they are bombing Berlin in the daytime as well as at night. Letters from home try to sound reassuring, but we can read between the lines. It's scary. And the Russians keep on driving westward. They have crossed the Dnieper. Odessa is back in their hands and they're pushing into Romania.

May 1944. Sevastopol falls. Every single day we have to move the pins, move them closer to the German border. It feels unreal, because here in Harrachsdorf the soggy brown meadow-rug has again turned into a joyous carpet. Wild flowers in exotic shapes and enchanting colours bloom again in mind-boggling profusion. The final touch in this glorious valley, the one thing that makes everything perfect: Mutti. Mutti is here.

I was allowed to pick her up at Polaun station. Mutti has five days of vacation. She needs two for travel. That leaves three with me.

'You mean you can't eat with me?' Mutti is stunned, but instantly takes courage. 'All right. You go have lunch in camp. I will come afterwards to pick you up and to introduce myself to Dr Pfaffenberger. It will be all right. Here I am, a working mother from bombarded Berlin, with only three days to spend with my daughter, whom I have not seen in a year and a half. How can she refuse me?'

I practically have to pull Pfaffi's skirt to make her stop. She is in a great hurry to go upstairs. She gives Mutti one cool, evaluating look and I know she's not going to be nice. These two women are so different, the one forceful, the other shy, fearful. Mutti, feminine, very attractive; Pfaffi stocky, attractive in personality but not in looks.

'Since it's Sunday,' says Pfaffi, 'Ilse may spend the afternoon with you, but she must be back here for dinner.' Pfaffi walks upstairs, leaves Mutti standing there, pleading, 'Can't Ilse at least have dinner with me?'

Pfaffi turned the corner, throwing a cold 'No' over her shoulder before she disappears.

Mutti cries all the way to Hotel Erlebach. 'Why? Why? How can she be so brutal?'

I tell her all the reasons, but how can I convince her when I myself am not convinced? Pfaffi's behaviour is haphazard in these matters. When Soo-y-ing's father came here, Soo-y-ing was allowed to stay a whole week with him at the Erlebach.

'Why, why, why?' Mutti repeats. 'What does she have against me? A woman who has children herself and will not allow another mother to be with hers!'

Mutti and I are miserable together, and separately while she eats at the Erlebach and I in camp. After dinner we have an hour, when I must inform her that I can be with her only one hour in the morning and another in the afternoon for the next two days. More tears.

Choir practice Monday morning. It's the first time I have seen Erika since Mutti's arrival. I sing, but tears are streaming down my face. I hope Erika will notice. She does — nothing much escapes Erika.

'No singing for you today *and* tomorrow! Run along, give your mother my regards ... Oh, don't worry about Pfaffi, I'll take care of that.'

'This Erika!' says Mutti. 'Can't we do something nice for her?'

I still have to eat all meals in camp, and what are three days? After a year and a half, it takes three days to reach a level on which to talk to each other. Our conversation consists of bits and pieces of information, fragments that are never finished. Then Mutti's suitcase is packed and I finally ask her, 'Have you seen Vati?' Her 'No' is so short and definite that it cuts off any further questions. It's time to say good-bye again. I cannot even see her off.

4 June 1944. The Führer has been generous, has declared

Rome an open city. The Allies are in Rome. Our pins move north on the map of Italy. North towards Germany.

6 June 1944. The Allies have landed on the shores of France. Will we be able to throw them back into the sea as the radio announcer says? Heavier and heavier raids on Berlin; to us the amazing thing is that there's so much still standing.

12 June 1944. The radio blares on about our secret weapon. A weapon that will turn the war around, erase the cities of the enemy. But on 25 June we lose the last big Russian city, Minsk. Yet, here in camp, choir practice has priority over everything else. It's also the only time we see Erika. The different voice groups practise separately now, the choir together for only two hours. Breathing exercises, enunciation. Erika has infinite patience. What happiness when she's satisfied. We are beginning to entertain dreams of becoming professional singers. Therefore we are not surprised when Erika declares us ready to entertain and starts to work out a programme. We are to sing for convalescing soldiers, and at other children's camps. While the Allies conquer Cherbourg and Caen, and the Russians Vilna and Bialystok, we are busy rehearsing. So busy, in fact, that parental visits now go practically unnoticed.

Suddenly, unannounced, Vati arrives, and I cannot even embrace him, have to wait until he is through talking to Pfaffi and Erika. Finally I'm in his arms, and we leave the hotel hand in hand.

'After what your mother told me,' he says, smiling, 'I had to come and see what's going on here. I told myself that, no matter what happens, they are not going to give *me* that kind of treatment. I have only a day and a half, so you are going to stay with me at the Erlebach. Don't look so frightened. It's all right, I have permission.'

Where has the time gone? Another hour and he has to leave. Gently but firmly, he pushes me into the chair opposite him. 'I have to talk to you,' he says and looks with detached interest at my uniform. 'You know how much I dislike uniforms, don't you?'

I know, and instantly I feel uneasy, guilty.

He goes on, 'Well, there's nothing we can do about it. You are still a child and everyone in your camp is wearing it, so it has to be all right. But you must promise me one thing.' He waits for me to nod. 'Never, *never* become a leader. Do not accept any official status.'

I nod and shake hands with him, but I worry. Worry because in a way I already am, unofficially, a leader. I'm in charge of our floor, and take over for Helga or Irene sometimes at flag-raising, line-up, group activities, all those little things that come up daily. He's still holding my hand. I muster up courage.

'Vati! I'm already on the list. At the next big ceremony they are going to make me a leader.'

'You must, under all circumstances, avoid it. I don't know how, but do it you must. Promise me.'

We look each other in the eye. I know he knows that it's not going to be easy.

'The war is not going well. No one knows what will happen.' His voice becomes a whisper. 'You do know that I and your whole family are opposed to Hitler. You will, of course, not mention this to anyone. I mean *anyone*, not even to your very best friend.' Then his voice softens. 'Remember, little Hedgehog, be on your guard! Keep your eyes and ears open!'

So many questions in my mind, but no time, no time. I wave until I can see the train no more. Vati is going back to Berlin, to the bombardments. Thousands are dying every day on the front, in the cities, and my only worry is how not to become a Hitler Youth leader. Ilse, you should be ashamed. I *am* ashamed of myself. Vati's going back to unimaginable horrors, and I walk through this idyllic valley of a million flowers, remote from it all.

'What did he say about the war? What does he think will happen?' Pfaffi and Erika bombard me with questions which I couldn't answer even if I were less confused than I am. 'When you write to him, give him our regards. Tell him that we will look after you.'

I believe this of Erika. For Pfaffi it somehow seems a strange thing to say. I admire her, at times even like her, but would she look after me especially? I have never thought that she regarded me as anything but one of her many charges. In this, however, I may be wrong.

21 July 1944. An attempt on the Führer's life has been made. The Führer himself goes on the radio, assuring the German people that he is alive and well, that he has not sustained more than a few cuts and bruises. Providence has intervened in his behalf, he says. The revolt, hatched by German generals, has been completely suppressed. All the conspirators have been killed or have committed suicide.

Outside of a gasp or an 'Oh, my god,' this particular newscast is met by us with stunned silence. There are almost no comments, except from some Super-Nazis, among them Sigrun, who heaves a deep sigh and says, 'Thank God the Führer lives.'

Ruth searches my eyes, but I look away. Yet, when she passes me on the staircase, she whispers something in my ear. Did she say 'Pity'? I think so, but I'm not sure.

August 1944. The Red Army reached the Baltic Sea. The American Eighth Army entered Florence, and the Russians crossed the border into East Prussia. That was where Uschi had been sent. Uschi Bohr. I had written her parents for her address – how long ago that seemed – but never received an answer. What would happen? They would have to move the camps, surely . . . Unthinkable thoughts!

'Total war' and 'total mobilization' were declared in Germany. 'Now with the enemy at the gates, the Nazi leaders bestirred themselves. Boys between fifteen and eighteen and men between fifty and sixty were called to the colours. Universities and high schools, offices and factories, were combed for recruits'* ... and the SS began rounding up the 'part-Jews', the Mischlings, First Degree. Vati's boss, the Little One, had been able to protect Vati as 'essential to the war effort' up to that time. There was nothing he could do now. Vati, unbeknownst to me, was arrested. He and five others from Hermsdorf – the youngest fifteen, and the oldest twenty-two years old – were sent to a labour camp of the OT (Organization Todt) at Zerbst, a small town about fifty miles southwest of Berlin, where an airport was being built.

We have entertained the soldiers with apparent success, were treated to coffee and cake and came home long past midnight. Pfaffi was furious, maybe because Erika had stayed behind and sent us home by ourselves. But the next morning they are happily sitting together at breakfast, planning more such evenings. Pfaffi seems to have forgotten that the night before she was 'never going to let us go out again'.

There is fierce fighting in and around the French seaport of Brest, Rennes, Le Mans, Chartres, Nantes. The Americans cross the Marne and the Seine. Like giant pincers, the enemy surrounds us, coming closer and closer. When I think about it, my insides ache as if that iron ring presses my body together.

It was one of Lauenstein's rare visits to our camp, and we knew something special was up. Sure enough, we were ordered to help the local farmers. He had it all worked out by lists. Sigrun and I are to help with the haying. The villagers of Harrachsdorf are poor. They plant some vegetables and potatoes by their houses and that's about all. Not much grows here during the short summers, so hay is about the only crop there is to harvest.

Our farmer is a frail old lady, her face a thousand wrinkles, a small, bent figure wrapped up in black woollens. She stands by her whitewashed hut every morning, expressionless, mute. She never even acknowledges our greeting, disappears instead into

* *The Rise and Fall of the Third Reich, A History of Nazi Germany,* William I. Shirer, Secker & Warburg, 1960, page 1087.

her hut to return with two glasses of ice-cold milk. It takes us an hour to reach her house, and by then we're looking forward to the cold milk. She can walk up that steep mountain without losing her breath, and she has shown us how to handle a heavy wooden rake. In her hands it looks light as a straw, in ours it feels impossibly heavy. The haystacks have to be evenly spaced, then raked out to dry, then bundled together again neatly. She spent the whole first day quietly watching us. Whenever we didn't do it right, she'd come over, take a rake from us and show how she wanted it done. When she did it, it looked easy. We now know how hard it is.

We work on high ground, far above her house, in the blazing sun. I'm amazed that we haven't suffered from sunstroke. Each day we are about ready to give up, but then, just at the right moment, she waves, motions us to come down. We run. One has to have been hot and exhausted to fully understand the meaning of ice-cold milk and a bowl of fresh blueberries that have all the aroma of the pine woods. We also get two slices of bread each, spread thickly with golden butter so cold that little drops form on it. The pleasure of this meal excludes feeling, thinking, anything but eating, and we don't leave the tiniest morsel.

There is never a chance to say thank you. The old woman comes and goes in and out of the dark entrance, quietly and quickly. She's there one moment, gone the next.

Slowly we walk back up. The rakes get heavier as the afternoon wears on. How often we look at our watches, grateful when it's five o'clock and we can go home.

25 August 1944. The Allies are in Paris. Romania has surrendered; they have their oilfields back. The 'Bolshevik hordes' rage through Latvia, Estonia, stand at the door of Warsaw. And Patton's army has taken Verdun.

We are too tired to worry, too tired to be afraid. We almost fall asleep at the dinner table. Every bone and muscle in our bodies aches. Our hands were so raw after the first week that we could hardly hold our coffee mugs. Now the blisters have turned to callouses, and in the morning we are too sleepy to even remember our intention to plead sick. So each day finds us on our way up again.

And she's there each morning, that fragile black-clad figure, with two glasses of milk. By the time we reach the house, she's gone and the glasses stand waiting on a stool, As we work in the sun, the rakes are instruments of torture, every leaf of grass a lead weight. Gather, lift, throw over, spread out, two steps, gather. What's to stop us from quitting? Why not just go over to the trees and sit down in the shade? We don't. We work and look forward to lunch, to the blueberries and buttered bread. Then we can cool our hurting hands in the river by her house.

Amid muffled boos, Pfaffi has declared that Saturday is letter-writing day. Pfaffi makes sure that we write home regularly. We are not allowed out of the house until we've shown her a finished letter. Saturday afternoon we have to mend and do laundry. Claims that all our chores have been done must be backed up by evidence, which no one can produce. There is always something else. Grumbling, we do as we are told. But tomorrow, Sunday, we intend to go to the Elbfall Lodge, to the Mummel waterfall, for a swim. What if the world is going to pieces? What can we do about it? We've worked hard enough. Let's go for a swim. Our group, the crazy skiers, is set on the idea. The others say, 'Swim? Where? Among the pine needles?' The Mummel is shallow, rocky, but higher up at the Lodge it makes a tourist spectacle of itself, falling thirty feet, straight down. We'll go there. 'Swim under the waterfall? You are out of your minds!'

Sunday-evening line-up. Everyone is in uniform, at attention, as on every other night. Ruth and I stand on either side of the flagpole, ready to haul the swastika down. Our dignitaries appear, Erika first, behind her Helga and Irene, then Pfaffi. Pfaffi? She never takes part in this ceremony. I have a hunch why she's here tonight. They stop and face us.

'Whose asinine idea was it?' Pfaffi thunders. As if you don't know, I think and raise my hand.

'Ilse! Ilse Koehn, of course. Good and – I am sorry to say – *bad*!'

'Ilse Koehn! Step forward!' Erika makes her voice sound harsh, official. 'You! Supposedly a leader! You have shown yourself unworthy! Incapable of handling responsibility!'

'How about that?' says a devilish little voice in my head. Here it is, handed to me on a silver platter, and I didn't even plan it. Above me the flag noisily wraps itself around the pole. To get it down is going to be a mess.

'You are herewith relieved of all your leadership responsibilities.' (See if I care, goes through my head) 'And divested of the symbol of honour.' (And I want to shout, 'Hurrah') when she grabs my black scarf, the Hitler Youth symbol of honour, and pulls it from my neck. 'These will have to be earned back again by exemplary behaviour. Do you understand?' I nod. 'To recklessly lead those who trust in you into what might have been a disaster is unworthy of a Hitler Youth leader – and unforgivable!'

(Just like Stalingrad . . . and anyway I wasn't in charge. In charge! Since when is anyone in charge when we all just play around? But never mind, you don't know what a favour you've done me. Oh, if only you knew. I almost grin. Almost but not quite.)

'Ilse, step back. Sigrun will take your place at the flag.'

(Good luck, Sigrun. You'll tangle it more and more because you've never done it. Ruth and I are old hands at this . . . and, my dear Sigrun, if you think that you'll take over all my other duties, you have another thought coming.)

'It was worth it, wasn't it?' Ruth asks, and the group, my group, looks at me anxiously. Soo-y-ing, rolling around in the pine needles, says, 'If I had one of those honour scarfs, I'd give it up gladly for just one more chance to stand behind that green water.' Soo-y-ing, because she's half Chinese, is allowed to wear the Hitler Youth uniform, but not the scarf and leather ring.

'Stand? You mean tread water!' Hanni says excitedly.

Then we all talk at once, talk about the wonderful cave we

discovered behind the waterfall. Ruth, after diving into the small basin, had disappeared. How scared we had been until we saw her hand momentarily poke through the tons of water that dropped roaring over the jagged rocks. Ruth had discovered the cave and how to get to it underwater. We all went into it, singly, since there was only room enough for one person. Inside you had to tread water, but you could breathe because there was a few feet of space above the water level. We try to relive our fantastic experience, describing to one another over and over again the eerie green-blue of that fairy-tale grotto. Sure, it had been dangerous – dangerous and marvellous. But by the end of the day, just as we had become quite expert at it, Hoffmann and Lenz had to appear. Hoffmann and Lenz on their Sunday walk.

'This whole honour bit,' says Ruth on our way back to the house, 'is a lot of you-know-what.'

Hanni adds, 'Soo-y-ing is honourable, and she doesn't have a scarf. Besides, a scarf – a lousy scarf a symbol of honour. Bah!'

I know they want to console me. It is, after all, about the worst thing that can happen to you in the Hitler Youth, just short of expulsion. But I am actually glad. I wish I could tell them why, and I almost do. But only almost.

Hay and more hay. I see hay, feel hay, breathe hay, dream hay. Will it ever end? And then one morning it's all gone, carted away to be stored for the winter.

We go to say good-bye to the graceful, silent old lady with the wrinkled face. She motions us to follow her to the stream behind her house. As she pulls a branch towards her, out of the stream comes a clay jar hanging on a string. Inside that jar is another one containing the delicious golden butter. For the first time we see her smile, smile because we are so surprised. We have wondered all the time how she managed to keep her butter so cold in this heat.

Back at her house, she brings out a big, round loaf of the bread we love so much. We are certain that she bakes it herself. She holds it against her bosom. As easily and gracefully as she handles the enormous rakes, she draws a big knife through the bread towards herself. She cuts as many slices as we can eat, and we thank her as well as we know how.

'You've done a fine job. I didn't think you would, or could, but you did. Thank you very much. May God bless you!'

She can talk! And fluent German at that!

A now-familiar black-clad fragile figure, she stands in front of her house, silhouetted against the white wall. We wave as long as we can see her, and that's for a whole hour, all the way down the bare mountain.

The end of September 1944. The pins that mark the Western Front move uncomfortably close to the German border, but then so do those showing the Eastern Front. Along with the 'honourable retreat' and 'orderly disengagement' messages in the news, we now hear an ever increasing amount of what we used to call 'gruesome propaganda' when the enemy broadcast it. Tales of unbelievable atrocities committed by the 'sub-human Bolshevik hordes'. Hair-raising accounts of rape, murder, torture and burning. They always end in a statement that sounds like a threat: 'No upright German will ever allow himself to be taken alive by these brutal beasts.'

And the Russians are close to the Czechoslovakian border! What if they come here? What will happen? What will become of us?

It's a quiet dinner. I imagine that all of us have more or less the same thoughts. I pay scant attention to Pfaffi, who has stood up and is in the midst of a speech about choosing a candidate to be sent to a training camp for leaders. She uses words like intelligent, industrious, talented, trustworthy, interested in arts and crafts. What will happen if the Russians come here? I think, my heart contracting. Suddenly I hear my name called out, and thunderous applause.

'Ilse! Ilse Koehn!' says Pfaffi. 'I don't think anyone here will disagree with my choice.'

Is all this clapping really for me? I have to get up, blushing, as Pfaffi, Erika, Helga, Irene and even Hoffmann shake my hand. Out of nowhere appears my black scarf, washed and ironed, and before I know it, it's around my neck again. I'm proud and at the same time very confused. It dawns on me that I'm going to a camp for Hitler Youth *leaders*. There are two days to get ready. Two days in which to figure out how to go to camp and *not* become a leader. It will be more than I can cope with. I'm frightened and there isn't a soul I can ask about what to do. Ilse, the best girl in camp. Ilse, you have done it again. Oh, shit! And they think I'm crying because I'm so happy . . .

Twenty girls, from different camps, we are met in Hirschberg by Helen and Irmchen, who run the training camp. They seem nice. We are to take the train to Tetschen Bodenbach, where the camp is located. The others disappear into the small compartments, but I remain in the corridor trying to straighten out my mixed feelings. I tell myself that Pfaffi had to choose someone, and since the stress was on arts and crafts, I was the logical choice. Our newspaper had relieved the boredom, and I had written a lot of sketches for the evening entertainments. There had been nothing special about what I did, except that I was the only one doing it. I'm trying hard to reason myself out of the pride I feel at having been selected. I tell myself that the one-eyed man is king among the blind. I almost say it out loud. And as the countryside rolls by, I see myself, standing by the flagpole as the scarf was ripped from my neck. That had been a blow, though I had been unwilling to admit it even to myself. I see Mutti in tears at the Erlebach and Vati in his old loden coat, and I can almost feel his strong, dry hand. Vati, I promise never to become a leader in the Hitler Youth. My face is getting hot. The joy of escaping the monotony of Harrachsdorf is gone. So is my pride. How can I keep that promise without making my life miserable? I stare out of the window, see nothing. I wish I were at home, but, thinking about it, I don't want to be in bombarded Berlin either. Vati and Mutti are there, and that isn't right either. I feel guilty, a coward. And in Luebars, Mutti is almost never there, and Vati is not home in Hermsdorf either. Always away, always working. And Oma. Oma gone, but left is that unknown something about her death. And now there is no one to talk to. No one to turn to. Standing at the

train window, I feel utterly lost. I can look into the compartments where the others are joking, laughing. I feel shut
out. Apart.

Helen comes out, puts her arm around my shoulder, says
nothing. Suddenly there's a feeling of such mutual sympathy
that I am baffled. When she finally speaks, she says, 'You are
not looking forward to the camp?' and I know she doesn't
expect an answer. But how can this young woman whom I have
never met before be so understanding? In perfect rhythm with
the clickety clacking wheels Helen continues. Her voice is low,
barely audible, yet clear. Discontent, can't stand uniforms, silly
to forbid lipstick and smoking, honour, cowardice, what is
heroism. He left ... fell in battle ... we were so close ...
regimentation. She keeps her voice monotonous. My mind
reels, I don't understand, hear only individual words. I am be-
wildered by her confidence, astonished, uncomprehending. And
yet, somewhere inside I understand it all. I grieve with her, for
myself, for the world at large, and before long both of us are
crying, until Helen finds a handkerchief – and laughter.

'I shouldn't do this to you, little friend. It isn't fair to burden
you with my heartaches. Forget what I said.'

As if on cue, the compartment door opens and excited girls
spill out into the corridor, swarming around us, imploring us
with great urgency to come inside and have our fortunes told
by an old woman. The one in the print dress. The spell is
broken.

The camp is a handsome two-storey mansion with a beautiful view over valley and town. There's no kitchen duty, no
menial chores. Czech maids do it all. They also cook and serve
our meals in a formal dining-room on a flawlessly polished
mahogany table large enough to seat all twenty-two of us.

The tall double doors to the music room are closed, but I can
hear Helen loud and clear: 'Let's do the Divertimento, Koechel
one hundred and thirty-six, from the beginning.'

I like that one. In my mind's eye, I see Helen behind her
cello, Eva, Inge and Gudrun with their recorders and Luise at

the baby grand. Luise, who wants to become a pianist. Luise from Aachen, her mother killed in an air raid, her father in battle.

Mozart, harmony, joy envelop us. How well they play, accomplished musicians all. We like it here, especially the evenings. Dinner by candlelight, candles in polished silver candlesticks, silver on spotless, shiny damask. The evenings are just cool enough for a fire in the huge fireplace. We sit around on the gorgeous Oriental carpet, surrounded by books in ornate oak bookcases, think, dream, while our musicians play. They play medieval recorder pieces, Praetorius, madrigals. They play Mozart, Haydn, Beethoven and, of course, Bach. Elfie sings cantatas. The Bach Cantata No. 82 is everyone's favourite; it has become our lullaby, the one Elfie sings every night before we turn in.

> 'Sweet slumber, my weary eyes close
> Gently into blessed rest.
> World, I cannot stay,
> I find nothing here
> to appease my soul.
> Here, all is misery,
> And there, there I may enjoy
> Soothing peace, sweet repose.'

I will hear it for the last time tonight. I wish I could stay here in this beautiful mansion, in this joyous atmosphere. But we leave tomorrow. The wonderful weeks are over. We have listened to music and made music. We have each taught the others one song. We have written a play and acted in it, and produced a puppet show for which we made the papier-mâché puppets. Each of us has given a talk about a book of her choice, and not a single one was Nazi literature. We have written and recited poems, and each acted as leader for part of a day. And we have all made toys. All kinds of toys. For once, all the necessary materials and tools were at hand. We also had concentration exercises. Concentration is regarded as essential to leadership. Our exercise consisted of having to listen to the fifteen-minute radio newscast from Berlin. It was broadcast at slow speed for those who wanted to write it down. I couldn't imagine anyone wanting to do that. Well, Irmchen did write it down while we sat around trying to memorize it. The first evening no one could remember more than the first five minutes. Now the average is about eight. Only once did I retain all of it.

All our activities are individually rated. Today everyone is feverishly completing assignments. I've made a dolls' house. I'm still sanding it, but am almost ready to polish it smooth with crumpled-up wrapping paper. I know my rating will be high. Too high. 'Promise me to never become a leader in the Hitler Youth.' But our activities here are so harmless. Completely apolitical, except for the newscasts. Our singing, plays, poetry and certainly the toys we made won't hurt anyone. And then I hear Vati say, 'It may be true that all they do is sing and play games. But these very songs and games are designed to teach you the Nazi philosophy.'

I shake myself back into reality. Tonight we hand in our work. Tomorrow we'll be told whether we've passed the course and are now leaders. Here I am, back again where I started. How will I get out of it?

One by one, we are called into Helen's and Irmchen's room. Except for the first two, who have not passed, everyone emerges triumphant, waving the status symbol, a red-and-white cord with whistle, to be worn with the scarf and leather ring. I am the last one to be called.

'We called you last because you were the best girl in the course.' Helen draws me close, hugs me, then turns to Irmchen.

'Oh, she knows.'

They both smile and I don't know what to say or do.

'You don't mind if we smoke?' from Helen.

I shake my head.

'Maybe she would like one?' Irmchen says, but Helen interrupts.

'Oh, don't be silly. She's still a child.'

'Yes,' says Irmchen, 'but a very bright one.'

'Sit down, little friend. Let's talk.'

They ask me about Harrachsdorf, Berlin, my parents. I am beginning to lose my timidity, manage to hold back the tears. And we talk about books until the gong sounds, announcing lunch. I wish I could stay here, didn't have to go back. I have just found two friends.

'We've enjoyed having you here. You know that you have passed with flying colours ... and here is your diploma and your cord. The symbols of your new status as a leader in the Hitler Youth.'

Silence.

'Maybe she doesn't want to become a leader. Have you asked her?' says Helen.

They both look at me. And I find it very easy to say, 'No, I don't want to.'

They both burst out laughing. A happy, roaring laughter, the last reaction I would have expected. They laugh so compellingly that I join in, even though I don't understand what's so funny. I finally manage to say apologetically. 'But I have so enjoyed it here. And ... well ...'

'It's all right,' Helen assures me. 'Don't worry about it. We'll fix it. You don't have to become a leader. You *are* one, whether you wear that silly cord or not. We understand. We will write a report to Dr Pfaffenberger and the Hitler Youth command saying that you've done so well that you should continue training for the next higher rank.' I look frightened, because they add, 'Who knows where and when that will be ... if ever?'

In the general happy and noisy mood of packing, I was asked few questions. It was just as Helen had predicted. Everybody seemed to think it perfectly natural that I should go on to higher training. Everyone congratulated me, and a few said that they envied me. And that was that.

I am alone on the train, clutching a book by Edgar Allan Poe – a gift from Helen and Irmchen, inscribed by both of them. I am crying. I have found two friends and lost them. I am crying because I have never felt so nowhere in my life. Where are Vati and Mutti? In Berlin, where bombs are falling. Trains pass our slow one. Trains carrying grey-faced, haggard soldiers, canvas-covered guns and the old slogan, scratched and marked up, 'Wheels must roll for victory'. For one moment the countryside appears in sparkling autumn colours, then is blocked out again by another troop train.

Hirschberg station. I am caught in a teeming sea of soldiers and Red Cross people running in all directions. Up and down staircases. There is a train on every track and the soldiers climb over the tracks, crawl through spaces between cars, even underneath. Shoved and pushed, I am glad when I spot Pfaffi and Hoffmann, who have come to meet me.

'We thought we'd take you to a little café,' Pfaffi says, lifting my suitcase. 'We have three hours between trains.'

'If we can find a seat!' says Hoffmann. 'It looks as if all the armies have descended on Hirschberg.'

'Well, they are needed, and badly,' Pfaffi answers.

Hoffmann looks furtively around. She looks more frightened than I've ever seen her. 'Let's not talk about it,' she says to Pfaffi. 'Not here!'

The little plaza in front of the station is crowded with heavy military trucks, guns, vehicles of all sorts and soldiers, hundreds of soldiers and Red Cross personnel. So many people and vehicles that the cobblestones are no longer visible. There's no laughter, there are no smiles. All the faces are weary, grey, haggard. I am startled to discover a huge gun entrenched near the station. Soldiers wearing battle helmets with guns on their shoulders guard it. Are they expecting air-raids here? But I suddenly realize what the gun means – the front is coming close. Fear forms a lump in my stomach. What if . . .? I am walking between Pfaffi and Hoffmann. Would they protect me, or run off and leave me alone? Suddenly I hate Hirschberg. I want to be back in safe Harrachsdorf. And the lump in my stomach gets bigger as I realize that there's no one there either – that is, no one to protect me. Well, maybe Erika, and at least the other girls are there too.

The small café is jammed with soldiers. Everyone is hidden

behind the cigarette and cigar smoke that fills the low-ceilinged room. There are few women, as far as I can make out. The waitresses use their elbows and hips to clear a path. They laugh and flirt over their shoulders, and the grinning men shout remarks.

'We should celebrate your return,' Pfaffi says. She has turned to me, which isn't easy since we're practically in each other's laps. 'I saved some ration cards for cake and tried to get hot chocolate, but there's neither cake nor chocolate. I guess you'll have to make do with coffee, like a grown-up.'

How nice of her, and how ungrateful of me to think she might just leave me, that she doesn't care. But that little devil inside my head keeps arguing, 'What else could they have done? Leave you alone at the station? They always come here. It's not because of you.' I try to block out the little devil's voice.

The chairs, already overlapping, are pushed even closer together as three officers insist on sitting with Pfaffi and Hoffmann.

It is late and dark when we arrive at Polaun station. Erlebach's horse and carriage are there to pick us up. The quiet here, after the noise and commotion in Hirschberg, is both soothing and ominous. The huge pines sway in the wind, stars shine brightly and the rubber wheels of the carriage make a funny whizzing sound. The horses snort. Soldiers and war. War coming close, but here it still seems far away. I fall asleep.

October–November 1944. The Allies are on German soil. Aachen! The Russians? Some say they are fifty kilometres away, others claim that they are already in Prague. We are about eighty kilometres north-east of Prague. Rumour has it that Herr Erlebach has a car all packed and ready for a fast getaway. Whatever you believe, one thing is certain: The front is coming close. We can hear it. When the wind is just right, we can hear the distant rumble of heavy artillery. At first we thought it was a thunderstorm. A thunderstorm – wouldn't that be nice! The mood in camp is as dark and grey as the fat clouds overhead that keep dumping snow. Snow, snow, snow. I hate snow. Sigrun has asked Pfaffi whether she can room with 'Stupid Gisela.' This would have been the talk of the camp only a few months ago. Now it's of small importance. I'm rather glad, because Renate Pfaffenberger now shares Room 28 with me. She arrived while I was away. Luckily, we liked each other right away. No one goes skiing any more. It's no fun unless you can climb into the mountains. The last time we did that, someone took potshots at us. No one was hit; still, it doesn't exactly make us feel like going into the woods. Besides, Pfaffi has strictly forbidden it. Also, there are two round holes, unmistakable bullet holes, in the entrance-hall window. You can almost touch the fear that has spread through the camp.

One morning at breakfast Ruth is missing. A few of us know that she ran away from the camp last night, helped by Hanni and me. She got out through the bathroom window. A carefully planned escape. She is now well on her way to Berlin with her older sister, who arrived yesterday. Pfaffi, of course, should send out an alarm so Ruth will be picked up and forced to return, if she's lucky. Pfaffi pretends not to notice Ruth's absence until the following morning, when someone really stupid actually tells her that Ruth is missing. Even then she says nothing, does nothing, questions no one. She knows that we're all hatching plans, either alone or in groups, to enable us to get out before the Russians arrive. Every whispered sentence begins with 'When the Russians come . . .' The horror stories of what the Russians do when they come can make anyone's hair stand on end.

Erika's plan to tour the front lines with our choir to entertain the soldiers has been turned down as too dangerous. The Eastern Front, that is. She still hopes that we can go to Norway. Norway? She's thinking of Norway, when all we can think about is how to save our skins! Well, wait a minute. Come to think of it, Norway may not be a bad idea. The fear is getting unbearable. We've finally decided to confront Pfaffi: Will we be going to Berlin? Has she heard anything about our camp being relocated? She takes her time before answering. She looks at all the worried faces around her. In the distance the guns grumble. At last she says, 'Don't worry. We'll stay together. If the camps are to be relocated, I promise to tell you at once. In the meantime, keep calm. There is no reason to worry. We are all here together.'

Never has she sounded less convincing, never looked so uneasy. We feel that she knows as little about the situation as we do.

'Vati! Vati! Vati!' He is here. Vati has come to take me home. Or has he only come to visit?

Pfaffi, Erika and Hoffmann instantly gather around him and insist that he talk with them in private. How I resent every minute he spends with them.

'Yes, I have come to take you home,' he says when we are finally alone. 'But it's not as easy as you seem to think. We must leave today. I have to be back tomorrow, come what may.' He sounds grave. 'No one at home knows that I'm here, except Mutti. She is well, but I have brought a certificate that she is ill and needs you. I doubt that this stupid piece of paper will work, but we'll try. If not, you'll have to manage to get out of camp without arousing suspicion. It is very important that no one finds out before I have a chance to get back. Otherwise . . .' He makes the motion of being hanged. 'I don't know your camp routine, so you'll have to work that out. Hedgehog, this is serious.' I want him to smile, but he doesn't.

'Now we'll go see Dr Lauenstein. He's the only one, according to Pfaffi, who can give us permission. If he doesn't give it . . . Well, we'll cross that bridge when we get to it.'

The few villagers we meet stare at us. An able-bodied man in civilian clothes without so much as Party insignia is a rare sight in Harrachsdorf. I am nervous and, as usual, afraid. Vati wants to know about Lauenstein, what kind of man he is, and he does not like what I tell him.

'But I think he likes me!' I say. 'Ever since I alone knew his favourite poem.'

Vati only shakes his head.

Lauenstein gave me a big smile when we entered his office. Now he shouts, 'No! No! Impossible!' over and over again. He refuses to even look at the doctor's certificate. Vati waves it in the air, repeating for the hundredth time how absolutely necessary I am to my mother. Their voices get louder, angrier. Vati neither begs nor pleads. He demands the release papers.

'No!' shouts Lauenstein. 'And this is my final word!'

Vati shouts back, 'I will not put up with either your behaviour or your decision! This is outrageous! My wife is sick and you, hiding behind your "orders", will not allow my daughter to be with her mother! I will go immediately to the Hitler Youth headquarters!'

Lauenstein has had time to catch his breath and study my father. He has been sitting, but now he rises slowly, leans over his desk and deliberately, menacingly, says, 'Who are you anyway? Where do you come from? Why aren't you in uniform? You don't even wear the Party emblem! It is your kind that knife our troops in the back!'

Vati has taken my hand and is pushing me through the door. He shouts, loud enough to be heard all over Harrachsdorf, 'You will find out soon enough, I assure you!'

We walk away quickly, as quickly as we can without actually running. I was frightened by Lauenstein's menacing voice as much as by Vati's bravado.

'Where is the nearest telephone? Might as well keep up the bluff!' says Vati.

'You mean you're really going to call Hitler Youth headquarters?'

'Why not? We have nothing to lose. We may bluff our way through yet, though I doubt it. But we had better try. Who knows what this super-Nazi may do?'

The small Czech restaurant where we look for a phone is shabby and, except for the old woman behind the counter, empty. She eyes us suspiciously, then points to a phone booth in the corner.

After many different operators and secretaries, the Herr Oberbannführer himself is on the line.

'Never mind who I am,' Vati says. 'I'm the father of a girl who is being detained in an evacuation camp, despite the fact that her mother is seriously ill. I demand her release. Right *now!*'

I can't hear the other side, but can tell that it's no again. Then I do hear, because the Oberbannführer is shouting just as Lauenstein did, 'It is necessary for one and all during this time of great struggle to remain at their posts and do their duty!'

That's enough for Vati. His pent-up anger erupts. 'Ridiculous rules! The only duty a child has is to be with her mother when she's needed.' Vati has raised his voice too. I get more frightened by the minute, noticing that the woman seems to be following every word. Vati opens the phone booth for air just as the voice at the other end thunders clearly through the room.

'Who are you to talk to me in such a manner? I will have you arrested immediately!'

Vati puts the receiver down, says something I have never heard him say before: 'Kiss my ass.'

The old woman looks at him, shakes her head, makes the sign of the cross and disappears into a back room.

'Sure he'd like to know who I am and where,' Vati chuckles, 'but we didn't do him the favour of telling him that. They're going crazy because they know that their days are numbered.'

'But, Vati! What if Lauenstein phones him?'

'There's nothing we can do. Besides, Lauenstein strikes me as a man with a big mouth and not much behind it. You will go back to camp now. Should anyone ask, just tell them that I had to leave.'

'But,' I interrupt, 'there is only one train today, the ten p.m. one!'

'Then say I got a ride with someone. Or, better still, you don't know. All you know is that I've left.'

'But where will you be?' I ask in dismay, shivering involuntarily at the sight of his thin loden coat and light shoes.

'At the Hotel Erlebach, of course,' says Vati with a big, reassuring smile. 'Where else? It's warm there.'

I am to be at the Erlebach at eight o'clock. Eight o'clock is late to make the train, but too early to get out of camp. Dinner will barely be over. What if I get caught? And only one piece of luggage – Vati was adamant on this point. Only warm, practical things, nothing but the bare essentials. It's silly, I know, but it does make me sad to have to leave so much behind – particularly my skis. I'll have to tell Soo-y-ing and Renate, even though Vati warned me not to take anyone into my confidence. I'll *have* to. Soo-y-ing will probably watch the door while Renate helps me pack. They will carry the suitcase down, hidden in their laundry, and then hide it in the bathroom. They will also have to push me through the narrow bathroom window there.

Dinner seems to last forever. The first one up, I race to our room and throw coat, shawl and mittens out into the night. I haven't quite closed the window when, of all people, Sigrun enters.

'You open the window in *this* weather?'

'Just checked to make sure it was tight.' I leave her standing there and run downstairs, right into the arms of Pfaffi.

'Your father is such an interesting man,' she says, obviously in the mood for a leisurely conversation. She goes on and on while I'm on pins and needles. Finally I hear her say, 'Please ask him to come and see me again tomorrow.'

'But he's already left,' I stammer.

'Well, give him my warmest regards when you see him.'

'But I won't see . . .'

'Well, then, when you write him.'

'Where on earth have you been?' Soo-y-ing and Renate whisper.

'Your mother – '

'Never mind. Be quick or you'll miss the train. I don't envy you the walk through the woods alone, at this hour and with that suitcase!'

I have a sudden urge to tell them the truth, that Vati will be with me, not waiting in Hirschberg as I have told them. But I'm already wedged into the window, unable to move until they give me a painful shove. Up to my armpits in snow. Six feet of it make a nice cushion. Here comes the suitcase. Plop. I hear the window being closed. Alone. Where the hell is my coat? I find it, the mittens too, but not the shawl. Decide to forget it.

Faster, Ilse, faster, I urge myself. It's eight o'clock already. But the suitcase is too heavy and walking on the icy sleigh grooves is impossible. I stumble towards the Erlebach.

The lobby of the Erlebach looks especially warm and friendly tonight. A fire is blazing in the huge fireplace, and smoke from cigars and pipes fills the room. The officers around the fire drink hot punch and laugh.

'Where have you been?' Vati raises his eyes towards the ceiling. 'I thought I'd have to storm your camp!'

Now that we are ready, we can't get away because Herr Erlebach wants to talk with Vati. He is about the same age and build as my father, a handsome man in spick-and-span uniform and shiny boots.

'I see you are leaving us, Herr Koehn! Please give my regards to the capital, and keep us supplied with electricity.' He shakes Vati's hand, slaps him on the back and pats me on the head. 'Should you ever come to our neck of the woods again, I hope you'll stay with us. Heil Hitler!' Snappy clicking of heels and Erlebach makes his way back to join the crowd of officers.

I had noticed their quizzical, suspicious looks, but they turn away to Erlebach. Why is the most prominent Nazi in town so friendly to Vati? But this is not the time to ask. We are leaving. Vati takes hold of our suitcases, but is left with only the handle of mine in his hand. Consternation, noisy drawing in of air through his nostrils. Someone offers to get string, but we don't wait.

Outside it is dark and bitter cold. Not another soul about. The snow, piled high on either side of the road, glistens. I am in front, Vati behind me, with one suitcase on his shoulder, the other in his hand. We skid and stumble towards the train. Will we make it?

We have to stop so Vati can switch the bag to his other shoulder. I hear the minutes clicking away. Slowly we leave Harrachsdorf. Much too slow. It's normally a two-hour walk. We have much less time. We'll have to take the short-cut, a trample-path up a steep hill that meets the road again on top. It's an icy, treacherous ascent. At times we move on all fours, careful to keep the bags between us. For God's sake, don't let go of the bags! Hold on! I'm holding on!

A dark figure appears, comes closer. Someone to bring us back? Have they found out already? It's a man with a briefcase, who politely asks us to let him pass.

'This is the way to Polaun Station, isn't it?' Vati inquires. I know what he has in mind.

'If you want to make the train,' comes the reply, 'you better hurry. Once you reach the top, you'll see the road. Can't miss it.'

Vati pleads for help and the man agrees to carry the suitcase with the handle. He is fast. We have trouble following him.

He reaches the road long before us and drops the bag there. 'Sorry,' he calls down, 'but I have to make the train, and I'll never make it with *this*!' He has disappeared into the darkness before we reach the abandoned bag.

Once more Vati shoulders it, picks up the other one and lurches forward on the ice. It looks as if he's doing some crazy kind of dance before he regains his balance. I stumble along behind. When we stop, he lets me carry his bag. I alternately carry, push and drag it. We are panting and hot despite the cold, our breaths visible clouds of steam. Stop. A huge, total silence. Darkness except for the eerie reflection of the snow. Startling, sudden creaks of frost-stiff firs sound like shots. Vati's voice sounds hollow and too loud.

'Good God! How far *is* this station?'

'Just another two or three turns of the road.' I try to sound convincing. But, like all mountain roads, this one winds and winds. Every time we round one turn, another one looms ahead and still no station in sight. We repeat the same question and answer:

'How many more?'

'Just one. Just one more.'

Vati stops, sighs. 'What do you have in here anyhow, bricks? Didn't I tell you to bring only the most essential things?' He sits down on the offending piece of luggage, about to light a cigarette. 'Let's face it, we'll never make it.'

I drag both bags now, and he comes after me.

'You know I can't let you do that!'

We are moving again and I talk and talk. The station *has* to be beyond the next bend. Just one more turn. We make three, then Vati refuses to go on and lights his cigarette. I try to convince him as much as myself: 'That funny-looking tree there, don't you see it? It's a landmark. We are almost there!'

He doesn't move. Mops his brow.

'Maybe the train is late. It must be, or we would have heard it by now.'

'Are you sure?'

'Positive! You can hear it all the way to Harrachsdorf.'

'Well, in that case, let's make an all-out effort.'

Faster than we've gone for the last hour, we make our way towards that last – we hope – turn.

'There it is!' I wish I could shout, but I have only enough breath to gasp, 'That lantern, the wooden house, it's the station!'

At the same instant a long-drawn-out hoot shatters the silence and bright lights come towards us. Huffing and puffing, the train halts at the station. Three hundred yards to go!

The conductor, hanging outside, looks along the cars, away from us. We have to catch his attention! I can't scream, so I run, run faster than I have ever run in my life. When I reach him, I can only point frantically towards the wood where Vati has just appeared.

'Please!' I gasp. 'Please wait . . . My father . . .'

'Hurry, man!' shouts the conductor. 'We're late already!'

154

Vati struggles to close the gap. The train begins to move, emitting big clouds of smoke.

The conductor yells, 'Hop on, man! Be quick!'

The engine passes. I can't do any more – no strength. Helpful hands reach out. I'm being lifted, dragged, feel hard, cold metal. I'm aboard. But Vati! Vati!'

He's running alongside, burdened with the damned bags. The train is moving faster. I get pushed inside, out of the way. Something hits me. The suitcase – two suitcases – and then Vati is next to me. Vati's aboard. We've made it.

We sway with the movement of the train, unable to move or speak. We've made the only train that can take us to Hirschberg, then on to Berlin – home!

The rest is a blur. People, soldiers, the maelstrom in Hirschberg. Finally we are on the train to Berlin, wedged into the toilet. The train is jammed, soldiers hanging out of the windows, out of the doors, absolutely jam-packed. No lights except for the SS patrols with their flashlights, who check everyone's papers. Everyone's but ours. We're behind the toilet door. Unbelievable stench, but we are undisturbed.

The train has stopped. We are not in Berlin, far from it, but since I can't see anything, I don't know where.

Vati whispers in my ear: 'From Gesundbrunnen Station do you know how to get home?'

I nod.

'Good. I have to leave now. I'll write.'

Before I can say anything, he has disappeared into the crowd.

Though his sudden disappearance baffles me, I am convinced that he had to do it, assuming, as I do, that he had left work without authorization ...

[Vati, as the only specialist on 100,000-kilowatt cables, had some freedom of movement and he'd used it to leave the forced-labour camp. He went back to Zerbst after getting me out of my camp. As he explained later, 'Where else could I go? Caught without papers, I would have been shot on the spot, and I knew of no place to hide.'

When he returned, the SS firing squad was ready for him. The OT

Bauführer, however, intervened. First he would have to fix the cables that had been damaged by the last air-raid. *Then* they could shoot him.

But the daily air-raids damaged the cables as soon as they were operational, and his execution was postponed again and again.]

11

1944-5 · Berlin

November–December 1944. Gesundbrunnen Station. Behind one of the ticket windows is Mutti, but I can't get to her. The pushing, shoving, impatient crowd won't let me.

'You brat! *You* wait in line like everyone else, d'you hear?' The fat officer blocks my way, and others follow, showering me with nasty stares and nastier remarks. Too tired to argue, I wait my turn. She's so busy! Too busy to recognize my voice at first. I say, 'Two tickets to Luebars, please!' and she answers automatically, 'Luebars has no sta . . . Ilse!'

Instantly, angry shouts from those behind me: 'Can't they play their family scenes somewhere else?' 'Of all times! Move! For heaven's sake! I have to make a train!' 'What's going on? Hurry! Hurry up!'

And then I sit next to her in the tiny cubicle for two eternally long hours. Two hours during which she doesn't have a single second to talk with me. When she finally does, on the way home, her first words are,

'Wait till you see the pig!'

The pig, the pig, the pig. While I'm still carrying my suitcase, Grossmutter drags me to what used to be a storage room, next to the veranda, to see Jolanthe, the pig.

'What do you think of the pig?' is Grossvater's first question when he gets home. All through dinner I have to listen to how many sausages and pounds of bacon and meat it will yield. How difficult it was to get permission to raise it, and then it was allowed only because the State gets two thirds of the pig when slaughtered and we get only the remaining third.

'Did Ernst bring you to Gesundbrunnen Station?' Grossvater

suddenly wants to know, and he doesn't believe me when I tell him that I don't know where Vati got off.

'How can you not know?' he shouts, then calms down. 'Well, you're here now. But what are we going to do with you? You can't stay here without ration cards! And you'll have to go to school.'

'Bah!' Grossmutter interrupts. 'We can always feed her. What are you talking about? And school?'

'I'm saying that I don't want any trouble.' He raises his voice again. 'I don't want any trouble with any of the Super-Nazis who snoop around. You're crazy if you think we can keep her here without anyone knowing about it. Grete has to apply for permission papers right away. Do you hear me, Grete?'

'I heard you. You don't have to shout,' Mutti answers wearily. 'I've arranged for someone to take over for me tomorrow so that I can go.'

'Make sure to take the pig's documents along. You can forget about those fake doctor certificates, particularly since you're working. But the pig may be a help. They need people like us to feed the army. God knows Grossmutter can use Ilse's help. That should do it. It's not that we can't feed her, but she can't stay without official permission. And she *has* to go to school.'

'The Russians may be here tomorrow, and you talk about school! School!' Grossmutter scoffs. 'Nothing but nonsense and humbug. What if Grete doesn't get the papers, hm? What are you going to do? Send her back? You know as well as I do we'll keep Ilse here.' Grossmutter gets up, starts clearing the table.

'All I said was that I don't want any trouble!' screams Grossvater, banging his fist on the table.

Mutti begins to cry. 'I *said* I am going to get the papers tomorrow,' she sobs. 'What else can I do? My God! Ilse has only just arrived and already you're yelling and screaming.'

'Oh, for heaven's sake, stop crying. Don't worry. Go to bed,' Grossmutter says from the kitchen.

Grossvater gets up. 'Stop this damned crying! Didn't you hear what she said? Can't I say anything in this house without everyone breaking out in tears?' He slams the bedroom door behind him.

Mutti, in the kitchen, is still crying. 'Why does he always have to be so gruff? What does he expect me to do?'

'You know how he is,' says Grossmutter. 'He doesn't mean it.'

Mutti and I hug each other in bed, hold hands in the darkness. 'At least we are together now.'

'Yes, we are together now.' Mutti's hand grows limp. She's asleep. I think of Hermsdorf and Vati. Where is he? Where did he go? No one in Hermsdorf anymore. I wish the war was over and then the three of us could be together again. I cry very, very quietly so as not to wake Mutti.

Mutti and Grossvater are gone when I awake. I find Grossmutter in the kitchen. A cherry-almond cake is cooling on the windowsill. A heavy iron pot sits on the coal fire. Its lid bobs up and down, sending waves of nauseating odour through the kitchen.

'It smells awful. What is it?'

'Pig fodder is no perfume,' she chuckles, handing me a piece of cake. The cake is delicious, like everything she bakes. How can she create such marvels and at the same time live with such ugliness? She leans against the rickety kitchen table with its scarred, crumbling linoleum top. Incisions from so many knives. A new wave of offensive odour pervades the kitchen as she takes the pot from the fire and pours the contents into a pail. I follow her into the pigsty, where she tosses the fodder into the trough and pushes the soiled straw aside with a pitchfork. Leaning on the pitchfork, she watches with obvious satisfaction as Jolanthe slobbers up her food. 'Come on, we'll take a walk. I'll show you the garden.'

The veranda, once a place to have coffee on week-ends, is full of wooden crates, baskets, pails and bowls. They are brimming over with bruised apples, beans, pears, lettuce, cabbage. Piles of cabbage.

'You can help me make sauerkraut. You see how much there

is to do? We have to make jam, too, before the plums and apples rot completely.'

Arm in arm, we walk the narrow garden path, and wherever I look I see the drooping brown tops of potato plants.

'Yes, we'll have to get them out before the frost comes.'

'You never planted under the trees before.'

'I know, but who knows what lies ahead? Whatever it is, it's not going to be good. We've tried to use every bit of land. If we live, we'll have to eat, right?'

The garden glows with lovely autumn colours. The trees and berry bushes are empty, but the string beans still hang on their poles.

'What's that over there?'

'Sugar beets. Don't you remember? But they're hardly worth the trouble. A hundred pounds of beets and a whole day lost for one pound of sugar. No, thank you, no more. This is the last batch; we'll feed some of it to Jolanthe and make molasses from the rest.'

Grossmutter waits as I climb into the boscop, my favourite apple tree. Here I have an unobstructed view over three gardens and the meadow and fields beyond. Twelve, fifteen miles of fields, all the way to the woods at the horizon, a colourful band against the blue sky. Two miles away, Luebars looks like a toy farming village. Farmer Neuendorff's hay wagon completes the rustic picture. The horses trot slowly up the road, the same road on which our house stands. Destruction, war and air raids seem unreal at this moment.

'Do you think there'll be an air-raid tonight?' I ask Grossmutter with a mixture of fear and the silly kind of hope that one dare not admit, hope that something will happen.

'Probably,' she answers evenly, as if we were talking about the weather.

'Are you ever afraid, Grossmutter? I mean in an air-raid?'

She shrugs her shoulders. 'Me? You know me. I'm not afraid. There's nothing you can do. If it's meant for you, you'll get it, whether you lie in bed or hide in the cellar.'

On the way back to the house she throws a handful of

kernels to the chickens, stuffs some hay into the rabbit hutches. 'I've been thinking,' she says. 'Why don't you run over to the Watzlawiks'? Eberhard must be home. He goes to school in Oranienburg. Let him tell you about it.'

'But I don't know him, and I only know Frau Watzlawik by sight.'

'What's that got to do with it?'

The Watzlawiks, mother, father and son, all three greet me, the mother and father as if I were their long-lost daughter. Frau Watzlawik, a tall, bosomy woman, hugs and kisses me, repeating over and over again, 'Oh, I'm so glad you're here. I'm so glad you're here.'

Herr Watzlawik, a foot shorter than his wife, is a thin, sad-looking man. I've never met him, but he too hugs me, saying, 'We worry so much about Eberhard. It's such a long way to travel by himself, and those air-raids . . .! If, God forbid, anything were to happen to him, we would not even know where to look. Now at least there'll be someone from the neighbourhood – better yet, from right across the street – to go to school with him.'

'Oh, I'm so happy you're here,' the mother repeats.

Eberhard, standing behind his parents, makes funny faces, shrugs his shoulders in a gesture of comical exasperation, while his parents question me, want to know all about my camp, how I came back, etc., I don't tell them that I've fled camp, only that Mutti is trying to get my papers today.

'You just go along with Eberhard tomorrow,' says Herr Watzlawik. 'Say that you'll bring the papers later. That's what we did with him. I was running from Pontius to Pilate to get permission for Eberhard to stay, and at the school they didn't even ask for his papers. Not once. The authorities make it so difficult, but in school no one seems to care. Isn't that right?' Eberhard nods as his father continues, 'He should not be here, but we brought him home from his aunt's in the country. The way things are going, we want to be together. At least we can die together.'

'Papa!' exclaims Frau Watzlawik, the smile vanishing from

her face. 'Papa, don't say that! I'm frightened enough as it is.'

'We have to face the facts, dear. No use sticking our heads in the sand. The fact is, we are losing the war. What's the use of denying it? The Russians are at Kuestrin, the Allies in Muehlhausen. In a matter of days, months at the most, they'll be here. If the Russians reach us before the Allies ...' He pauses. 'Well, I'd rather be dead than fall into their hands alive.'

'Papa! Papa!' Eberhard's mother cries out. 'Don't say such things or we'll be dead before *anyone* gets here.' Frau Watzlawik sits down and covers her face with her hands.

'Mama! Mama! He doesn't mean it.' Eberhard has put his arm around his mother. Now he turns angrily and faces his father. 'You know how it upsets her when you talk like this.'

His father stands at the window, his back towards us, clenching his fists. I know that everybody is afraid, no one knows exactly what will happen, but everyone feels that the end is near. But at the Watzlawiks!? It's something more, something different, but I don't know what.

Eberhard walks me out. 'I so hope that the western Allies will be here before the Russians, don't you? Because if the Russians come here first, my father will kill us all.'

'He doesn't mean it. He can't.' I can't believe that.

'Yes, he does. He really does,' Eberhard says earnestly, then suddenly smiles. 'Anyway, I'm glad we'll be going to school together. I take the seven-o'clock train from Waidmannslust, which means the six-thirty-five bus from here. You *are* coming, aren't you?'

'Yes, I guess. I think so.'

Grossvater and Mutti are both home when I get back. I can tell by their faces that Mutti did not get the papers. She looks frustrated and very, very tired. They gave her the run-around at the Hitler Youth headquarters, sent her from office to office, but never, it seems, to the right one. 'How rude they were,' she says. 'No one has *ever* treated me like that! Those *pigs!*' and

Mutti cries – as much from anger and frustration, I'm sure, as from exhaustion.

'Eh, Grete, eat!' Grossmutter urges. 'Eat before your food gets cold.'

But Mutti pushes the plate away. 'I'm too tired to eat. I think I'll go to bed. Wake me at six, in case I don't hear the alarm. I won't be home until day after tomorrow because I've switched shifts, remember? And all that without accomplishing anything! I wish it was all over. All of it.'

'The Watzlawiks say that I should just go along with Eberhard tomorrow.'

Mutti nods. 'I suppose it's all right. What else can we do?' Then suddenly her eyes open wide with fear. 'But what if they've already heard that Ilse ran away? What if there's an alarm out for her? We can't let her go alone!'

'What if? What if?' Grossvater mocks. 'Of course she can go alone. Besides, she's going with Eberhard. She's old enough. When I was her age . . .'

Mutti's shriek interrupts him. 'We know all that, Father! We know what you did, but there was no war then and no Nazis!'

'I would go with her,' Grossmutter says, 'But I'm expecting a coal delivery tomorrow, and you know we'll have no coal all winter if there's no one here when it comes. Besides, I was never much good in school,' she chuckles. 'Learning does not fill your belly.'

'Ilse will go alone. That's that,' says Grossvater, and adds, 'And supposing they do find out she ran away? What can they do to a child?' Turning to me, he announces, 'You will say what Herr Watzlawik told you to say, that you'll bring the papers later. And don't mention your father! Do you hear? Don't mention your father. If they ask you, you came home by yourself.'

Mutti is asleep. I want to talk to her, ask her so many things, but . . . the shrill sound of sirens, early warning. Full alarm immediately follows and already the air is vibrating with the hum of planes, the noise of anti-aircraft guns. We grab our bags, scramble half-dressed to the cellar. The house shakes. Grossvater comes running, slams the door, gasps,

'They've dropped Christmas trees to indicate the target area and we're right in the middle, God help us.'

'Christmas trees?'

'Green light bombs that look like firework trees,' Grossmutter explains. 'The reconnaissance planes drop them to guide the oncoming bombers. But we can't be sure they'll be coming close. It's hard to tell at night.' She grabs a handful of beans from a nearby basket, opens the pods with the nail of her thumb and flicks the black-flecked beans into a bowl.

A barrage of noise and shooting rolls in, grows loud, louder, reaches ear-splitting level. New, frightening sounds mingle with the familiar flak. Never will I wish for an alarm again if we live through this night. Now there is a hoarse, rolling noise like a giant chain being dragged over a metal roof. Warrroooom! Bombs fall, the detonations shake the foundation, the lights go out, plaster falls.

'That was close,' says Grossmutter without a trace of emotion in her voice. 'Where's the candle?' She finds it herself and lights it. The candle flickers, eerie shadows dance around. The noise outside makes new crescendos, ebbs away. Fire engines scream in the distance. All Clear. We've survived. But the school is burning, the grammar school that is now a hospital has been hit.

We haven't been in bed for more than an hour when another alarm sounds. But they bomb somewhere else. It's four thirty by the time we can go to sleep. Sleep for an hour and a half.

Of course we oversleep, or rather, stay in bed too long. Eberhard and I have to run for the bus and then almost don't get on because it's so crowded. The same with the train. A mass of haggard people packed like cattle, we sway as the train bumps along. I had expected excited talk about last night's raids, but hear only scattered sentences.

'Man! This time the north [of Berlin] got it for a change.'

'Nah! That was a mistake. It was all meant for the centre of town, as usual. Maybe their markers drifted — it was very windy. Or someone goofed.'

'Yeah!' from another corner. 'Some fireworks last night, great spectacle and all they hit were gardens – and the school in Luebars. Small yield, I say. They had the fire under control in no time flat, nothing lost. No one hurt.'

'But Anhalter Station! Holy-God-be-with-us! That got it on the second round. The shelter. Three hundred people. They were still digging an hour ago when I passed by.'

'That was a direct hit, I know. They could save themselves the trouble of digging, all they're going to find is corpses.'

'Right! And they'll only have to bury them again.'

The voices are sleepy, detached, matter-of-fact.

Oranienburg is the last stop. The school, an old brick building, is right by the station. A giant red cross on a white square is painted on the wall. Only the main building is still used as a school; the rest – annexes, gym and assembly hall – have been turned into a hospital. On the roof, at each corner, looms a giant flak cannon flanked by machine-guns.

Eberhard leaves me at the headmaster's office. The headmaster, a very old man with grey hair, scarcely looks up.

'I'm new here, my mother will get the pa – '

'What grade are you in?'

'Five – I think!'

'Second floor on the right as you go down the stairs.' He waves me away. Out. Admitted.

School. Real school again. I'll be so far behind. What will it be like? One moment's hesitation before I open the door.

'Ilse!'

'Ruth!' It's my friend Ruth Schubert. We're the only ones there, and we dance around and hop up and down with joy.

An officer, Dr Martin, sticks his head through the door, 'No use starting with two. I'll wait for the others,' and he withdraws.

'That's Martin,' says Ruth. 'Absolute asshole. He is supposed to teach us German. Oh, don't look so shocked. You should hear the language the boys use. Asshole is nothing. But tell me about camp, about Pfaffi and Hanni. I want to hear everything.' We talk, and slowly the classroom fills with boys and girls.

There are many more students than desks, and those who don't have a seat lean against the walls, sit on the desks of others and on the windowsills. Almost everyone is smoking or rolling cigarettes. The air is thick with smoke and a loud and lively discussion is under way about whether the majority of the planes last night were Lancasters or Liberators, Spitfires or Mustangs. Dr Martin enters, but the noise and arguments continue. A new group arrives and instantly joins in the discussion.

The last boy in nonchalantly says to Martin, 'Couldn't make the earlier train. My whole block was burning. Still is.'

Martin shouts into the din, makes gestures as if they could sweep it all away, clenches a fist and shakes it at the ceiling. Finally, he thunders, 'Never! Never will the enemy succeed in undermining our morale or our determination to fight to the victorious end!'

Sudden silence, into which a voice from the back booms, 'The propeller's on the tail.'

The class roars with laughter, but Martin continues as if he still has an audience. 'These insidious attacks against helpless women and children and . . .'

'Should have seen it. And the smell!'

'We will fight to the last man, woman and child if need be,' from Martin.

'Carried her away in a pail, that was all that –'

'But we will be victorious.' The bell rings and from the back comes one last sentence:

'That's where the detonation mechanism is, stupid.'

'Heil Hitler,' says Martin. He clicks his heels and departs.

The boys have started a poker game, some girls knit, others tease the boys. All this goes on not only during recess but also during Art, Geography, Science. All except Latin. Ruth has told me about seventy-five-year-old Dr Graefe, who's come out of retirement to replace drafted teachers. When this small, fragile-looking man enters, there is instant and total silence. As he begins to ask questions, I'm amazed that everyone seems to have done the assigned homework. The others conjugate verbs until my head swims. I'll have a lot of boning up to do, but Dr Graefe, handing me a beginner's book, promises to help.

Ruth leaves early. 'Sorry, but I'm going to the country with my mother. You know, to see what we can get. We may be gone a day or so. It depends. The farmers are stingy. Last time we only got potatoes and we had to dig those up ourselves.'

Throughout the forty-five-minute train ride back to Waidmannslust, Eberhard whispers into my ear. He points out all the spots in the countryside where, he says, we could take cover if the train is bombarded. A trench, a cluster of bushes, underneath the span of a small bridge – he has picked out places all along the way, debating with himself the pros and cons of every single one. He tells me his reasons excitedly, but quietly and with an occasional anxious glance at the other passengers. I know it's all meant to comfort me, but it doesn't.

'Can you come over this afternoon?' he asks. 'I would like to show you something.'

'Maybe. Maybe if I tell Grossmutter that you have to help me with my Latin.'

'Please come! You see ... Well, all the other kids on our block are away and I ... I've been very lonely, but now you will be my friend, won't you?'

'Yes. I want to be your friend. I'm lonely too.' It sounds strange when I say it, and suddenly I realize how desperately I too need a friend.

'Let's shake hands,' Eberhard says. 'Friends until we die. Until death.'

'Until death.'

Eberhard and I solemnly shake hands and look into each other's eyes. I like him very much. Skipping through the chickenyard, I want to shout, 'I have a friend! I have a friend!'

Eberhard has an attic room all to himself. It's nice and cosy. I would like it for the books in it alone. He spreads a map of Europe on the floor and then shows me a funny-looking box that has all kinds of wires and a handle and a tube.

'My father and I put this radio together,' he says proudly.

'You'll have to promise not to tell anyone, not *anyone*, about what you're going to hear.'

The contraption emits beeps and squeals as he fumbles with it. 'If my watch is right, we should catch it. Here! Here it is! Listen!'

'Boom-boom-boomboom. London calling. London calling.'

And I suddenly feel very close to Vati. Vati's radio was much better. Here we have to listen very hard to catch any words over the other noises. We are bent intently over the radio, our noses almost touching. If it were possible to crawl into this box, I know we would.

Eberhard circles areas on the map. It is already full of marks. When the broadcast is over, he says, 'As usual, our newscasts are way off. See here! Strasbourg fell on November twenty-three, Saarlautern on December three. Yet this very morning Goebbels said that we are still holding out heroically. And here in the east – see how close Kuestrin is to us? Less than a hundred kilometres. And that's where Zhukov's army stands.

'Oh, yes, my parents know that I listen,' he says when I ask him. 'I told you, my father helped me build this radio. It's just that it upsets my mother so. You saw her yesterday! Why do you think my father is so gloomy? To know what's really going on is enough to depress anyone. We are losing fast. All that talk about secret weapons – don't believe a word of it. But, of course, you can't say this out loud. My father says that when the end comes, the Nazi brass will fight to their last breath and take as many of us along as they can. But I don't think, as he does, that we should commit suicide. After all, we may survive. Isn't there always a chance?' He pauses and, when I only nod, goes on. 'The Russians are people too. Human beings. Aren't they? They can't kill all of us.'

'No . . . well, no, they can't. Not possibly. Not all.' I'm frightened. Kuestrin. They're already in Kuestrin. A chill runs down my spine. What will happen? At least I can reassure Eberhard that his secret is safe with me. I say, 'I used to listen to this station with my father.

Eberhard smiles, looks relieved. 'I knew it. You and I were meant to be friends. By the way, where is your father?'

'I've been afraid of this question. 'I don't know,' I stammer, 'honestly, I don't know.' And, like a silly girl, I start to cry.

Eberhard puts an arm around my shoulder, very lightly, shyly and tenderly. 'I'm sorry. I shouldn't have asked. Oh, Ilse, I hope everything is going to be all right. Here, I have something else for you. Take it home and copy it, but you have to give it back because I have only this one. You know what it is, don't you? Maybe you have one already.'

'What is it? What's it for?'

'When you tune into the special station – it's ninety-five point four on your dial – you'll get the so-called weather report. It reports on the conditions in the airspace over Germany – whether there are any enemy planes and, if so, where and how many. See, here over the North Sea, that's zero-five north; the British come from there. When the announcer reports, "Enemy bomber squadrons in zero-five north on south-south-east course,' they usually come here. And you'll soon be able to tell pretty well. The planes are so fast that nowadays the alert doesn't sound till the planes are practically above us. But with this map you'll know in advance. When they're coming from the west or the south, it's usually the Americans. They're day raids. I hate those.'

January 1945. Mutti did finally get my papers, and the very next day I almost got thrown out of school. Martin caught me writing a letter to Hanni and had one of his furious fits. It wasn't the letter so much as that in it I had called him 'stupid Martin'. I still shudder at the thought of what Grossvater would have said. The headmaster was understanding, though. He let me off with a warning. Luckily, it was only 'stupid Martin'. I could have written 'asshole' – but no, I guess I couldn't. I can barely say the word. Shame, I guess. *Scheisse* – well, that's different. I've said that often enough.

Now that I finally have ration cards, they're just about useless. You can't get anything. Twenty-five grams of sugar a week, fifty grams of butter. Grossmutter says that's not enough to fill a hollow tooth. Anyway, they're always out of whatever it is. Or if there's been a delivery, you stand in line for hours and by the time it's your turn there is no more left. But we have enough food. Grossmutter has managed. The only thing we don't have is coal. I'm always cold. So, when she asks me to come along with her and help with the cart because Coal Neuendorff, the brother of Farmer Neuendorff, has got a delivery, I'm eager to go.

It's the same old scene. The line is a mile long and we can't even find out whether there's going to be any coal or not. Some of the people waiting have handcarts like ours, others empty baby carriages, some only nets or huge shopping bags. The very old woman in front of us is supporting herself on crutches and she talks to Grossmutter.

'Yes, yes, I have a cart just like yours at home, but what good does it do me? I'll be lucky if I can carry a net of coals home. I've been standing here for over an hour and they haven't even opened up yet. Three sons and a husband! Only one is left, and I haven't heard from him in months. Three big, strapping sons and a husband, and a tall, handsome one he was. All gone. Nothing to live for. But wouldn't you know they pester me to come down to the cellar during the raids? It's the law – as if it mattered what happens to me!'

The line moves as a murmur runs along, a murmur mixed with exclamations! 'We have to fill the sacks ourselves.'

'What? What?' says someone. 'Put the coal into sacks ourselves? What will they think of next?'

'Next you'll have to go into the coalmine, of course,' a voice exclaims. Laughter. 'In the mine you'll at least be safe from the bombs.' More laughter.

'Open up, Neuendorff!' someone shouts, and the line echoes, 'Open up! Open up!'

'These fat farmers,' says someone behind us. 'They only want to get rich fast. God forbid they should get their hands dirty. Asking us to fill the sacks ourselves!'

'It's true,' says a tired voice somewhere, 'these farmers have everything. The Neuendorffs have the coal and the fields. The Quades have the cows and the dairy and the grocery store. Why, only the other day I begged for one cup of milk, one lousy little cup of milk for my baby. Not a drop would they give me. "I can't do that," she said to me. "If I give you any, they'll all come running and we don't even have enough for ourselves." And I'm expected to believe her?'

Angry voices begin to overlap. Staccato sounds of wrath and frustration. Feet stomp, hands clap to get warm, to move, do something. The temperature is about twenty degrees Fahrenheit.

'Come on,' says Grossmutter, 'let's go home.' And just then Neuendorff's head appears over the yard gate. Afraid to open the gate, he must have climbed on something to be seen.

'Go home! There is no coal! I don't know where you got the idea that I have coal. Go home. I don't have any.'

Grossvater's mood at night is worse than usual. He is now a fire warden and must spend one night of every week at his factory. He works for the Mergenthaler typesetting company.

'I'm sixty years old,' he grumbles. 'Some of the others are even older. Fire watch! What do they expect us to do with a couple of pails of sand and water? Yes, there are some cots in the cellar,' he replies to Grossmutter's question. 'I want to take a basket of apples along for Walter tomorrow. Maybe you can get it out for me.' As usual, it is not a question but a command.

Grossmutter retorts angrily, 'You didn't bring back the last basket I gave you! How many empty baskets do you think I have? Do you want to listen to the news?'

'Naw! We'll know when the Russians are on our doorstep. I bet even then *they* will still be winning. 'Night!'

'Grossmutter? If I keep it real low, may I listen to the radio? There's a special station.' I show her my map. We listen as the announcer gives the co-ordinates. Bomber on south-south-west course in zero-five north. She seems interested. We hear the announcer say, 'A raid on the Reich capital may be expected.' We look at each other.

'How long will it take them to get here?' she wants to know.

'Fifteen, maybe twenty minutes. That's what Eberhard said.'

'Just enough time to do the dishes. Come on, you can dry.'

But we don't do the dishes, because we are glued to the radio as more and more bomber formations are announced. We listen until the sirens go off. 'Looks as if we are in for quite a night!' she says.

'Mutti?'

'Don't worry, she'll be all right. They go to the bunker.'

Two alarms that night, during which Grossmutter knits continuously. The sky is red over the centre of town. Oh, dear God, please let Vati and Mutti be alive! If at least Eberhard and I could be together during air-raids. But he's across the street, and during a raid that's the same as being at the other end of the world.

Everyone is happy tonight, Mutti and I because tomorrow is her day off, and because we got some sugar and can bake a cake. Even Grossvater smiles, but he can't refrain from making his usual speech: It didn't come from nothing – work, hard work, etc., etc.

He's already half-way into the bedroom when he delivers the blow. 'Don't forget,' he says to Grossmutter rather than to me, 'Ilse has to go to Tegel tomorrow – for the pig fodder.'

'Tomorrow?' both Mutti and I ask.

'It has to be tomorrow. Between nine and ten. No later than eleven. Make sure of that. It's the only time Paul and Otto are alone there. No one must know.'

'What's all this?' asks Mutti.

Grossmutter shrugs her shoulders. 'I can't help it,' she whispers. 'He made the arrangement. His friends Paul and Otto are with the Home Guard at Tegel Lake. They save the kitchen scraps for pig fodder, hoping that they'll get a piece of Jolanthe when we kill her.'

'But, Grossmutter, Jolanthe has plenty of food! You don't even give her all of *our* table scraps!'

'I know. But what can I do? You know how he is. They're his old friends.'

'A full pail is too heavy for Ilse,' says Mutti desperately.

'Nonsense! She can hang it on her bike.'

'She's not going to Tegel by bike! It's too far! I won't allow it!' Mutti is upset, and Grossmutter tries to pacify her.

'Maybe you are right. It's too far. But by bus she'll be there in no time and then it's only a ten-minute walk.'

'Ten minutes?' exclaims Mutti. 'It's half an hour at least, and you know it! Ilse can't carry a full pail that long. She's still a child. The whole thing is ridiculous!'

Grossvater suddenly screams from the bedroom, 'She bloody well *can* carry a pail! She's not made of sugar. Let her take the bus. Otto and Paul are breaking their backs to collect the stuff, and she's too lazy to pick it up? Quiet now. Go to bed. How can I sleep with all this chatter?' He continues to grumble. 'Bad enough that *they* don't let us sleep.'

'It's not much,' Grossmutter whispers. 'You'll be back by noon. And, Grete, you can start on the dress from Frau Ruhl. Then you'll both be busy and won't miss each other.' She follows this announcement with one of her cackles.

Sirens. Air-raid. Every single night! And Grossvater has to harass me about the damn pig fodder. Finally, the All Clear and a few hours sleep.

It's one of those exceptionally bright, sunny days that make one want to skip a step and whistle. On the way down to the lake I try my best to fill the empty winter streets with images from long ago. Colourful stands that sold toys used to line this one. That is where Vati bought me balloons. I remember the café with swings and seesaws that we used to 'visit'. Grossvater said the shelter is right behind it. Are they going to defend Tegel Lake? There's the big bridge where I learned to count to a thousand. A thousand steps on either side. Or was it only nine hundred and eighty? I'll count again.

Sirens! A drill? An alert? Probably one or two recon-naissance planes. But I look for a shelter just in case. The tiny houses of old Tegel village look far from safe, and, anyway, all the garden gates I try are locked. I keep on walking, hoping to reach the shelter before there's a full alarm. The sirens blare, howl. Full alarm! Oh my God, where is everyone? The only being in sight is a little girl pushing a doll carriage. She can't be more than six years old. I run, catch up with her and see that there's a live baby in the carriage.

'Where do you go? Where's your shelter during air-raids?'

'The bunker.' She points to the other side of the bridge.

Thank God, a bunker. Bunkers are safe. God, how slow she is! 'Come on, come on, hurry up!' I carry the baby, with my pail banging against my side. She has only to pull the empty carriage, but it's slow going up the steps to the bridge. Steps, more steps, damn these steps! Finally, the top. We race on to the bridge, stop for breath in the middle of the hundred-yard span. What's that noise? A swarm of hornets? Where? And then we see them, and for one long moment we stand frozen.

'Oh my God!' What a sight! Hundreds, thousands of aeroplanes are coming towards us! The whole sky is aglitter with planes. Planes flying undisturbed in perfect V formation, their metal bodies sparkling in the sun. And no anti-aircraft guns. Only the terrifying, quickly intensifying hum of engines, thousands of engines. The air vibrates, seems to shiver; the water, the ground and the bridge under us begin to tremble. It's unearthly, a tremendously beautiful sight! A whole blue sky full of silver planes.

We run. The first formation is already overhead. All hell breaks loose. The anti-aircraft guns shoot and bombs fall like rain. Millions of long, rounded shapes come tumbling down around us. The sky turns grey, black, the earth erupts. The detonations begin to sound like continuous thunder.

A house! Shelter from this nightmare. We reach it, though I don't know how. I collide with the old lady who is standing in the door. She tries to take the baby away from me. We stand in the doorway, entangled by the pail, and I see the bomb, watch it hit the roof, and see the house cave in behind her.

'*God in Heaven!*' she screams. '*God in Heaven!*'

174

'Grandma! Grandma!', wails the little girl, pulling at her skirt. 'Grandma, let's go to the bunker, please, please, Grandma!'

I'm flat on the ground. Bombs, bombs, bombs fall all around me. It can't be. It's a dream. There aren't that many bombs in the whole world. Maybe I'm dead? I get up, drag pail, old woman and girl with me towards a porch, a concrete porch with space underneath. Above the detonations, flak fire, shattering glass rises the old woman's high-pitched voice: '*God in Heaven! God in Heaven!*' And now the baby is wailing too.

Hang on to the earth. It heaves as if we are on a trampoline, but I cling to it, dig my nails into it.

Why is it so dark? The old woman crouches over the baby. She shakes a fist at the little girl, then screams:

'God in Heaven forgive her. Forgive her her ugliness, her sin ... O Lord, I know she didn't say her prayers!' Her fist comes down on the little girl's head.

A sizzling piece of shrapnel embeds itself in the concrete of the porch. The little girl grabs me, her nails dig into my neck. Her voice, as if in excruciating pain, pierces my eardrums:

'*Mama! Mama! Where are you, Mama?*'

A clod of soil hits me in the face. I'm still alive. Alive with fear and ready to promise any powers that be that I'll become a better person if only my life is spared.

Warrrooom. Warrrooomwarroomwaroom. My whole body is lifted off the ground, dropped again, up and down again. This is beginning to be fun, if only the earth wasn't so cold. Woweeee! But this sets the old lady off again.

'You wicked girl ... O Lord! ... Why didn't you say your prayers?' Over and over again. Can't she think of anything else?

'Mama! Mama! Mama!'

'Rrrahrrahrrahhhhh!'

Grandma, little girl and baby wailing over the bombs, the flak. Will this ever end?

Suddenly it's quiet. Dead quiet. A spine-chilling, eerie quiet.

I'm breathing. We're all breathing. Strange to hear our breaths. What's that? Oh, only a fire engine. Sirens. Sirens again? All Clear. That means I can leave.

'I'm sorry, but I have to go. I have to collect some pig fodder,' I say.

'Of course, my dear,' the old lady replies. 'I'm sorry you have to leave so soon. You must come again. Come visit us. We'll have tea. It's very nice to have met you.' We shake hands very formally.

Pig fodder, shelter. Where's the shelter? Where am I? I walk, stumble, get up, feel nothing, no legs. Funny to walk and not feel your legs. They look all right, I just don't feel them. Bomb craters everywhere. Amazingly, there are still some houses standing. What's this? A bomb. Interesting. I must take a look. Ah, it's probably only the twenty-kilo type. Relatively harmless. No wonder there were so many of them.

There's the restaurant, the swings. Now I know exactly where I am. The roof looks fallen in. Bombs? Maybe it's just old age. It was so long ago. I feel sorry for the boats. Such beautiful boats, ripped apart, varnished mahogany splintered. Ugly bombs.

'You must be Ilse!' two old men in steel helmets say to me. One takes my pail, disappears with it into the shelter. Oh, that's where it is. He comes back, hands me the pail full of something grey and slimy. Did he have to make it so full?

Step carefully, Ilse. Your grandfather will be mad if you lose any of it. Why did they have to throw all that junk on the road? A whole kitchen range. Glass, pieces of furniture, parts of houses. I climb over it, walk around, always take the easiest way. The bridge – good. But this time I'm going to count.

Seven hundred. Seven hundred and ... And now I have forgotten again. Never mind, I can do it on the way down. Tegel village, and I have forgotten again to count the steps. At least there are people here. A thought occurs to me. I forgot to say thank you. I should have said thank you for the pig fodder. Maybe Grossvater can tell them. He can say that I had to catch a bus or something.

Now, there! That's a sight. The house is cut in half, a historic Tegel house nine hundred years old. And the old church, nothing but a skeleton. Someone with a chair bumps into me. 'Can't you look where you're going?'

There's the bus stop. No bus. Typical. I'll probably have to wait for an hour. A piece of burning wood sails by my ear.

'Move!' someone yells.

'Sorry.' I hadn't noticed that I had walked into the middle of a human chain. Pails are being passed from one to another. Maybe there is no bus. I might as well walk. Walk, walk, walk. The pail is heavy. Why do they make pail handles so thin?

When I pass the large housing development, I walk in the middle of the street. All the houses are burning. Flames crackle; there is a terrible smell. People are running in all directions. Fire engines, ambulances, police. I barely avoid a police car, step in a hole, trip, but somehow manage to keep the pail upright. I only lose a little bit of the slop. Grossvater won't even notice it.

Good God, but this policeman can scream. He'll burst his lungs. He comes towards me, gesticulates. What does he want?

'Out! Out! Get away from here! Get away!'

He points at my feet. I look, uncomprehending. What is it? I'm standing on something – something large, about thirty feet long, and a good part of it is buried in the ground.

And then I understand. I run towards the policeman, don't care that the pig fodder is splashing all over me. An aerial mine. My God I had been standing on an unexploded aerial mine. I have long since passed the policeman, firemen, people, but I'm still running. I run until my legs seem to buckle under me. Stop to catch my breath. Look back. They've cordoned off the area.

The apartment houses around Waidmannslust Station are burning too. A huge crowd of people stand in front of the movie theatre. They too are screaming and yelling.

'Look at the fire! Look at it! The roof won't hold.'

I can't stay to look. I must go home.

'Two hundred people trapped in the cellar of the movie . . .'

I have to get home. Walk, run, trot, stumble, it doesn't matter. Have to get home, home to Mutti.

Our street. Everyone seems to be out in the street talking. But the houses are still standing.

I stop, stand rooted to the ground, don't even feel the pail in my hand. I see it all, and yet don't see or hear anything until I'm in Mutti's arms.

That's when the tears come. The tears and the terrible shaking. The tears stop, but the shaking doesn't. I shiver, shake, tremble as if I had fever chills.

'Today, 3 February 1945, one thousand US bombers attacked the northern part of Berlin in a day raid,' Lindley Frazer announces on the BBC.

Everything is so nice here, so orderly. The Watzlawiks' is a cultured household, Grossmutter said. Cultured? Anyway, it feels particularly comfortable today after all the debris, the burning houses. If only Frau Watzlawik would let go of me. I'm buried in her arms and bosom.

'Mother!' How stern Eberhard can sound. 'Let her go. You'll only make her cry again. Would you like me to play the piano?'

'Oh, yes, please do. Play something happy.' He knows that I like to listen to him play. His mother disappears into the kitchen, comes back again when he plays:

> 'For one night of bliss
> I'd give everything.'

'Eberhard! That's unseemly. You are both much too young for . . .'

'Mother, please! You were the one who took me to see that movie.'

Finally she leaves us alone. There's room for both of us on the piano bench. He plays, sings. I sing along. All the hit tunes.

'You are the woman of my dreams . . .' He isn't looking at the keys any more. He's looking at me. Our eyes are inches apart, and then he kisses me. Two closed pairs of lips meet for a second and then his mother enters with two cups of soup.

'Don't weep for love.' A quick, awkward embrace in the corridor.

'Think of me tonight.'

Tonight, tonight. I begin to shake again – tonight another air-raid . . .

Beep – beepbeep – beep. That's all. Beep – beepbeep. No enemy planes over German territory. 'Leave it on, please, Grossvater. May I keep the radio on?'

'If there's an air-raid tonight.' says Mutti, 'Ilse and I will go to the bunker. And you and Grossmutter should come too.'

God we have gone over this so many times, but they have said it's foolish. The bunkers are too far away. The streets are dark. Our house is as safe as anything. 'But if you want to go, go.'

'I know our cellar is safe,' Mutti says apologetically, 'except – '

'I told you, go.' Grossvater raises his voice. 'But I'm staying right here. If Mutter wants to go . . .'

'Me?' she says mockingly. 'With my old legs? No, thank you. But *they* should go.'

'I said go!' Grossvater repeats. 'But I will not let them go if there is a full alarm right away. They will have to leave with the alert.'

Yesterday he yelled and screamed at the mere mention of the word bunker, but today's happenings have visibly shaken him. How glad I am for the gridiron map. We'll know early.

Beep. Silence, then the cool, detached voice of the announcer: 'Incoming flight in zero-five north, course south-south-east.'

Even Grossvater gets up, his stubby finger traces the co-ordinates. Our fingers meet on the North Sea.

'Hamburg,' he says. 'They'll probably stay there.'

My heart beats, and the uncontrollable shaking takes over.

'They'll stay there, and you'll run to the bunker for nothing,' says Grossmutter.

There is the voice again. 'The bomber formations have now passed Hamburg, still flying east-south-east. An attack on the capital is to be expected.'

We are in our coats, out on the street with the bike in no time at all. The bike will be faster. The bags are easier to carry this way, and on the even stretches of road Mutti can sit on the baggage rack. She protests, but gives in to Grossmutter, who practically puts her on it. Grossmutter wants us to take all the family papers, the documents of house and pig. Two more bags go on the handlebars. All four together must weigh thirty or forty pounds, plus Mutti! I pedal hard, furiously, with the strength of fear.

House doors slam, garden gates squeak, dark figures hurry through the night. They come from everywhere, out of every street. A constantly swelling stream that turns into a solid black mass. Like a flood-swollen river at springtime, it moves with irresistible force towards the bunker. Individual faces become visible for a second when a red flare illuminates the sky. No, they are not faces, they are spooky masks, frightened, frightening. The sirens howl 'Alert' and without any interval switch to the 'Full Alarm' signal. White beams of searchlights finger the sky, criss-cross each other in search of enemy planes. Tracers add giant basting stitches.

Still three hundred yards to go over an open field. Hundreds race towards the one door.

Luckily, the door is at the side, right next to the fence, where I leave my bike, even lock it. And then we are catapulted, sluiced, past the soldier guards with their rifles at the ready, pushed by those behind us, through the steel door. Inside, we are forced against those already there. There's no room, and still we get packed tighter. A little more and we won't be able to breathe. Flattened, squeezed to death in the fight to stay alive. Screams, flak, planes and shouting outside. The guards have closed and locked the door and it's suddenly quiet.

The shoving and shifting continues until we have breathing space. Too bad that breathing is a necessity even in this foul air.

The interior of the bunker looks like a battleship. Grey concrete walls, supposedly nine feet thick. Narrow corridors lined with cubicles. Open steel doors every ten feet. Most of the cubicle doors are open too, allowing the fortunate bunk-bed inhabitants to peer sleepily at us. The bunks are stacked in tiers of four, with barely a foot of space in between the beds, and that space is occupied by relatives or friends. At least they have enough room in there to sit on their bags. That's more than we have.

Where do they come from, all these tired, shabby, oddly dressed people? All the frayed coats, trodden-down pumps? Fur collars of moth-eaten martens that bite each other around the wearer's neck. There are a few boots, slim ski pants, reminders of peacetime vacations, and a few Persian-lamb coats, the ultimate status symbols in our area. And everyone wears a scarf, except, of course, the few soldiers in the crowd, who get dirty looks from those around them.

'To take away room from women and children!'

The crowd shifts, makes way for the unending procession to and from the toilet. Angry words. One baby begins to cry, triggers others. The air is not improving.

Time passes, minutes, hours, Lethargy has settled on us like a stone. Inside someone's bag an alarm clock suddenly goes off, startling everyone.

'Good God! What time is it?'

'Only two thirty,' stammers the owner of the clock apologetically.

'*Only* two thirty! She has some nerve – *only* two thirty! That's all right for her. *She* doesn't have to get up early.'

There would have been an argument, had it not been for the All Clear. One huge sigh from all, and the next instant a simultaneous scramble for the exit. Ferocious shoving accompanied by shouts, screams and curses. We spill out into the clear, cold night.

Over the city the sky is red, billowing smoke, wavering flames. We hurry home through our unharmed streets. Within minutes we are alone. Swallowed up by the darkness are the thousands who almost suffocated us only minutes ago.

The house is quiet except for Grossvater's snoring as we tiptoe upstairs.

March 1945. The station platform in Waidmannslust is even more crowded than usual. Some people have been waiting for two hours. At last the train comes. Ah, forget it. Passengers are already hanging on the outside. We'll never get on. There is, nevertheless, almost a stampede when the train comes to a stop. Those outside hanging on to the doors want to make sure they get in. Those who want to get off have to fight the solid wall of people wanting to get on.

'Let me through! I *have* to get to work!'

'Do you think *we're* going on a picnic, you nitwit?'

'Come closer, Mother – and if you inhale, there'll be room for three more!'

'Let the kids in. Make sure to get the kids aboard, they have to go to school. We have to ensure our future!' Laughter.

'One more, one more. Come on, everyone, raise your hands. Lift your arms and shout "Heil Hitler" and there'll be even more room.' Laughter.

It's this so-called gallows humour that, miraculously as it may seem, gets everyone aboard. The electrically operated doors close, but even then the train doesn't move. It seems to be waiting for one last remark.

'What's the matter? Someone sitting on the track?'

The train begins to move. Eberhard and I, separated by many people, wink and make faces at each other. By the time we get to school, we are over an hour late, but still we're the first ones there. Ruth has probably overslept, as usual, but she'll come. We all come to school every day, no matter how late. And it really doesn't matter. Most of the teachers don't begin until everyone is present, and then we pay little attention. We come because we have to. There's been talk about 'court-martialling' students who play hookey. We come, too, because we have a desire to be with others our own age. Though no one admits it, we are afraid – we live with fear. Fear of the next alarm, fear for our own and our parents' lives, fear for the roof over our heads. Those who have already lost theirs feel this most acutely. We, the 'guarantors of the future', as the Führer calls us, are all afraid of being caught by an air-raid in an unknown part of town. We hide our panic with bravado. We know everything. We know how to get ahead in any line, how to squeeze into overpacked trains. We know where and how to get things. The way we talk, it would seem that each and every one of us is an expert on incendiary bombs. We discuss the comparative merits of German, Russian and American tanks in precise technical terms and with the air of authority befitting a major general. Most important, we all know the one place to be during an air-raid: any bunker.

Irregular verbs are meaningless by comparison. Who cares about drawing Frau Kunst's old flower pot? The history of the Nazi movement – are you kidding? Incessant talk, clicking of knitting needles, shuffling of cards as well as the calls of the card-players accompany every lecture.

Here comes Ruth, her dark-brown hair tousled as usual, deep-blue eyes flashing. How handsome she is, in a sturdy, solid kind of way. She has enough energy for three, never stands still, always moving, talking.

'Hi!' she says, plopping down into her seat. 'Just missed the train.' Already she's up again – someone has called her name. Then she's back in her seat in a flash.

Sudden, total quiet. Everyone rises. Dr Graefe has come in. After a barely audible 'Good morning, ladies and gentlemen,' he begins his lesson.

We all want to do well. We've tried, but it's obvious that no one has done the homework properly. Only a few hands go up, fewer every day. And most of the answers are only half right, if that.

Dr Graefe puts down his book, looks at us, smiling sadly. The class hang their heads.

'Ladies and gentlemen,' he starts, 'it's no use. We will proceed no further today. And from now on you will do your homework here in class.'

A loud, unanimous '*Hurrah!*' interrupts him.

'Children! This is nothing to rejoice over, I assure you. It is obvious that you are all tired and unable to ignore what's going on outside of the classroom.' He pauses, and thirty-six pairs of eyes follow his towards the one window with glass in it; all the others have been blown out and have been replaced by wood. 'It all seems singularly pointless.' He halts again, looks down at his desk. His hands grip the edges as if he were holding it down against some great force. 'That's why I agreed to come out of retirement – to give you something lasting – a bit of education. But now some of you are going to be educated on a subject that is not my speciality – cannon. Too soon. Much too soon. Which brings me to the sad duty I must perform.' He does not look up, which is unlike him, but shuffles through his papers until he has found what he wants. Holding them in shaky hands, he continues: 'Today your Fatherland has called the class of 1929. 3 March 1945, you who were born in 1929 are called up to bear arms. Those whose names I will read will report for duty as flak helpers in the assembly hall tomorrow morning at nine a.m. Breller, Choenbach, Gerhard, Mertens, Mons, Mueller, Schubach and Tetzlaff.' His voice is toneless. Then he gathers his books, crumples the paper, drops it, mumbles, 'Insanity . . .' Shabby briefcase under his arm, Dr Graefe leaves the room.

Momentary, stunned silence until Tetzlaff jumps up and shouts jubilantly, 'Finally! *Finally!*' He tosses a book in the air. 'Who needs this silly Latin? Did you see that the old fool was actually crying?' Tetzlaff, Mertens and Schubach are clearly overjoyed. They feel like men. They don't notice the silence, don't notice that the rest of us leave without saying a word.

'We must find Eberhard at once.' Ruth is voicing my thoughts. Eberhard is already waiting for us at our meeting place. He answers our question before we have a chance to ask it.

'They won't make me a soldier! Never! I have a weak heart. I

184

can prove it.' He has to bend down to whisper to us. How helpless and weak he looks. No, not weak . . . vulnerable. 'I'm scared,' he says. 'If they ever put me behind one of those flak guns, I'll drop dead from fear alone.'

'I think everyone is scared,' says Ruth, 'but no one wants to admit it. Only stupid people are not afraid. Look at that ass-hole Tetzlaff. I bet he's the first one to have his trousers full. My father says the real heroes are not the soldiers, but those who refuse to fight. Especially now.' She takes a deep breath, goes on in a low, conspiratorial voice. 'It's always the ordinary, common people who have to take the hot chestnuts out of the fire. They have to pay for everything. They have had to pay for every war all through history . . . pay with everything they had, including their lives. The rulers always survived and got fatter. The big Nazis *have*. They don't care whether everyone else starves or freezes or dies. The common soldiers have nothing. Look at them when you see a troop train. Their lives are all they've left to give. But if they'd refused in the beginning, the Nazis couldn't have even started this insanity.'

'It's too late now,' says Eberhard. 'We're down to the wire – everyone has to save his own skin. And I'm not going to shoot anyone or anything. I'm not even going to touch a gun.'

'You see?' Ruth interrupts him. 'That's just what I mean! What you're doing takes much more courage. Everyone thinks you're a sissy just because you like playing the piano and you like books and that sort of thing. But you have so much more strength than they do.'

Eberhard's normally pale face flushes; even his ears turn red.

Ruth, who notices, hurries on, 'I mean it. Really, Eberhard, I mean it. Physical strength is not the only strength. The mind is much stronger.'

I'm amazed at the authority and fearlessness with which Ruth talks. She puts it all so clearly and precisely.

'I know Ilse agrees with me, even though we've never really talked about it. Right, Ilse?'

'I wanted to, thought about it often, but . . .'

'I know.' Ruth looks at me. 'I knew all along, but somehow I too wasn't sure. I bet your dad told you, just as mine did, to keep your mouth shut, not to breathe a word to anyone about what was spoken at home.'

I nod fervently, wanting to say something, wanting to talk about my father, something I cannot do at home. I wonder, as I have so often before, what my grandparents have against him. I know it's not that he is anti-Nazi. They are against Hitler too. But before I can say anything, Ruth continues.

'And then, don't forget, we were so much younger – children still. But now it's different, we're grown-up. You both listen to the BBC, don't you?'

Eberhard and I exchange a glance, one that says, 'I didn't tell her but of course we *should* tell her.' We both nod earnestly.

'Well,' Ruth continues, 'then you know where the front really is. The front is in Germany. The Russians are practically in Frankfurt on the Oder, the Allies in Frankfurt on Main. Gosh, I wish the western Allies would step up their offensives. Then once more Germany will be free. There are so many people waiting for this moment – Communists, Social Democrats, Catholics, even Jehovah's Witnesses. They couldn't get together, so Hitler came to power. Now we're all in the same boat . . . Well, see you tomorrow. Stay alive!'

At the station, we scramble, rush, push aboard with the thousands of others.

'Eberhard,' I ask later, 'what are you going to do? I mean, how are you going to get out of it?'

'Do? Nothing,' comes his reply. 'That's just it. I'm going to do nothing. Nothing at all.'

I think that he hasn't looked so cheerful since I don't remember when. And now he starts coughing and his whole, thin frame shakes violently. The effort drives tears into his eyes.

'Got to see a doctor,' he sputters between coughs. 'Will you tell my classroom teacher tomorrow that I had to go to the doctor?'

March–April 1945. Eberhard is home sick. But his type of pneumonia allows him to move about quite freely, doesn't interfere with his piano-playing or anything else, for that matter. But it's turned his mother into a nervous wreck. Every door is locked twice, three times. Even I have to use a special code, whistle a certain tune and use a two-short-two-long knock to get into the house. Every noise makes her rush to the window and each time anyone walks down the street, Eberhard has to jump into bed. Even when the mailman comes.

> Night and destruction surround us
> On the edge of this yawning abyss.
> Still hope – hope
> For a tomorrow
> Because of you – with you.

A four-times folded slip of paper. The poem Eberhard wrote for me. I carry it with me wherever I go.

Jolanthe, the pig, is big and fat. The neighbours sneered. Almost everyone around here keeps chickens, rabbits, even geese or ducks, but the general opinion has been that a pig, like cows or horses, belongs on a farm. Yet now that Jolanthe is about to be slaughtered, the pig is the matter of greatest interest to our neighbours. Word of mouth has obviously spread to other parts of Luebars too. People whom I don't even know stop me in the street and inquire after my health and about the well-being of our pig. The bold ones want to know the exact date of the killing, and then they add with a somewhat uneasy laugh, 'I hope there'll be a piece for me,' or 'You can't eat it all yourselves. Don't forget, I'm willing to help.'

Most people, though, after hearing that we and the pig are well, tell of their troubles in apologetic tones.

'My boy hasn't been well for so long, the doctor says if he could only get some meat . . .'

Mutti hears everyone out to the end.

Grossmutter never waits long enough to hear the whole story, tells everyone right away, 'We'll make a lot of fresh blood and liverwurst. There'll be a bowl for you too. Just come around.'

I know that at least a hundred people in our neighbourhood have been promised 'a little bowl'. I'm beginning to fear a stampede. How can Jolanthe, that one pig, fill all those bowls, especially as the State is entitled to two thirds of her?

Grossvater and Grossmutter worry about all the details involved, and not about filling the bowls. They both grew up on farms and have set things up with experienced care.

Everything except the actual killing is to be done in the cellar. No one seriously considers that there might even be a single night without air-raids. Grossvater has finished building a smoke-room into the chimney. His workbenches have been cleared and a gigantic meat-grinder is mounted on one of them. Additional tables have been set up for meat-cutting and the preparation of sausages. Neat bundles of wooden sticks have been made ready to close Jolanthe's guts once they're filled with sausage meat. By the door stands a stack of not so little bowls. Eager neighbours have brought them, expect them to be filled. Firewood is piled high by the copper kettle, normally Grossmutter's washtub.

Eberhard and I, hands over our ears, nevertheless hear Jolanthe's last, frightened squeal and a few curses from Grossvater. Jolanthe the pig is dead at three in the afternoon. The professional butcher, the state controller and the meat inspector come inside and have a few slugs of schnapps before they sign their statements that Jolanthe is fit to eat.

'Seven hundred pounds!' The message travels through garden, yard, cellar, reaches every part of the house, because there are 'helpers' everywhere. At least fifty, I'm sure. I'm also sure that the only ones who know what they are doing are my grandparents and one friend of Grossvater's who used to be a butcher. Eberhard and I make and hand out coffee. Enormous amounts of coffee. Ersatz coffee, to be sure, but even that is hard to come by. Mutti is in charge of two large pots, our biggest filled with vegetable soup. The helpers have to be fed. The mood in our house is joyous, almost festive. The smell of blood, meat and sausage is all-pervading.

In the cellar, the meat-grinder groans and clanks. Impossible to say how many people are there. Some take turns at the grinder, since it's hand-operated; others carry away the mountains of meat it chews up and spews out, then stuff it into the guts, which have been cut into sausage-size lengths. The sausages, row upon row, pile up on the table, neatly looped at each end and kept closed by one of the wooden sticks. They are ready to be smoked.

'More wood, we need more wood. The fire must be kept going.' It crackles under the big copper vat. Night falls. The first batch of blood sausage is ready. And here comes everybody, the whole neighbourhood. The line stretches through the kitchen and corridor, down the front steps, through the garden and out into the street. Mutti, with beaming smiles, ladles the blood sausage into the oddest receptacles, chosen, we soon can tell, after long and serious deliberation. Someone actually comes with a pail! Mutti is forced to say, 'No, I am sorry. There would be none left for anyone else. Don't you have anything smaller?'

The woman only shrugs her shoulders, and Mutti pours a few ladlefuls into the bottom of the pail.

Alarm! Everyone scurries down into the cellar. It's never been so crowded, or so happy. Laughter, as rare as fresh, unrationed wurst now, fills it, drowning out the sound of flak and planes overhead.

'If we have to die, at least we'll die with a full stomach,' says a man sitting next to Eberhard and me. He noisily alternates bites of warm wurst and chunks from an enormous loaf of bread. 'Here!' he urges us. 'Take as much as you like. My wife baked it. You won't get anything like this very often, not even with a cook like your grandmother in the house.'

Eberhard and I refuse. We've stuffed ourselves with cake and agree that we couldn't eat any of the meat even if they paid us. The smell alone is almost too much for us.

The work continues at a frantic pace. Everyone eats, jokes, watches the pig become ham, lard, sausage. There's enough noise to almost drown out the All Clear. When Eberhard's mother appears, we finally let go of each other's hands.

'Oh, I've been so worried!'

'What's there to worry about?' asks Grossmutter. 'You knew he was here. Come, I'll give you some sausage. There may not be much left after this.'

At seven in the morning it is all gone. The feast is over.

Our share of the pig, in the form of bacon, sausages and lard, is stashed away. Only Grossmutter knows where. We now have bunk beds in the cellar. Grossvater made them. There's no point in trying to go to sleep upstairs, or in taking off all our clothes. I think sometimes how nice it must feel to sleep in only one's nightgown, and undisturbed at that. But I can't take my clothes off any more than I can get rid of my fear. At any moment the house may be hit. We have to be ready. Cold, gnawing fear still makes me shake uncontrollably every time the cool radio voice announces incoming flights. I want to run to the bunker, but Grossmutter won't go. Grossmutter and I are alone much of the time. Mutti works thirty, forty, forty-eight hours at a stretch, and Grossvater does too, staying at least two, often three nights at the factory on fire duty.

We are encircled, and the territory around us shrinks daily. Berlin is the goal, the final prize of the victors. Hitler has given the order to destroy everything. Nobody, nothing must fall into the hands of the enemy. 'Scorched earth,' he said, 'is what we'll leave them.'

At least Eberhard is coming to school with me again. He doesn't have to man an anti-aircraft gun. Though he's trying hard to hide it, he really is sick. That terrible coughing, being out of breath after a few normal steps, is real. It also means that we can't run if our train is bombarded and they start machine-gunning those who try to scramble to safety.

There isn't any security at school either. We are supposed to go to a shelter, but teachers and students alike prefer the sturdy old building to the three feet of dirt overhead in the shelter.

We've reached the point where we don't know why we come to school. No one keeps attendance records. Classes? They are nothing more than a rumour-spreading and debating society.

No one has seen Dr Graefe. Someone claims that his whole block was burned down, but no one knows for sure. Nothing is certain. Ruth and I have written letters to the camp in Harrachsdorf. No answer. Did they get out before the Russians got there? No one knows. We know that if we don't see each other in school any more, communications between us will be cut. We have no telephones, and even if we did, how much longer would they work? The mail? Some comes through, a lot burns in the air-raids or is left behind on disabled trains and trucks.

'Everything is coming apart at the seams,' says Ruth. She's right, yet, surprisingly, the city still functions. Gas, water, electricity all work, except for short periods when one of the main lines is hit. Trains run, though with enormous delays. People go to work. The radio blares daily messages that those found guilty of leaving their assigned posts will be court-martialled. And in case some mothers might be under the delusion that children cannot be court-martialled, children who do not attend school will be drafted for defence work, says the radio announcer. Eberhard, Ruth and I have made a pact. We've promised each other to keep in touch with whatever means are available. Even as we make this solemn agreement, we all know it will be impossible. We hear heavy artillery day and night. It's the front. We are surrounded, almost. How will it all end? Soon, dear Lord, we say like everyone else, let it be soon. Rather an end with horror than horror without end.

'Stay alive!'
'Stay alive!'
'Stay alive!'

Ruth, Eberhard and I shake hands, part at the train station as usual.

Eberhard's parents have come over with him. They are debating with my grandparents and Mutti about whether to keep us home from now on. Mutti and the Watzlawiks hesitate, are afraid of the official threats. Grossvater isn't sure. But Grossmutter, apparently as unconcerned about State decrees as ever, says, 'The children will stay home. Only place to be from now on. If someone comes and inquires, they're sick. *Basta!* ' She looks into the uncertain faces around her and adds, 'I don't understand why you make such faces. Just listen . . . That's not only artillery; that's tank cannon and machine-guns that you hear – and you *wonder* whether the children should go to school?' She taps her finger against her forehead. 'Really!'

Now there are planes overhead. We hear the anti-aircraft guns. The Watzlawiks have to wait quite a while before they can cross the street to go home. Through the cellar window I watch them disappear around the corner of their house. They've just made it. Now the sirens howl. Alarm.

Another air raid, it's just another air raid. We've already lived through so many, but this one – I don't know, it seems especially severe. Mutti and I bend closer to the concrete floor, as if this would help. Grossmutter peels apples, her knife evenly cutting the skin in spirals. Rooooom. The house shakes on its foundation. The glass storm windows standing here in the cellar, protected by rags, make a peculiar, high-pitched sound. Every item in the house rattles, clanks, vibrates. The preserves on the shelves move in their glasses. Suddenly there is a succession of loud but dull thuds. Grossmutter drops knife and apples, races upstairs, shouts,

'Fire! The kitchen is burning!'

We all run upstairs, rip down burning curtains and towels, push the square incendiary bombs into the metal dustpans Grossmutter has handy, and then shove them out into the garden through the open windows. We are oblivious to the flak and the continuing rain of bombs. The often cursed pails filled with water and sand, always in the way, come in handy now! We race up and down feverishly, getting rid of the mean grey canisters that seem to be all over the place. Everything is under control by the time the All Clear sounds. All the fires are out. We run into the street to see whether anyone needs help.

The whole neighbourhood has been showered with these incendiary bombs, one foot square and two feet long. Everyone has had some, but since they are relatively easy to handle, not much damage has been done.

'Well,' says Grossmutter, 'got away with no more than a black eye – again.'

It takes a whole day to clean up the mess, sweep up the glass from the broken windows and board them up. Grossvater fixes all the holes in the roof, at least temporarily.

Two days later he comes home looking like an Egyptian mummy. His arms, completely bandaged, are stretched out in front of him. His head too is covered, with only slits for eyes and nose.

'Don't touch me! Don't touch me!' His desperate whispers are really muffled shouts. 'Ouch!' He screams when he inadvertently comes in contact with a chair.

It's a shock to see him this way, yet somehow it seems in keeping with everything else that's going on. He says the bandages make him look worse than he really is.

'We tried to put out the fire. Then there was an explosion. The doctor says these are only first-degree burns. They will all heal.'

'At least you can stay at home now,' Grossmutter says stoically. 'There's good in everything. Just in time, too. The end can be no more than a few days away and it's best we should all be together at home. I wish I knew of a way to keep Grete home. Grete! Do you know how to walk home from Gesundbrunnen?'

'Grossmutter!' Mutti answers with exasperation. 'You know we have the bunker!'

'I'm not talking about air raids!' she retorts angrily. 'I'm talking about Russians! You should come home *before* they get to you! If I had my way, you'd stay home from now on!'

'Don't be ridiculous! I can't just stay home! And I can't run away from work either. You know that.'

'That's not doing one's duty. That's being utterly stupid,' Grossmutter grumbles.

'Don't let her go in those flimsy shoes! Make her wear something solid,' comes Grossvater's voice from behind the bandages.

'Everyone is still working,' Mutti says defiantly. 'And so am

193

I! They have military police and SS all over the station, controlling everyone, not only soldiers. They check our papers even when we are in uniform. Everyone must remain at his post. Those who don't will be regarded as traitors and will be executed immediately. You just don't know what it's like out there. Barricades in the centre of Berlin. Soldiers hanging from lamp-posts, and around their necks are signs that say "TRAITOR". You just don't know what it's like. Every entrance and exit, every platform is patrolled. I need a special pass to come home. How can I just walk out? You have no idea.'

'Oh, yes, I have.' Grossmutter comes as close to shouting as I've ever heard her. 'I have a very good idea. A much better one than you do. It's going to be everyone for himself. Save your own skin. That's what it's going to be. And, my dear Grete, the big Nazi wheels will be the first to run and save themselves. *Your* best chance for survival is *here*! Right here at home! They will trample each other to death in your bunker.' Grossmutter pauses. Grossvater gesticulates, but she continues, a little calmer now. 'At the first sign of disintegration, leave! Come home, but *walk*! Do you hear me? Listen to me! *Walk*! Don't rely on trains and buses, even if they are still running. It may be a matter of hours – who knows? – before everything breaks down. *Walk*! Your feet are the most reliable transportation. How many hours do you think it will take you?'

'Five, maybe six. I really don't know.' Mutti is barely audible.

'Grete! Promise me that you will keep your eyes and ears open and, at the right moment, leave. There *is* such a thing as the right moment, and I hope you will be able to sense it. When it comes, just leave, walk out and *no one* will stop you. And . . . Grossvater is right. Unless you put on your other shoes, you're not going at all.'

'Come on, I've already told Hertha,' says Grossvater. 'We'll make that opening in the cellar wall. Grete, you'll have to help. Grossmutter and Ilse can't do it alone.'

Gathering in front of the brick wall that separates our cellar from the Ruhls', we hear Hertha banging away on the other side. We have all agreed that we must be able to get to each other without having to go out into the street or garden. That's too dangerous. In case of fire or whatever other calamity might befall us, we want to be able to help each other. I can't imagine old Herr Ruhl in his wheelchair being of any help, nor his seventy-year-old wife, but Hertha, their daughter, might be. Anyway, it will feel good to have more people around.

'Use the chisel, the other one – not there, in between the bricks!' Grossvater's commands come out muffled through his bandages.

We work on either side, attacking the wall with all our might, in turn encouraged, cursed and directed by Grossvater, until we have a hole large enough for a person to crawl through.

Mutti helps, but we could have done it without her. Once I got the knack, it wasn't so hard, particularly with the big sledgehammer. Mutti has to leave. She has put on her uniform and, obediently, her walking shoes. We watch her walk down the street towards the bus. I hope there won't be a bus so that she will have to come back.

Vavarooom, varroom. Instinctively we duck. Berlin is being shelled.

'And she insists on going to work!' Grossmutter shakes her head as Mutti waves once more before disappearing around the bend.

18 April 1945. Berlin is under attack, artillery shelling a constant noise and low-flying Russian planes an ever present threat, since they machine-gun everything that moves.

If I only knew where Vati is! I don't even know whether he is still alive. I sometimes think of the Gerstens, all the friends in Hermsdorf, especially the 'Roosters'. I have neither seen them nor heard from them in years. These thoughts come and go, leaving my head as soon as something explodes nearby.

[Axel Hahn, the 'Rooster', arrested for underground work against the Nazis, was hanged in Oranienburg concentration camp on 18 April 1945, two hours before the arrival of the Russian Army. It would have given me courage to know that on this day Vati, and with him the five young men, escaped the OT camp and that they would arrive safely two days later in Hermsdorf.]

If only Mutti would come home. Goebbels, our propaganda minister, screams hysterically on the radio: 'Berlin will be defended to the last house, to the last woman and child, to our last breath.' The slim hope that they might declare Berlin an open city is gone. The unbelievable, the seemingly impossible has become a reality. Old men and young boys are erecting barricades on Berlin's famous thoroughfares. They are made to carry rifles that they don't even know how to fire. They rip up the asphalt and cobblestones and dig trenches. And still trains and buses are running, and people stand in line in front of stores. They wait pressed against walls, ducking only when an explosion is really close. They wait to get a bit of food, anything edible.

'The potatoes have to go into the ground,' says Grossmutter.

Typical, I think. The city is under fire, but she has to plant potatoes. We take turns digging, halving potatoes and putting them in the ground. Every few minutes we must drop everything and run to the trees for cover from the low-flying planes. This time we were a bit slow.

'Maybe they saw us?'

'Come on, come on!' Grossmutter answers. She is already digging again. 'We still have so much to do!'

I follow reluctantly, then scream, 'They are coming back!' I see her run, hear the MG, see the earth squirt up beside me as I dive into the entrance of the old shelter, landing on my side because I've hit the rim of the metal rain barrel. For one short second I clearly see the pilot, his helmet, goggles and gun.

They're gone as fast as they came. When I pick myself up, my leg is bleeding and the rain barrel has two neat bullet holes. I tie Grossmutter's handkerchief around my leg, and even though the blood seeps right through, we continue.

'We've got to get them in. If we survive, what's in the ground may be all we'll have.'

The shooting is so intense that I just have to climb a tree to find out if I can see anything.

'Grossmutter! Grossmutter!' I jump down and flee into her arms. 'Tanks, Russian tanks! They are lined up at the edge of the woods. There must be hundreds of them!'

'Yes, yes.' She hurries to a spot where she can see beyond the three gardens. 'It'll soon be over.' Her voice is flat. 'All the more reason to hurry,' she says after a pause. 'Come on, we only have a few left.'

When we get back to the house, we find an excited crowd in our kitchen: Eberhard, his mother, the Ruhls and most of the women who used to meet for coffee and cake. They are breathless, near panic.

'Platanenstrasse. The SS has moved into Platanenstrasse!' Else Gerlitz is shaking and the low tone of her voice conveys more horror than a scream. 'Those SS pigs have moved in to defend the street with a handful of "Werewolves", children twelve or fourteen years old. They are throwing a couple of sandbags in front of the cellar windows of houses, and that's what they call fortification. It would be funny if it weren't so serious.' Else Gerlitz twists her apron nervously and, between sobs, continues. 'All my life I've known Hedwig. We went to school together and now she's trapped on that street. Oh, to have it all end like this! These bloody pigs!'

'Else, stop shouting. My God, if someone heard you!' Eberhard's mother says, herself close to tears.

Defiantly, Else says, 'Who can hear anything over this din?'

'Why Platanenstrasse?' asks Trude Kort, our neighbour on the other side. 'Do you think they'll come down here too?'

'Don't paint the devil on the wall,' says Grossmutter.

'He'll kill us all! He'll kill us!' wails Eberhard's mother.

'No, he won't. No man kills his own family.' Grossmutter sounds stern, convincing. 'He was no Nazi bigwig. What does he have to fear?'

Frau Watzawik mutters between sobs, 'I know he has the pistol. He's shown it to me. I know he means what he says.'

Both Eberhard and Else, who has dried her own tears, put their arms around Frau Watzlawik.

'Stop crying. That won't do any good. Can't you hide the pistol?'

'I don't know where he keeps it. I've looked all over. Oh my God, what can we do?'

Else is sobbing again as she talks. 'It's all sealed off up there now. I climbed over the back fences, or I'd have been trapped there too. Children with a few anti-tank weapons and hand grenades, trying to stop the Russian army. Not one stone will be left on another. And I've know her all my life, all my life!'

'Else!' Grossmutter commands. 'Don't talk as if they're already dead.' She stirs the soup. The women surround her as she works, unconsciously, it seems, making room for her as she moves about the kitchen.

'Alma,' Else says to her, 'I don't understand you. How can you cook soup and wash dishes when the Russian tanks are in Luebars?'

They all look at her in bafflement and consternation.

'They're not in the village yet,' Grossmutter replies. 'And besides, what else is there to do? What do you want me to do? Run out and keep the Russians away with my apron? As long as I am in this house, I'll do my work – and there's plenty of it. I suggest you do the same.'

Varoom! A close detonation.

'Oh, God!' screams Eberhard's mother. 'Eberhard, let's go home! Let's go home to Papa!'

They leave, all of them. Eberhard and I don't even say goodbye, don't even have a chance to arrange when we'll see each other again.

Outside, the din continues undiminished. Is it coming closer? Perhaps not. I'm lying on my bunk, fully dressed. Grossmutter's eyes are closed, but I don't think she's sleeping. Grossvater makes snoring noises, but that's because the bandage doesn't allow him to breathe properly. He shifts uneasily, turns, mumbles. He too must be awake. Who can sleep?

I wish Mutti would come home. If only she hadn't gone to

work! What will happen if she doesn't get back before the Russians come? I think of those rows of tanks I saw. All my insides are one big lump of solid fear. I have to go to the toilet. I don't dare go upstairs alone, don't want to go on the pail in Grossvater's work cellar either. I'll wait. If Grossmutter moves or speaks, I'll ask her to come upstairs with me.

Old Herr Ruhl, sleeping in his wheelchair, makes strange wheezing noises. He has asthma. Three more people have come, relatives of the Ruhls. They have fled from the Russians and arrived tearful and moaning only a few hours before. The woman is small, birdlike, the man short and squat. He has said hardly a word. Their seventeen-year-old daughter is lame. They're quiet now.

19 April 1945. Grossvater has gone to the doctor in Waid-mannslust. The Russians haven't come. Not yet. I want to run away from it all, but I don't know where to go. I have to talk, talk, talk to silence the mounting panic inside me.

'Grossmutter! What's it going to be like? What will they do? Shouldn't we try to leave?'

She pays no attention to my questions. 'I wish your mother would come home,' she says. 'Grossvater too. I could have re-bandaged him myself. Maybe he shouldn't have gone. And Grete! Why doesn't Grete come?'

For the first time Grossmutter looks worried, I realize with a shock. She is worried!

'They may not let her go,' she adds.

'They have to let her go home after her shift,' I say.

'The trouble is, child, *they* don't have to do anything but save their own skins. You're shaking, Ilse. Can't you stop it? What good does it do? *Don't* put the cups there! Look at what you're doing! Don't think about the rumours!'

'I can't think of anything else.'

'You don't have to think to know where the cups belong. We're still all right, still in our own house. There! That must be Grossvater.'

'Is Grete back?' As usual, his worry shows itself in anger.

'Why isn't she back. What's keeping her now? Everything is disintegrating fast. The train crews are abandoning the trains. I caught a bus, but the driver said it would be his last run. Where is she? Where the hell is she?'

He paces back and forth in the kitchen, his bandaged head a white globe, his shaking hands, stiff white mittens. 'Time and time again we've told her to leave at the first sign of trouble. That's *now*. Why do you think it took *me* so long? There are grenades flying overhead. I could actually see them. And the planes strafe anything that moves on the street and there's nowhere to take cover. I almost got hit at the bus stop, the one in front of the butcher. We knocked, but they're boarded up. Won't let anyone in. Afraid someone might get a look at what they've hoarded over the years ... Ilse had better run to Tante Martha and phone Grete.'

'I'd hate to send her. You said yourself there's too much shooting. Listen!' *Rayatatatatattttta*. 'Do you hear that? She won't get farther than the garden gate.'

Another volley of machine-gun fire and with it the door bursts open. Mutti! Even Grossvater embraces her, forgetting his burns, and then screams in pain.

'Thank God you're home. How did you manage? What's happening?' we all ask at once, and Mutti, clearly exhausted and nervous, needs a while to calm down before she can talk.

'It was madness, absolute madness. Thousands of people at the station. Children alone, with backpacks large enough to make a man stagger. How good it is to have Ilse home! You can't imagine the chaos! Soldiers and civilians carrying what looked like whole households. SS and MP still checking papers, grabbing men and marching them off to be shot. Everyone shouting, screaming, pushing, yelling above the gun-fire — and I'm still selling tickets. Selling tickets and don't even know whether there are still trains. Suddenly someone says, "Two to Luebars" just as Ilse did when she came home, and I'm so stupefied I say, "That's no station" before I realize that it's Herr Ahl, my colleague, the one who lives right behind Tante Martha. "Come on," he says, "the air is getting thick" and he puts a finger over his mouth and rolls his eyes. I don't know what to do because an SS officer is standing behind Ahl and my supervisor is behind me and I'm sure they've heard him.'

We can tell that Mutti is reliving the scene as she tells it.

'Then my supervisor pushes me away from the window, says loud enough for the SS officer to hear, "Take an hour off, Frau Koehn. Three shifts in a row without a break! Go get yourself a cup of coffee. Here's your pass." And as he hands it to me, he whispers, "Make yourself scarce! Good luck. Report back tomorrow . . . if there is such a thing." Wasn't that decent? Ahl was waiting, he had a pass too. God knows how he got it. Without the passes, we would never have been able to leave the station, let alone come home. I wanted to take the train, but Ahl insisted we walk.'

'What did we tell you?' Grossmutter interrupts. 'Isn't that what we told you?'

Mutti slumps into a chair, but keeps on talking about trucks burning in the streets, barricades, people not being allowed into cellars, a boy shot by the SS in front of their eyes. 'They said he'd defected. He couldn't have been more than fourteen.' Her voice trails off. She has fallen asleep, still wearing her uniform and the 'sensible walking shoes'.

Grossvater too is asleep. Asleep sitting up. I follow Grossmutter into the kitchen and see her kneeling in front of the stove.

'What are you doing down there?'

She looks up, grins like a kid who's been caught with its hand in the cookie jar. 'Oh, nothing, nothing. Just getting some lard.'

'Lard? What's it doing down there?'

'Psst' she says, after taking a few spoonfuls out of a clay jar. She puts the jar back under the stove, carefully replacing a tile. 'I know the Russians! Those Muzhiks have nothing to eat themselves.' Grinning triumphantly, she adds, 'You wouldn't have thought of that, I bet. We won't starve – not as long as I live.'

I'm still staring at the tile. Grossmutter giggles slyly. 'Go get potatoes and help me grate them. I thought I would make pancakes tonight to cheer everyone up a bit.'

'Pancakes! Oh, great! My favourite meal. May I invite Eberhard, please?'

'Of course, of course. Invite his parents too.'

Grossmutter starts making cakes and the smell wakes up Grossvater and Mutti. 'Leave the doors open,' they tell me. 'Run fast! Watch out for planes!' As I cross the street, I see Eberhard, who waves frantically and points to the sky. Then I see the low-flying Russian planes, and race towards the Watzlawik house. Safe.

'I don't understand! I don't understand why they stay there!' Eberhard says even before saying hello. I don't know what he's talking about. 'The western Allies, of course,' he says impatiently. 'They have been at the Elbe for days, should have been here by now. What are they waiting for? And now we're encircled by the Russians. My father says they will be here tonight. Actually, they could be here any moment. Have you seen the tanks?' Eberhard seems more upset, more frightened even than I am. His face is white and drawn. I can't think of anything to say, then remember what I came for.

'We're having pancakes tonight. I came to invite you and your parents.'

The word 'pancakes,' the very idea of them, brings some colour back to his face. I repeat my invitation to his mother, who has just appeared.

'Oh, no. Thank you, no,' she says in a funny kind of voice. Her eyes are red and swollen, her hands fluttering. In that same strange voice, she adds, 'Thank your grandmother, but no, I couldn't possibly.'

'Can't Eberhard come?' I plead.

'Yes, yes, of course. He can go.' Now her voice is different, tired, resigned. 'He can go, but only for half an hour.'

Eberhard seems undecided. I drag him by the arm, we race back across the street and sit down to an enormous pile of pancakes with apple sauce and sugar. Grossmutter has even filled the sugarbowl, an act so unusual that it sends shivers of fear down my spine. I think this meal may be our last. The last meal and then . . . the Russians.

Eberhard eats and eats, but his head is sinking lower. Finally he can neither hide nor stop his despairing sobs.

'Eberhard, what's the matter? It won't be all *that* bad,' Grossmutter says soothingly. 'You'll live to be a happy old man.'

Eberhard shakes his head furiously. 'My father! My father is going to shoot us tonight.' He gets up, tries to control himself, but when Grossmutter gives him her handkerchief, he suddenly flings himself into her arms and hides his head on her shoulder. Grossmutter says soothingly. 'You'll live to be a happy old what's to come, Eberhard! Don't even say such things. Your father is a reasonable man, a nice, quiet man who's never hurt anyone in his life. Why should he be so scared of the Russians?'

'I don't know, I don't know. All I know is, he is going to shoot us. I know for sure.' Eberhard dries his tears, has himself under control again. 'I have to go now. Thank you. Thank you very much.' Solemnly he walks over to Mutti, bows and shakes hands. Bows in front of Grossvater, then to Grossmutter once more. 'Good-bye.'

'Wait a minute. I want you to take this to your parents.' Grossmutter hands him a large bowl filled with pancakes.

Alone in the corridor, we face each other, and Eberhard says, 'Ilse, I want to thank you. Thank you for everything. It was so nice to be your friend.' One fast, hard embrace, one kiss and we even miss each other's lips. He dashes out.

And only then does it hit me. 'It was so nice . . .' He used the past tense. What if his father . . . I don't dare complete the thought. There he is, rounding the corner of his house. How could he not be here tomorrow? But then, I might not be here either. The knowledge shocks me as much as the grenade that comes down at the end of the street. It is the first close one in a while. Unable to move, I stand in the doorway, staring at the blood-red sky, the deserted street, the Watzlawiks' house.

Emotions, like an avalanche, sweep over me. Crying, I flee into the relative safety of our house.

Night of 19 April 1945–morning of 20 April 1945. Mutti is pacing back and forth, nervously wringing her hands. 'What are we going to do? What are we going to do?'

'Do? What is there to do but wait and see?' Grossmutter and Grossvater answer in unison. 'We are lucky not to be in town,' she goes on. 'Why don't you lie down and try to sleep for a while?'

'Sleep?' cries Mutti. 'When the Russians can be here any minute!' She starts her nervous pacing again.

Grossvater reads. Doesn't he know we can see he's holding the book upside down? Grossmutter pretends to knit, but finds one excuse after another to get up. She stokes the coals in the stove, goes out to the veranda. The shooting outside intensifies. We hurry to the cellar. Our neighbours are already there.

No one can sit still. We mill around, talk, but don't make sense.

And then a different sound mixes with the shooting – a strange rumble. There is commotion in the street. We run upstairs. The dark street is crowded with running, rushing people. There are bicycles, handcarts, baby carriages. A bright red flare illuminates the ghostly sight. 'The Russians are coming!' a woman with a heavy rucksack gasps. 'They're coming, they're right behind us!'

In panic, Mutti and I run down to the cellar. We want to leave. We have our coats on and bunker bags in hand before Grossvater can stop us. We cry, shout, scream, until he and Grossmutter, brooms in hand, physically block our way. Grossvater, despite his bandages, suddenly looks formidable.

Grossmutter, having put her broom aside, pulls at our coats. 'Grete! Ilse! Be sensible! Can't you see that there's no place to go? You'll be overtaken on the open road. That's suicide!'

Grossvater too puts his broom aside as we meekly take off our coats. He goes upstairs to the window, returns. 'They're all gone. The street is deserted, empty. Completely empty and . . . Luebars village is burning.'

Everyone goes upstairs. We crowd around our small attic window. The seven-hundred-year-old village is burning brightly. Orange flames shoot up. That must be Quade's . . . and look, look, Neuendorff's – God, all that straw! The next barrage of shells sends us back to the cellar.

'Their cannon must be right by the church, to judge by the flashes.'

'Yes. How soon do you think they'll be here?'

'Maybe they won't come tonight, but wait till morning?'

We're all in our cellar, all except for the old Ruhls. We can't get the wheelchair through the small opening. We sit anxiously listening to the shooting, the noises outside. Everyone jumps when we hear footsteps on the stairs. It's Else Gerlitz, who wants to check whether we are all right.

'No fighting for me,' she says. 'Do you have your bedsheets ready? I'm going to hang mine out at the sight of the first Russian. Not before, though. One of those fanatic Nazis might still come by before it's all over. Anyway, I'd better get back. Glad to see no one here is ready to die for Führer and Fatherland. Let's keep in touch. Take care!'

'Be careful going back.'

'Don't worry. I'll go the way I came, over the fences. I'm not fool enough to run around on the street.'

'Well,' Grossmutter says after a while, 'it looks as if they're waiting for morning. We may as well try to get some sleep.' But not even she is serious about that.

We have another visitor: young Schmid, the only known Super-Nazi on our street. He is wearing his uniform under his civilian coat. He's very cheerful.

'Glad to see everything's all right here. We better stick together. There are only a couple of men on this street anyway. Guess there aren't enough of us left to fight the Russians, eh?'

Only Grossmutter answers. 'You can't be *that* insane!'

He looks around, says, 'Oh, no, not just us right here. Not unless we can get some more men and arms together.'

As soon as he's gone, everyone starts in on Grossmutter. Grossvater yells, 'Woman, are you out of your mind? This Nazi can have us hanged at the last minute! How could you say that to him?'

'Don't you know what that was all about, you fools? Didn't you see that, for all practical purposes, he was already in civilian clothes? He's trying to make last-minute friends. For years everyone has been scared of him and his father. Now *he*'s the one who's scared. If he wants to fight, let him go to Platanenstrasse. They've always hung their shirts in the wind, the Schmids. They'll have a white sheet out even before Else will. You want to bet? Ah, that twenty-four-year-old snot. I've known him since he shit in his diapers. How important he felt in his uniform, and always "Heil Hitler, Frau Dereck!" Suddenly he's our good old friend and neighbour.'

Mutti presses close to Grossmutter and whispers something. All I can hear is 'Hertha.' We'd always thought of Hertha Ruhl as a Nazi. She'd bored everyone to tears with her 'absolute belief' in the Führer. But Hertha now sits quietly, staring into space.

They won't come tonight. Hertha has decided to go back to their own cellar to lie down. The three relatives follow. It's not easy for the lame girl, but eventually she too gets through the opening. We sit and wait. Wait to die? It's different from air raids, more frightening.

Grossmutter gets a stack of bowls and opens two glasses of her precious preserved peaches so that everyone can have some. I climb with her through the opening to take peaches to the Ruhls and their relatives. They are astounded. The lame girl can't thank Grossmutter enough, all but kisses her hand. 'God has sent you. We will never forget this.'

Grossmutter, as if lecturing a child, interrupts. 'I don't believe God has anything to do with my peaches. My husband and I planted them, watered them, picked them. I cooked and preserved them and God didn't help me one bit. But go ahead — pray if it makes you feel better. Maybe He'll help you. He's never helped me.'

For the first time in hours it is quiet. Nervously, aimlessly, we move around the cellar.

Our cellar windows are slightly above ground, and except for one small slit they are carefully boarded up and covered with sand. Grossmutter, who is looking through this crack, startles us with, 'Look, look!'

Someone, we can't tell who it is in the dark, comes running out of the Niebisches' house and climbs the fence towards the Watzlawiks' and disappears.

'Must be Niebisch, Watzlawik's cousin. Probably checking to see if they're all right. No – wait a minute!'

We watch the figure, whoever it is, reappear with two large bundles, throw them over the fence, pick them up and disappear through the Niebisches' front door. Back and forth, back and forth he goes. Over to the Watzlawiks' empty-handed and returning with bundles, things. Suddenly there are two figures. Frau Niebisch? No one says a word. We watch them drag, lift and carry what looks like a piece of furniture. Strange. Is everyone thinking what I think and dare not say?

'Over there. Look on the other side! That's Seifert. They are also related, aren't they?' Grossvater says. 'Maybe . . .'

All three come into view again. All three are carrying various articles.

'Do you suppose,' says Grossvater, 'that I should go over and . . .'

'No!' says Grossmutter sharply. 'You can go tomorrow in daylight. Leave the spoils to the relatives.'

'You don't mean . . .?'

'What else can I mean? Come away from the window. I've seen enough. They can't even wait until the bodies are cold. People!'

Eberhard. Your best friend, Eberhard, is dead. My mind forms precise sentences, tells me that I should cry. But I feel nothing. I am numb. No one says a word. We sit in our small cellar world waiting for the Russians.

20 April 1945. 'The war is over! My God, the war is over!'

Hertha shouts. We are all in each other's arms, embracing, crying in a frenzy of hysterical joy.

Only half an hour before, we had waited in cold fear as we watched Grossvater cross the deserted street to the Watzlawiks' house. We watched him return and stop in the middle of the street and slowly raise his bandaged hands. A Russian jeep stopped in front of him. Four Russians talked to him, smiling. Grossvater shook his bandaged head and they turned around and drove back towards Luebars village.

Russians, the first Russians. Grossvater says they spoke fluent German. They wanted to know what happened to him and whether there were any soldiers, any Werewolves around. Yes, Grossvater told us, the Watzlawiks were dead. Lying in their living-room, shot through the head. Watzlawik must have shot his wife and son first, then himself. The house looked ransacked.

'Someone will have to bury them,' Grossmutter says.

The street has come to life. Russians everywhere. Jeeps, bicycles, soldiers on foot laying down telephone cables. Everyone is out, talking, laughing with the Russians. Hertha screams over and over again, 'The war is over! The war is over!'

In the happy frenzy only Grossmutter's face and manner do not change. 'Looks too good to be true,' she says.

Mutti and I, the Ruhls, their relatives are all talking at once. 'They are people, just like us. Look at them! All those awful stories – nothing but a pack of Nazi lies.'

Grossmutter looks doubtful and doesn't allow us to leave the cellar and go up into the street. But then Grossvater comes downstairs with Miele, Tante Martha's crippled helper, and tells us to go to Tante Martha's store.

'The Russian commandant has ordered all shopkeepers to sell out their food supplies. Tante Martha needs help. Grete and Ilse must help her. Go! Go on!' he says and urges us nervously towards the staircase.

Never have I seen our street so crowded. More and more Russians are pouring in. We pass the Schmids, father and son, just as the son is slapping a Russian on the back, laughing uproariously. To see Nazi Schmid so friendly with the Russians makes me trip over a wire, which prompts the young Russian who is working on it to shake a mocking finger at me.

What commotion, and no one seems to care that there is shooting again. No one seems to mind the howling grenades overhead, or the machine-gun fire.

Hundreds of people crowd around the bakery, showing not the slightest concern that the Russians are setting up a grenade-launcher next to it. If Miele hadn't led us through the gardens nearby and then through a rear entrance, we would never have got through to Tante Martha's. The shop is one solid mass of screaming, shoving people.

Tante Martha sighs with relief when she sees us. There is no time for anything else. Without stopping, she points to the sacks of flour and sugar on the floor, gives us trowels, continues to fill paper bags and hand them out. We are caught up in the chaos instantly. I see nothing but outstretched hands.

In the middle stands one Russian. He is being pushed around, elbowed, but he shouts out at the top of his lungs, 'One pound! One pound per person. Hitler said one pound!'

There are a few short laughs. But the crowd is intent on the food and almost crushes him in the effort to get something, anything.

Just as I reach the bottom of one sack, two more are lifted over the waiting heads and dropped down next to me. Two men carrying sacks come out of Tante Martha's storeroom. Just for a moment I wonder how it is that Tante Martha, who has always claimed that she alone of all the shopkeepers hoarded nothing, is suddenly able to supply all of this. But there's no time to think. Mutti and I, working side by side, exchange a fast, knowing glance. We scoop, fill, hand out bags like robots.

Fill a bag, hand it up, bend down to fill the next. I don't recognize Grossmutter until she all but pushes her face into mine. She grabs my hand, holds on to it.

'Come home! Come home immediately!' she insists in a voice that allows no questioning. Still she has to repeat her words for us to hear her. 'Grete! Ilse! Come home! Now!'

We have to battle our way out. It takes an agonizingly long time to push, shove and beat our way through the crowd. How on earth did small, plump, old Grossmutter manage to get in? There's no chance to ask her. The street looks and feels different. There are Russians everywhere. They are going into the houses. The street, the sidewalks are crowded with every imaginable kind of vehicle. There are no Germans in sight.

'Run! Run ahead! The looting has begun!' Grossmutter urges, but we hesitate. 'Run, I said. Don't worry. I'll catch up with you.'

The shooting is wild. Impossible to say where it's coming from except that it's all around us. There are planes in the sky. Even a German one. Am I seeing correctly? But already the tank behind us is firing, and we fling ourselves to the ground as everything seems to explode. Red-hot metal fragments whizz through the air. I don't want to get up. But then I hear Grossmutter's voice right behind me.

'Take the back road and keep to the fences! Run!'

We don't get far. The planes strafe the ground. I find a garden gate open, and run to the house. The door is locked. Behind me, Grossmutter at the gate shouts, 'Come out of there! Keep moving! To the Rieders' fence, from there to our back fence!'

Gardens, rusty fences, thorny berry bushes, compost heaps. Panting we run, stumble, fling ourselves to the ground. Finally the Rieders' garden. A Russian comes out of house clutching, of all things, a grandfather clock. He flings himself to the ground, clock and all, as a grenade howls over our heads. I don't look back, don't care what happens to him. I reach our fence and climb over it.

I take a fraction of a second to glance back over our three gardens with the now leafless trees that stand between us, the open fields and the road to Luebars village.

'Grossmutter!' is all I manage to say. She pushes us to the ground, away from a sight I know I will never forget. For six, ten, fifteen miles, as far as the eye can see – and that's way past

Luebars village – the road is filled with what seems to be the whole Russian army. Tanks, cannon, horses and carts, infantry, cavalry. A snake much wider than the road, on its way towards our house. Grossmutter allows us no time for a second look, but races ahead, half crouched. We get to our veranda and there collide with Gerda Walter. She is holding a large rucksack in front of her and is trying to push us back.

'The Russians!' She points to the kitchen.

'Into the cellar,' whispers Grossmutter, wheeling around and heading for the outside entrance to the cellar. She waits there for us to go in first, then changes her mind and pushes past us. Three Russians come out. They let us pass in.

Our dark, small cellar is filled with Russians. They seem to be coming from every direction. Grossmutter, though smaller than I, resolutely puts herself in front of me and Mutti and pushes us back against a wall. 'Wait, wait just a minute,' she whispers without moving her head. 'There'll be a moment when no one is around.'

That moment is long in coming. Thank God the cellar is so dark. Grossmutter slowly manoeuvres us into the part of the cellar closest to the Ruhls'. It's a tight spot and we almost block the connecting hole. I want to step aside to let some Russians through, but Grossmutter, reaching behind her, clutches my throat so firmly that I think I'll choke, so I stay where I am. Men and women in uniform come and go. They speak to each other, laugh. It sounds friendly, polite. They even step aside to let each other pass. Strange voices. Russian voices. Russian boots clomping up and down our staircase. Russian tanks rattling in the street, Russian artillery, Russian planes overhead.

A gun. Anti-aircraft? Grenade-launcher? It sounds as if they've stationed it right behind us. The house trembles, shakes, everything in the cellar reverberates.

A tall, heavy officer squeezes himself through the hole and sighs with relief when he's made it. He smiles at me. 'Soldiers? No?'

When he leaves, we are suddenly alone in the cellar. Grossmutter turns, pushes me aside, opens a kind of hatch in the wall behind me that I never knew existed. The opening is about three feet off the ground and only about two feet square. She manages to get me through it before I know what is happening. I find myself lying flat on cold, damp sand, because there is only about ten inches of space above me. I'm forced in further as Mutti and Gerda Walter come in after me. Grossmutter closes the hatch before Gerda has even straightened out. She struggles in the dark, and her boot hits my face. Then she too lies flat. Only the tiniest sliver of light comes through.

20 April–22 May 1945. We are lying in a crawlspace under the house, but we don't know exactly where. We listen to the peculiar howl of the Russian grenade-launchers. They're called Stalin Organs because of the arrangement of their five barrels. They fire one after the other.

When the Stalin Organ stops, we hear shrieks, Russian commands, roaring laughter, clomping boots, barrages of artillery, machine-gun fire and the clankety-clankety-clank of tank treads over the staccato of horses' hoofs, until the Stalin Organ drowns it all out again. The noises reach new heights. It is impossible to distinguish or separate them, much less associate them with familiar sounds. The dark, hollow space distorts them. Only our fear and imagination have room in this tiny prison.

Those thuds? That scream? Male and female Russian voices. Are they shouting angrily? Joking? Screams, shouts, laughter intermingle with explosions, single rifle shots, commands and the noise of an army on the move. It goes on and on and on. A particularly high-pitched, blood-curdling scream. Thuds and the hysterical voice of the lame girl's mother: 'No! No! No! Go next door! That's where the women are! Next door!'

I freeze, stop breathing. Nothing. Nothing happens. The hatch remains closed. Boots stomp up and down, up and down. Growls, glass breaks, objects are thrown about, shouts, then laughter. There goes the Stalin Organ again.

My boots hurt, probably laced too tight. I want to loosen

them, bang my head painfully, turn over, lie on my side, my knees raised to my chin.

'Ouch,' says Mutti. 'You hit me in the head.'

'I'm sorry,' I whisper into the darkness and grope for her, but my hands find only sand. Cold, damp grains of sand stick to my fingers, which are clammy with fear. I couldn't be more uncomfortable, but I dare not move. The wrinkled coat under me feels like rocks. Two pairs of long pants, one over the other, numerous sweaters, everything binding, hurting. The total darkness, the narrow space! Movements in the sand. We try to find more comfortable positions without hurting each other or making noise. Will it ever stop? Long ago, it seems, Grossmutter drummed against the hatch and whispered frantically, 'A watch! Give me one! Quick, quick or they're going to shoot Grossvater!' Gerda Walter, closest to the opening, gave hers. That was long ago. Mutti and I have given ours too, one after the other.

There has been no finger-drumming from Grossmutter, nor the sound of her voice, for an eternity. The shooting continues.

I inch forward on my belly, creep into the farthest corner like an animal. Even in this blackness I am ashamed to have to do the necessary, struggle with all the clothing, creep back until I lie next to Mutti and clasp her hand. Our fingers are intertwined, each clawing the other when it seems that the house is going to come down on top of us.

My mind roams, reaches desperately for an image, a happy, sunny one, to block out the present horror. I see young people, boys and girls my own age playing ball on a lawn. Did I once see it in a magazine, a book? I don't remember, but I force it into focus and transport myself there. I'm sitting in the shade of a tree. There's a beach. Soon I will go for a swim with the others. Suddenly it's as if someone has stabbed me, the thought that a scene like this is actually taking place somewhere in the world.

It is the fourth night. Three and a half days and this the fourth night, and the tanks keep rolling, the Russian voices continue laughing, cursing, commanding. There must be some

Russians in our backyard. They're so close we can hear them breathe.

Hours pass. Horribly, frighteningly long hours. Finally, Grossmutter's signal. Her fingers drum, then her voice, the most welcome sound ever: 'Get ready to come out. But be quick. The sentry may come back any minute. No noise! Don't make any noise!'

Stiff limbs, paralysed with cold, with cramps. We try to move, try to be swift and silent. What's that noise? My heart beats so loud that I think it can be heard through the whole house. But it's Grossvater, who in a low, urgent voice commands, 'Quick! For heaven's sake, be quick. We'll get you into the pigsty.'

Through the dark cellar, out into the courtyard. Though the pigsty is attached to the house, the only entrance is through the courtyard. We catch a glimpse of the ominous silhouette of the Stalin Organ, unattended among Grossmutter's beanpoles. Five of us in the empty pigsty. Grossvater and Grossmutter hold the ladder while we climb up and squeeze through a trap-door in the ceiling.

'Up, up! Pull the ladder up!' They urge in whispers.

We pull the ladder up, put the board that covers the opening in its place. Our ears strain for the fading sounds of Grossvater's and Grossmutter's hurrying footsteps. We hear the familiar squeak of the veranda door. Then all is quiet.

We are in the hayloft. We call it that even though it never contained hay or anything else. My grandparents have always had enough room without using it. It's a full-sized room with a slanting, unfinished ceiling. The floor is rough planking and there is no window. One brick has been taken out for ventilation. We find blankets, pillows, a basket containing hot soup. We have not eaten in days. Grossmutter has thought of everything. We find plates and spoons. fresh underwear and in the corner a most welcome, necessary item. A pail with a lid.

Incredible joy to be able to stand up, stretch, eat. Enough to forget everything else for one moment.

A sentry's heavy boots crunch on the gravel. He strikes a match, inhales slowly and with obvious pleasure blows out the smoke. If we can hear him, then *he* can ... We stop breathing before this thought can be completed. Boots. Russians come running through the yard. We hear orders and again the eerie howl of the Stalin Organ. We seize this chance to cough. All three of us cough as if on cue.

We've caught colds. If only we could cough! I *have* to, can't stand it any longer, oh my God, why don't they shoot that thing again? There ... *Horooom*. The ghastly howl is welcome. Still, we use pillows to muffle the sound of our coughing. Four days, four nights. It seems an eternity. We thought the war was over. But it's continuing, the shooting, the occasional machine-gun fire and rifle shots. Will it ever stop?

Morning dawns. We can see through the brick hole. We see them, as far back as Luebars village, all streaming towards us. They are spilling over into the fields and, near us, into the front gardens, an incredible army of tanks and jeeps, trucks in between herds of cows, peasant carts drawn by horses. There are field kitchens surrounded by soldiers on foot and on bicycles. There are motorized guns and cavalry, groups of foot soldiers, one of them chasing two pigs. A motley, slow-moving army. The tanks get stuck on the fences. One, straddled on Else Gerlitz's fence, keeps churning away. Cars, out of gas, are left behind. Finally, machinery, animals, people, ranks all come to a grinding halt. It's too much for the road. Shouts, curses. Nothing can move. Soldiers who were on vehicles get off. They all make for the houses. Blood-curdling screams! Was that Grossvater? Grossmutter? A neighbour? Last desperate protests against a threatened life, punctuated by rifle shots.

Russian commands, roaring laughter, curses, stomping feet, thuds. Things being smashed. But now the mass is moving again. Soldiers come out of the houses carrying everything imaginable. Infantry, trucks, tanks, cows, bicycles, peasant carts, on and on, and again it all comes to a standstill. A horse has fallen down in front of a gun. The driver beats the horse relentlessly, but it doesn't get up, only its head sways, then that too stops. It lies still, open-eyed with foaming mouth. The tank that has tried to bypass the horse is wedged in between the Watzlawiks' fence and the gun. The gunner in the open turret curses. The driver shoots the horse, fires all his bullets into it, then they kick and drag it to the side.

Night falls and fires illuminate soldiers and armour in the fields. An accordion in our house! The sound of an accordion prods, urges, leads the foreign, guttural voices until they rise above it. The clamour and stomping in the house have stopped. Instead the walls vibrate with deep masculine voices. Beautiful, almost unearthly sounds carry us away from here and now. Flickering fires in the fields and these wonderful voices, harmonicas and accordions lull our fears away, lull us into sleep. Almost. Hour after hour they keep singing, playing. The songs become louder, wilder. The moody, longing notes give way to aggressively triumphant music.

'They must be dancing,' whispers Mutti, her eyes black and wide in the semi-darkness. Huddled close together, we feel the walls, then the whole house shaking to the rhythm of the songs. Incredible energy unleashed.

'They're drunk! My God, they're drunk. What will they do?'

Glass shatters, followed by an outburst of laughter. Rifle shots, pistol shots, finally quiet except for one shrill '*Nein!*' in the distance.

In the morning, the army is on the move again. No sign of Grossvater or Grossmutter, only occasional howls from the Stalin Organ.

Day passes and night. Another day, another night and it doesn't let up. Still no sign of Grossmutter. Once we thought we heard her footsteps in the yard, but we weren't sure. She didn't come. But the seemingly endless Russian army keeps rolling. It rattles, roars, marches past our house. Finally, it's beginning to thin out. The Stalin Organ is dragged away and, best of all, Grossmutter comes, unharmed, and with news and food.

'Everyone has survived. Everyone in our house. Old Frau Ruhl sprained an ankle when they threw her against the kitchen wall. They threatened to shoot Grossvater a couple of times because he didn't have a watch, but Vladimir saved him each time. He saved Hertha too, when they almost raped her. This man has been running around, I tell you! Who knows when he sleeps? He certainly hasn't had any time for Lisa. Oh, that's right – ' Grossmutter interrupts herself – 'you don't know about him at all. Vladimir is a young Russian lieutenant, handsome too, who has taken a liking to Lisa – you know, pretty Lisa Gerber. He lives at the Gerbers' now. Ach, what a guardian angel he has been around here. Thanks to him, we got away with no more than a black eye. Everyone runs to him for help, and he always comes. Do you know that at one point I counted three hundred and fourteen Russians in our small house? Three hundred and fourteen! They made me cook for them. One of them gave me half a loaf of bread. You wouldn't think so, but they really have nothing to eat themselves. The house, of course, looks like Sodom and Gomorrah, but I'm going to leave it that way, at least for a while. Otherwise, whoever else comes in might get the idea that it hasn't been looted yet. Can't take any chances. It looks much worse than it is. The chairs and table are broken, but Grossvater can probably fix them. The glass in the étagère and almost all the glasses and dishes and all the pictures are smashed. But you didn't like them anyway.' Sly glance at me. 'No, they didn't take much. What do we have? Old rags in the closet. Oh, you should have seen the women! They sure are strapping figures, and busty, almost bursting out of their uniforms. One of them tried to get herself into Grossvater's old leather coat. You should have seen her, prancing around in front of the mirror, viewing herself from this side and that.'

'Did she take it?'

'Of course she took it. Walked right out with it. Their women are something, though. I did my best to look like an old peasant woman.' Grossmutter chuckles. 'Can't trust these rascals. And most of them did call me "Matka," Mother. Wait till you see the cellar! Not one glass left. What a mess! All the cider bottles broken too. Smashed them when they were looking for schnapps. Thank God, we didn't have any. They were drunk enough as it was. But wouldn't you know it, one of them found my lardpot, the one I hid under the stove. Ate it.'

She stops, listens to a tank that seems to have halted in front of the house, and continues when the iron treads roll on.

'Yes, he ate it right then and there. All of it. Sure. I have others. Still, it irks me that he found that one. And Gerda! The rucksack you left on the veranda . . .'

'The rucksack! My rucksack!' exclaims Gerda. 'Oh, my God, it contained all our papers! My parents', my own, the title to our house, everything! And . . .' Gerda tries in vain to hold back her tears. 'The jewellery, all my mother's jewellery and the silver. Everything, simply everything! I carried it everywhere, only to leave it behind at the worst possible moment. Oh, my God!'

'There was no time, Gerda,' says Grossmutter. 'Later everyone knows what they should have done. As it was, you were lucky to get to us – you could have been caught on the open road. And lucky again that we could hide you. Papers!' Grossmutter says, with her typical sneer. 'Papers! You can always get papers. There'll be plenty of people without papers. I wouldn't worry about that. The main thing is, you're alive and well.'

'That's true, Frau Dereck. Please don't think me ungrateful. You have done so much, but –'

'But nothing,' Grossmutter interrupts. 'What's gone is gone. Doesn't pay to worry. I will try later to go over to my sister-in-law's and also to your parents'. They must be worried and will be happy to hear that you are well, papers or no papers.'

'Maybe I should come along?'

'Oh, no! You stay right here. All of you. Though the worst seems to be over, there are still plenty of marauding soldiers around, and at night even the regular troops go through the houses looking for women.'

'But you've not only been hiding me, you've been feeding me as well,' Gerda protests weakly.

'What food? That one bowl of soup? We still have a few

potatoes left and a cabbage or two. Don't wor – Quick, close the hatch!'

Footsteps in the yard. Feet in boots. Rough Russian voices questioning, urging, demanding, over and over again. 'Frau! Frau! Frau!'

Grossmutter's voice: 'No. No one here. No Frau. Only me, old woman, very old woman!'

Proclamations have been posted all over. A member of each family must go to the Russian Commandatura to register each person in the household, and ration cards will be issued accordingly. My grandparents decide to wait a few days before registering Mutti and me.

We remain in our hideout, but Gerda, despite warnings from my grandparents, insists on going home. They both accompany her. Officially, at least, the days of looting and rape are over, yet bands of soldiers still come to the house looking for women and valuables. We've seen a whole group of soldiers attack two women who were peacefully walking down the road. We saw what they did, heard the women scream. It's enough to make me want to stay here until there isn't a single Russian within miles.

When Grossvater guards the front of the house and Grossmutter the garden side, we sometimes leave our hideout for short periods, just to walk and breathe a bit.

Days later, I don't know how many, on a bright sunny morning, Russian tanks roll by the house, the first ones in quite a while. They seem to have stopped, and suddenly there's a great commotion. Mingled with the Russian voices I suddenly hear Grossvater's. He screams, shouts: 'Knives! Knives! Quick, bring some knives!'

German and Russian voices intermingle, but the only distinguishable word is 'knives'. To our frustration, the brick hole is too small. We can't see what's going on. But whatever is happening is taking place right below us in our chicken yard.

Soon it sounds as if there must be hundreds of people involved in a knife fight with drunken Russians. A shot rings out. The crowd moans. Metal clangs on metal. The sound of more and more people joining what must be a melee. We hear shrieks of 'There! There!'

'No, here! Stab here!'

'Give *me* the knife!'

A Russian voice rises above all the others and shouts in German, 'Get in line! Everybody get in line!' Eventually all is quiet once more. Only then does Grossmutter remember us and call us down, and the mystery is solved.

A tank crew has been herding some cows. One of the cows jumped our fence and broke a leg. Grossvater and Grossmutter instantly saw the food possibilities. Grossmutter hurried to the Russian commandant to get permission to slaughter the cow. The commandant, she said, took his time, but finally did give the necessary permission.

The tank crew, with Grossvater's help, in the meantime took matters into their own hands. They dragged the cow into our yard and tried to kill the poor beast with knives. It didn't work, so one of the Russians shot it. When Grossmutter returned, she saw a line of people stretching the full length of our street. She only discovered what was going on when she reached the beginning of the line and the great cluster of people in her own yard.

'Everybody carried bowls and pails, just as they did when we killed Jolanthe. Can you imagine?' Grossmutter laughs. 'Here I was running to get permission, and when I finally got it, there was no more cow. I barely got this.' She holds up a bloody chunk of meat.

'They were decent fellows, though,' Grossvater says. 'Goodness, if I hadn't seen to it, they wouldn't have got anything.'

'It's true,' Grossmutter agrees. 'They would have come away empty-handed. I gave the tall blond one half of what I originally had. He looked so hungry.'

'The tall blond one? Why, I had already given him the best piece of the thigh!' Grossvater exclaimed. They both laugh and shake their heads.

Days later, up in our loft, Mutti says, 'Today is the twenty-second of May. We've been in hiding for four weeks. Do you know that? Four weeks! Germany surrendered unconditionally on the seventh of May, and we are still hiding.'

Just then we hear Grossmutter banging with the broomstick.

'Open up! Come down!' she shouts. 'I have a surprise for you.'

I'm half-way down the ladder before I see him. But then I'm there in a flash, shouting.

'Vati! Vati! Vati!'

Mutti and I both cling to him, knowing we'll never let him go again.

He says, 'You are coming home with me,' and everyone knows he means us both.

Vati in the middle, Mutti and I as close as possible on either side of him, we walk to Hermsdorf.

Everything has to be good from now on. I know it. For me the war is over.

Some other Puffins for Older Readers